# THE ART OF CONSULTATION

## PUBLIC DIALOGUES IN A NOISY WORLD

# THE ART OF CONSULTATION

## PUBLIC DIALOGUES IN A NOISY WORLD

RHION JONES
AND ELIZABETH GAMMELL

First published in Great Britain in 2009 by
Biteback Publishing Ltd
Heal House
375 Kennington Lane
London
SE11 5QY

ISBN 978-1-84954-002-5

10 9 8 7 6 5 4 3 2 1

A CIP catalogue record for this book is available from the British Library.

Set in Minion and Trade Gothic by SoapBox
Printed and bound in Great Britain by TJ International, Padstow

# CONTENTS

## PART THREE: WHAT GOES RIGHT?

# ABOUT THE AUTHORS

**Rhion Jones** was educated at the University of Wales and Balliol College, Oxford. He became involved in personnel management before it was rechristened 'HR', gaining experience in the motor industry, the (then) public water industry and information technology. He subsequently spent several years advising suppliers and users of customer service systems. For over twenty years Rhion has specialised in helping public bodies interact with a wide range of stakeholders, authoring more than forty White Papers and briefings on all aspects of this relationship. He is co-founder of the Consultation Institute.

**Elizabeth Gammell** originally trained as a ballet teacher, before raising a family and later becoming an enthusiast for new technology in the public affairs industry. She pioneered contact management applications through the LOBBYcontact suite of political databases in the days before the internet provided instant access. As development and standards director of the Consultation Institute she designs and builds training courses in public engagement and consultation.

# PREFACE

Never intended to be a weighty, academic tome, this book is our attempt to tell the story of the emergence of the culture of consultation over the past few years and to unravel some of the misconceptions and myths that have grown up around it. From our personal experience, gained through considerable practical research and listening to thousands of individuals engaged in the myriad methods of enacting consultations, we have distilled much knowledge. This is what we've set out to share – but not in a dry manner. We hope this book will make you smile occasionally too, for the issues span those of critical national importance through to the most local on our doorstep and which can involve us all.

Our sincerest thanks go to everyone who has generously shared their many experiences, especially to all the participants on Consultation Institute courses and those who have attended events. We are extremely grateful to Jonathan Wadman for his meticulous editing of this book, and to everyone at Biteback for their help. Also thanks to Quintin Oliver, Howard Kendall and Paul Rodrigues, who have been so supportive, but most of all to Lesley and Alistair, who have had to live with the creation of this book.

**Rhion Jones and Elizabeth Gammell**
*September 2009*

# PART ONE
# THE CONSULTATION
# CULTURE

# 1. HERE, THERE AND EVERYWHERE

## CONSULTATION CRAZY?

At every turn, someone wants to know what we think. We're promised a say in decisions we'd never heard of; we're invited to influence matters well beyond our immediate knowledge. Isn't it flattering? Isn't it impressive?

But is it real?

Just because something is all-pervasive doesn't make it good. And although the worldwide trend towards greater public participation is generally seen as positive, there are disadvantages as well. The consultation culture is far from an idyllic state of benign democracy with stakeholder organisations and the general public happily rejoicing that governments and quangos condescend to ask them their opinions. Instead, it is a rather uncomfortable half-way house between mass participation or direct democratic models and the traditional way we always took important decisions – namely to elect or appoint someone competent and let them get on with it.

Probably the first thing to appreciate about consultation is what it isn't. It is not a vote, nor is it a referendum. Many of those who are consulted and are called 'consultees' would like it to be a vote. Then if a case arises where, for example, the local council asks a hundred people what they think of its new car-parking regime and eighty of them say they don't like it, this would effectively kill the proposal. Under such circumstances, a council that still goes ahead with its plans may be foolish, but is well within its rights. The essential characteristic of consultation is that opinions are solicited, but the decision-maker is not necessarily bound to abide by what is said.

In a consultation, power remains firmly in the hands of those who mount the exercise. Maybe that is why the subject has failed to catch the attention of academics who write so much about the future of democracy. Consultation is probably not radical enough and leaves the establishment very much in charge. Nevertheless, the truth is that consultation is about holding a dialogue and encouraging a debate. It is about making choices and listening to people discuss the pros and cons of various options: the broader the range of participants, the more inclusive the debate. The greater the influence exerted by the debate on subsequent decisions, the greater the likelihood that stakeholders and others will take the dialogue seriously next time around.

This book looks at the art of consultation and recognises how difficult it is to organise such meaningful dialogues when so much else goes on. The ambient noise of a modern democracy, with a free press, 24-hour news and instant web commentaries, threatens to obscure the more considered debates which good consultation demands. Perversely, the greater the amount of public dialogue the less effective it might be!

## CUTTING THROUGH THE JARGON

Despite our best intentions, we haven't found it possible to write this book without using a few classic items of jargon. To make it easier, here is a handful that we will use repeatedly, so it's worth getting to know what they mean.

- *Consultation*: The dynamic process of dialogue between individuals or groups, based upon a genuine exchange of views, with the clear objective of influencing decisions, policies or programmes of action. (See detailed discussion on pages 115–16.)
- *Consultee*: The individual or organisation who responds to a consultation or participates in consultation exercises.
- *Consultor*: The individual or organisation initiating a consultation exercise and who will normally be responsible for acting upon its findings.

■ *Stakeholder*: An individual, group or party that either affects or is affected by an organisation, policy, programme or decision. (See detailed discussion on page 71.)

## IN THE NEWS

Those interested in current affairs might like to try this simple test. Switch on to BBC Radio 4's *Today* programme any morning, set your watch and start counting how long it takes before you hear the word 'consultation'.

We think that consultation provides journalists and broadcasters with an almost limitless supply of stories. Consider these fictitious but realistic examples.

| THE STORY | WHAT'S HAPPENED? |
| --- | --- |
| 'There is speculation tonight that the Government may (after all) go to consultation on the Chancellor's proposals for VAT.' | Classic pre-consultation spin to make the consultor look good and spread the 'We're going to listen' message. |
| 'Today the Strategic Rail Authority launches its consultation on introducing female-only railway carriages.' | Great opportunity to put two rival protagonists head to head and hope for some fireworks to enliven the morning. |
| 'Disturbing claims are made today that the Government isn't listening properly. Furious campaigning pressure group Friends of Sheffield Asylum Seekers have had their request for a meeting turned down.' | Crafty campaigner's press release seeks to bounce the consultor into giving favourable treatment to the complainant. |
| 'Today is the closing date for Boris Johnson's consultation on restricting the area covered by the congestion charge scheme.' | A chance to rerun exactly the same debate as was held weeks ago. . . but, hopefully, even more heated! |
| 'Council chief's gaffe throws public consultation into chaos.' | An opinion expressed by one of the eventual decision-makers gives opponents ammunition to rubbish the consultation. |
| 'Today, the Office of Fair Trading announces the long-awaited outcome of its consultation on the new consumer rights.' | Stock item from official press release highlighting the consultation in order to make its proposals more acceptable. |
| 'Angry health campaigners accuse NHS bosses of bad faith over hospital closure consultation.' | Disappointed stakeholders unhappy with outcome! |

Lest it seem that this shows disrespect for the ladies and gentlemen of the press, we need to stress that such coverage is good, not bad. All of these are solid, legitimate stories and they can be found on the pages of local newspapers even more often than they are heard on national radio. Cumulatively they create an impression of consultation as a battleground between grassroots campaigners and officialdom; the bigger the row, the better the story.

Through the prism of news values, this is fair enough. For every consultation that becomes a story, there are dozens that are less interesting and receive little or no coverage. But the sheer volume is still enough to reinforce the idea that consultation is now everywhere. Indeed, it seems as if public bodies or councils are powerless to act unless they first go through this opinion-gathering process.

At times, this is technically true. There is a long list of statutory requirements which mean that various administrative actions cannot be taken without first undertaking some form of consultation. For example, you cannot merge two schools without first consulting parents; you cannot designate a neighbourhood conservation area without consulting the residents; you cannot reroute a bus service; you cannot replace GP surgeries, and so on. Then there are public institutions which have been set up by Parliament with a legal obligation to consult us all. NHS trusts, under the Health and Social Care Act 2008, or crime and disorder partnerships, under Sections 5 and 6 of the Crime and Disorder Act 1998, are two cases in point. There are countless others.

But this is not always the case. Managers don't just consult because they have to – it can be among the worst kinds of 'tick-in-the-box' tokenism – but because they choose to. This form of 'elective' consultation is a bit like elective surgery – not something you necessarily enjoy but you go through it because you think it will do you good! And it comes about in two ways.

The better trigger is the realisation that without knowing the views of those who are to be affected by your decisions, you might get it wrong. Managers or politicians who grasp this point are the ideal consultors; they are doing it for the right reasons – one could even describe them as selfish reasons. But at least they are going to be motivated to listen.

The other trigger is what can be called the me-too phenomenon. Maybe a better cliché is 'jumping on the bandwagon'. Some of this is inevitable given that *participation, involvement, public engagement* and *active citizenship* are such fabulous, voter-friendly concepts that appeal to every grandstanding aspirant for high office. There is even a danger that enthusiasts for consultation can spark off a Dutch auction of ever more elaborate promises of greater public participation. All this increases the pressure on officials further down the chain to be seen to consult!

## CRITICS

Not everyone is impressed by the results. In 2005, Matthew Parris wrote a stinging critique of the consultation culture in the columns of *The Times* with the headline 'Don't ask my opinion; don't consult, engage or include; just lead'. It's definitely one of the most wonderful debunkings of consultation and includes this terrific paragraph:

> My argument is against tipping bucketloads of participation over every community, every group and every question – at every stage. The reason this can be unwise is simple. Big questions in politics are usually tangled into a wider web. They can rarely have a neat line circled around them . . . The besetting sin of modern British politics . . . is to quail in the face of the ancient truth that politics is about the clash of interests, and political leadership is about having the guts to arbitrate, . . . and instead [to] start jabbering and whimpering about consultation.

While Parris has to be careful not to throw out the baby with the bathwater, his overall scepticism is well placed. He wrote in the wake of Edinburgh Council's ill-fated consultation on a proposal to introduce a congestion charge. In a classic example of the perils of reducing a complex argument to a simple yes or no, the people of Edinburgh unsurprisingly voted against paying for the privilege of driving into their fine city. Four years later, people in Greater Manchester followed suit. In his entertaining polemic, Parris rails against Edinburgh's lack of leadership and the use of consultation as a cop-out. Frankly, many consultations are somewhat like this – a way of passing the buck or avoiding difficult decisions.

But although journalists find such exercises to be soft targets – yet another opportunity to poke fun at politicians and civil servants – there is a real problem here. Officials are damned if they do and damned if they don't. Ridicule follows the launch of a consultation if the press think they are just playing for time. But even worse criticism follows if they proceed with unpopular decisions without appearing to ask citizens what they want.

In the pages that follow, we will look beyond the headlines and try to understand the dynamics at work in this seemingly ubiquitous world of non-stop consultation.

## 2. NOW AND FOREVER?

### PASSING FAD OR HERE TO STAY?

Experienced readers will know that management ideas come and go with amazing speed. Who remembers Management by Objectives? Where did Quality Circles go? Tom Peters made a fortune with his volume *In Search of Excellence*, and then made another fortune explaining how he got it wrong! Michael Porter wrote a wonderful book called *Competitive Strategy*, and then another one titled *Competitive Advantage*, but by the time you're reading this book there will have been a clutch of even newer concepts.

Unlike Francis Wheen, who features such business ideas in his work *How Mumbo-jumbo Conquered the World: A Short History of Modern Delusions*, we think that many of these ideas have made a valuable contribution to our understanding of what works and what doesn't in modern society. Many of the more successful books in the last twenty years have chronicled the shift in power from the supplier to the consumer, and it is this irreversible trend that makes us think that consultation is more than a transient diversion.

What may well be temporary is the terminology. After all, an easy way to make money is to invent a new label. If we called this book *Hyper-dialogue: Next Generation Community Consultation*, we might attract the curious, those who always buy the latest of everything and also probably those about to board a long flight to the Antipodes. But we might also be adding to the bonfire of here-today, gone-tomorrow buzz-phrases, which so rightly antagonised Matthew Parris.

We need to distinguish between labels, which may change with the fancies of fashion, and underlying ideas, which may well be more stable. So, in trying to figure out whether the consultation culture is here to stay, we will try to avoid being too precious about the use of the precise term. Instead we will look at the broad range of public participation practices and examine the factors that make them an increasingly prevalent part of our lives. We believe there are four distinct but related forces that will make consultation a permanent feature of the twenty-first century.

## GROWING AWARENESS OF THE DEMOCRATIC DEFICIT

Turnouts at elections are falling, but this can be explained in more than one way. One analysis says that people don't care; provided their lives are secure, their jobs are safe and their incomes reasonable, they can't be bothered. Others argue that voters have finally figured out that if you want to influence public policy, voting three times a decade doesn't achieve very much.

Given the nature of the UK's first-past-the-post system, you have to be resident in one of a relatively small number of marginal seats for your vote to make a serious difference. So again, why bother? But even where proportional representation is used, the public's disaffection with electoral politics still applies; witness the depressing turnouts at European elections. It can't just be down to the arithmetic.

More persuasive may be a consensus that conventional politics has ceased to be a respectable profession. Soured by sleaze, with town halls and parliaments alike undermined by incessant media muck-raking, citizens take their revenge by simply staying away. This is tough on honest hard-working MPs or councillors, but it cannot fail to erode their confidence. Gone is the municipal swagger that built our city halls in the nineteenth century. Today's leaders are often cowed and nervous, aware that their mandate has never been weaker. Whenever they attempt to do something bold or courageous, opponents will cite their dubious legitimacy: that's one way to describe the democratic deficit.

Yet another variant is the analysis that organisations which influence our lives on a day-to-day basis simply aren't accountable; all the quangos, non-departmental public bodies, executive agencies and the bewildering list of hybrid public–private partnerships are run by people who can't be removed through the ballot box. It is this that fuels anti-EU sentiment and the idea that Brussels Eurocrats are beyond any form of political control.

What all this shows is that there are several kinds of democratic deficit, and that there is premium in finding ways to overcome the problems they cause. Many have a vested interest in finding solutions; hence the flirtation with direct participation, with eDemocracy and a whole toolkit of methods, many of which we will consider later in this book.

What makes consultation a firm favourite to last the course is that few decision-makers are willing to relinquish their power completely. They may talk the talk of community involvement, but ideally they would like to stop short of handing over their authority, no matter how weakened it may be, to a town meeting or a glorified focus group. The consultation model suits them nicely: learn to be really effective in asking for people's opinions, but keep the final decision-making to themselves. That's why it is here to stay.

## THE RISE OF 'EVIDENCE-BASED POLICY-MAKING'

This was a popular catch-phrase in the early days of New Labour and has spawned a variety of websites and training courses for civil servants, think-tankers and policy wonks ever since.

One can't argue with the general proposition. Of course it's better if public policy is made following rigorous analysis and the search for evidence. One can say the same for our courts. Obviously it's best if the verdict results from a rational evaluation of the evidence. But just as informed commentators could make a serious critique of the judicial process, so can the development of public policy, evidence based or not, be subject to serious question. Both cases beg the question 'What is evidence?' And is the quality or credibility of that evidence affected by the skill with which it is articulated or presented? Our prisons are full of convicted felons who believe they are there because their barrister was incompetent!

The trouble with evidence is that it is rarely conclusive. Gathering the facts about any situation is seldom as easy as it sounds and, as few policies ever start from a clean sheet of paper, we are usually influenced by our perception of what happens now. If we take a simple example, consider the policy on attainment-testing in schools. Your view on the policy would depend in large measure upon whether you were a teacher with experience of testing in recent years and maybe with a perception that the disadvantages outweighed any benefits, or whether you were an employer desperate for better information about school-leavers' capabilities.

In both cases, there is scope to structure an evidence-gathering research project that would reinforce the pre-determined views of the protagonists. No wonder that the phrase is sometimes twisted to read 'policy-based evidence-making', for it is clear to many that it is often possible to find evidence to support any proposition, provided one uses one's imagination and searches for long enough.

The problem is made worse by the great delight with which the media seizes upon eye-catching surveys or other sexy bits of evidence. In a fierce debate, as, for example, on fox-hunting, newspapers openly engage in the controversy; they can be unashamedly partisan when choosing what evidence to publish.

The rise and rise of Citizens' Juries is at least in part explained by the realisation that so much is based upon how you read the evidence. A consultation run by a top-flight specialist firm in 2008 crossed swords with the Market Research Society's adjudication panel when Greenpeace complained that it had not given a totally balanced account of the arguments about aspects of nuclear power. What a surprise! Very few people agree on the evidence. What's important is to hear it.

## THE TRANSPARENCY TREND

In the world of *Citizen Kane* or the folklore of early twentieth-century municipal politics in Europe or the USA, we conjure up images of power-brokers conferring in smoke-filled rooms. In his 1977 TV mini-series *Washington: Behind Closed Doors*, the director, Gary Nelson, skilfully depicted the Watergate scandal as the ultimate consequence of the corrupting influence of power in the American capital. But note the title. The inference is that the only reason such shenanigans happened is that they were hidden. In this case the irony was that, unbeknown to many, Nixon had the hubris to record all his conversations and effectively made public so much of his own wrongdoing.

Many Americans of a certain age see the Watergate scandal as a turning point in their country's history. This was the moment when their eyes were opened to the potential evils of untrammelled power; this was the point when transparency became an important goal.

In reality, this is all so much hype. The case for more openness and for greater accountability has been around for years. It's neither new nor particularly revolutionary. In fact, in most countries there's an ongoing debate about the best way to eradicate corruption.* In the UK it took the form of the anti-sleaze campaign. It is this that inspired such innovations as Parliament's Register of Members' Interests and its local equivalents. It led to the Commission for Standards in Public Life and the 'Nolan rules', circumscribing what elected representatives can and can't do. The idea is that if there is universal disclosure and if we know that a particular Member of Parliament is retained by this company or that trade association, it should eliminate the worst excesses.

Note that we don't outlaw lobbying. The influence business still exists; indeed, it is thriving! But greater transparency changes it forever. Once upon a time the added value of lobbyists lay with what they knew but others didn't. They knew who ultimately took certain decisions; they knew who would be making the technical recommendations; they knew who had the financial say-so. Not only did they know who these people were, for an appropriate fee they could arrange a suitable introduction, organise a lunch, prepare some private briefings and so on.

None of these practices has disappeared, but these days they take place in a climate of greater disclosure, not least because we have a Freedom of Information Act. As a consequence, those who are lobbied have to be more careful. Who they meet, under what circumstances, can become a matter of public disclosure. It is, therefore, unsurprising that

---

* The annual Corruption Perceptions Index (CPI), first released in 1995, is the best known of Transparency International's tools. It has been widely credited with putting TI and the issue of corruption on the international policy agenda. The CPI ranks 180 countries by their perceived levels of corruption, as determined by expert assessments and opinion surveys.

if a controversial decision is required, the safest course of action is to ask everyone openly for their views – rather than be accused of talking confidentially to a few stakeholders.

Transparency is still prone to be cosmetic. In the example we quoted above, the launch of a consultation exercise does not of itself reduce the risk that a small number of influential lobbyists could ultimately hold sway. A meticulous decision-maker ensures that the views expressed in that exercise are seen to be taken into account. She might involve a trusted third party or a university department; she might publish everything that is submitted. Indeed there are many things she can do to demonstrate this transparency.

But the salient point is that such regard for 'best practice' only arises because of the inexorable trend towards ever greater transparency. This is much assisted by the ability of the internet to offer a cheap and limitless publication method, so that virtually all calling notices, agendas and minutes of meetings can be found on an appropriate website.

In theory, we suppose it might be possible for this transparency juggernaut to be halted. The 21st-century citizen in a post-participative age could decide that it was high time that politicians and civil servants simply got on with things and stopped having to look over their shoulders all the time. We might decide that we don't want to delve into the minutiae of public bodies; the press might possibly decide that whereas entertainers and celebrities are interesting, boring bureaucracy is not.

On balance we think this is unlikely. We think the transparency trend will continue and as long as it does so, people with responsibilities will need to demonstrate that they are listening and will consult.

## CHANGING STAKEHOLDER EXPECTATIONS

This is basically a case of cause and effect. If what's discussed above in terms of the democratic deficit, or evidence-based policy-making and transparency, amounts to anything, then it is hardly surprising if stakeholders begin to notice. The result is that people now expect to be consulted.

There is more to it than that. Experienced stakeholders respond to so many consultations that they know precisely what to expect and will drive up standards, simply because an exercise that falls below a certain minimum will lead them to complain. There are probably several thousand professional responders, working in the bureaucratic agencies or for NGOs (non-governmental organisations), who can tell a good 'un from a bad 'un.

What the general public might expect is more complicated. On one hand, the average citizen is rarely moved to political action unless something threatens his or her immediate interests. However, on the other hand, whenever an important decision looms, the natural reflex now is to demand an element of consultation. Indeed, there is a ratchet-like escalator of expectations. If a local authority launches a formal consultation in advance of a particular decision, it makes life difficult for a neighbouring council should the latter fail to do the same in a comparable situation.

This ability to benchmark one consultor's approach with another is a feature of modern civic society. Intelligence networks and information exchanges are particular strengths of the voluntary and community sector; public bodies are vulnerable to unflattering comparisons if they insist on doing their own thing with little regard to what others have done.

Some organisations may not need encouragement. Remember that the competitive instinct is also alive and well among managers. In the current climate there is kudos for running an effective participation project. There is also the potential reward of improved relationships with stakeholders. After all, it is often in everyone's interest to ensure a good dialogue between decision-makers and those affected by their decisions. It is not, therefore, against the grain of modern management thinking to encourage a participative style of behaviour. So if that's what customers, suppliers, investors, employees and all the other stakeholders have come to expect, then so be it.

# 3. THE WHOLE WIDE WORLD

Consultation is not just found in the UK. In fact, like many political practices, our local variant is a peculiarly British pragmatic compromise with few rules and a pretty haphazard approach to standards. For years, consultation has been just something that happens rather than a process that is constitutionally inbuilt, and as such has tended to spawn a wide variety of species. In short, to put it in a biodiversity context, the UK is unusually rich.

## THE WORLD WIDE WEB OF CONSULTATION

We took a small sample of consultations from Google Alerts, covering the period from the end of December 2008 to the first days of January 2009, just to see what was happening beyond the United Kingdom. Given that this was over Christmas and New Year, it might have been reasonable to assume that little was going on, but the number of consultations was remarkable. Another search, using the terms 'European union' and 'public consultation', yielded 725,000 entries – fertile ground for any researcher.

The European Union has a website where all its consultations are listed.* There is a title and description, policy field, target group and the closing date for each consultation – excellent practice. You can also 'have your say in debates on the European Union and its future, discuss issues directly with leading figures and exchange views with other citizens interested in the same topics'. Online forums feature

---

* http://ec.europa.eu/yourvoice/consultations/index_en.htm.

the future of Europe, the EU budget, youth and multilingualism, and there are blogs which enable you to 'discuss current EU affairs with European Commission leaders', should you be so minded. A side panel allows access to thirty-four separate policy activities on everything from agriculture to transport and the consultations happening there.

Leaving Europe, our sampled consultations show a familiar picture: everything from the highly technical to the simplest human issue comes up for scrutiny and comment. In China, the business newspaper *The Standard*, explaining a public consultation, 'On amendments to the Land Titles Bill and the transition from the Land Registration Ordinance to the Land Titles Ordinance', told readers where they can view the relevant papers and gives the closing date for a twelve-week consultation. In Malta, a dispute over the employment of shipyard workers escalated to the point where 'the management has now committed itself also to inform the union and consult with it in every case of termination of employment'. In Pakistan, another employment issue resulted in the President, Asif Ali Zardari, calling for a privatisation process 'only after consulting all stakeholders, especially the workers and labour unions'. The police in Tonga launched their first public consultation 'to enable the police to know what the public was expecting of them' and stated: 'We will be working hard to accurately capture the public's perceptions and expectations.'

Community consultation clearly happens frequently – or is called for when it isn't happening and there is a demand for it. In Queensland, Australia, a story in the *Gympie Times* headlined 'Multi-purpose facility plan needs consultation' demanded community input into a feasibility study. In the United States, although cities are curiously lacking in visible evidence of public engagement, and the Obama-related online craze appears to be making public dialogue an exclusively internet-based experience, under the surface there is much activity, often linked to major infrastructure developments and a groundswell of community politics demanding a greater say in decisions.

These last consultations are largely concerned with planning, an area that raises a high proportion of disputed consultations – and not just in the UK. The mayor of Caracas, for example, announced a consultation on the future of the Sambil mall in the central district of La Candelaria because a new building 'contravenes any urban discipline', while, returning to Australia, a public consultation on reviving Hobart's Princes Wharf was criticised, with calls for action rather than more debate: 'We'll believe it when we see it, the Government has been all talk and no action for ten years.'

Consultation on health issues occurs worldwide too. In the Canadian province of Saskatchewan, the Patient First Review was announced in November 2008, 'to find out what Saskatchewan residents feel about the way health care services are delivered', with details of focus groups plus a website where people can tell their stories. Sounds familiar?

## THE IMPACT OF CULTURE

What many people fail to realise is how consultation can be influenced by cultural factors.

Even within the UK, regional differences abound. The way in which public participation is organised differs between Lancashire, say, and London. The Celtic fringe and the new devolved administrations in Edinburgh, Cardiff and Belfast reflect deep-seated differences in political culture that are particularly visible in relation to consultation. Stated simply, the Scottish, Welsh and Irish come from strong traditions of verbal and literary disputation. The art of argument and debate is the stuff of conversation; there is a psychological pre-disposition to challenge those in authority to make their case. No wonder that the new Scottish Parliament, the new National Assembly for Wales and the new Stormont Assembly reverberate to the sound of Celtic wit and, occasionally, wisdom.

Part of this is the belief that everyone has a right to be heard. The coal-mining culture of south Wales and its counterparts in Scotland and the north of England were particularly egalitarian and found artistic expression in eisteddfods, brass bands and adult education movements. Note this word 'expression', for it goes to the heart of the consultation culture. We are talking about the way in which communities communicate what they think. It affects the way in which intermediaries, representatives or 'gatekeepers' are perceived: in some communities they are respected; in some they are tolerated; in others they are passively ignored and in yet others they are openly vilified.

When the American Senate leader Tip O'Neill remarked that 'all politics is local', he may have been thinking of the pork-barrel 'tit for tat' favours for which the US is famous. He could equally have applied his comment to the impossibility of making universal assumptions about the use of political power and decision-making in large democracies. There are just too many variables and the presence of one larger-than-life figure in a city or county for a period can skew the system by influencing everyone's mindset about how to achieve change.

Apply this to public consultation. If a long-standing leader adopts a highly consultative style, his or her opponents will complain about the inevitable delays to decisions, and they will call for the 'smack of firm leadership': don't pussyfoot around seeking unlikely consensus, be bold, and so on. But if, on the other hand, our long-established leader is autocratic, the opposition will surely argue for a more consensual approach. Stakeholders will complain that they have no opportunity to express their views; any mistakes will be attributed to a failure to consult. In both these scenarios, when change arrives, the pendulum will swing in the opposite direction.

It's not just personalities that affect the local political culture. Ipsos MORI has demonstrated that the desire to become involved is highest in local authorities with severe problems and lowest in areas where the council is performing well. This is another face of the proposition that contentment breeds apathy, a much-disputed explanation for our ever-reducing turnouts at elections.

Another factor can be the socio-economic or the racial/ethnic mix in a community. We know, again from sound research, that general citizen satisfaction with council services is lowest in areas of high ethnic diversity and highest in stable, indigenous populations. This will affect the propensity to become involved in civic responsibilities, complaint levels and also the overall level of trust in public bodies.

What all this shows is that it is virtually impossible to generalise about a particular community's likely approach to consultation. There simply cannot be a successful 'one size fits all' formula that makes equal sense everywhere. Attempts to graft theoretical best practice without regard to local circumstances are unlikely to work well and may lead to indifference or even provoke antagonism.

So whether it is Sheffield or Shanghai, Swansea or Soweto, the precise form of public participation will reflect local political cultures and the locally accepted ways of involving stakeholders. The mechanics will be different and the outcomes may be very different. What will be the same is for someone to decide, consciously or unconsciously, when a consultation is required and, having undertaken it, to make use of what has come out of the exercise.

# 4. CONSULTATION IN THE PUBLIC POLICY ENVIRONMENT

There is no single overarching motivation that leads governments or companies to consult us. Different organisations have their own imperatives based upon their roles and responsibilities; given how varied they are, it is somewhat surprising that they often emerge using remarkably similar techniques to organise apparently very disparate objectives.

To understand the phenomenon of consultation it is necessary to recognise how 'old hat' it really is. What is new about consultation is its widespread use and persistent misuse.

## COMPLEX ORGANISATIONS AND THE FOUR ENVIRONMENTS OF CONSULTATION

We have identified four separate consultation environments:

- Public policy
- Employee
- Corporate
- Customer

All four environments represent classic scenarios where consultation has been used, is being used and will continue to play a significant role. In this book we focus firmly on the public policy environment, but before doing so it might serve well to understand the wider picture and to reflect a little on the other applications of consultation.

In fact the best starting point is to consider the modern-day organisation. In almost all respects it is a far cry from the early twentieth-century model. Private companies may still carry the same label, but in so many other respects, they have very different kinds of structure. Public bodies are probably unrecognisable. In between we have a range of hybrids occupying a strange twilight world where public finance and private initiatives intermingle, where the hope is for the best of both worlds – and the risk is of the worst. Meanwhile the 'third sector' slowly but surely encroaches upon both. But they all have three characteristics that oblige them to indulge in one form or another of consultation.

Firstly, they are all image conscious. Private companies may be obsessed by their valuation and the ups and downs of their share price. They will accordingly spend heavily on investor relations and other means of influencing informed opinion in their favour. Indeed, protecting and enhancing the reputation of companies, and the individuals who lead them, has led to a multi-million-pound industry in its own right – corporate social responsibility (CSR).

CSR is sometimes characterised just as the private sector's social conscience. Indulging in good works and trying to appear as a good corporate citizen is viewed as a hallmark of a mature, responsible, worldly-wise company. But because it is often associated with the high-profile philanthropy of American business leaders, the detailed nitty-gritty of CSR is sometimes overlooked. In our view, the core of CSR is the building and maintenance of stakeholder relationships and the conduct of effective dialogues that are helpful to the business. That is why top companies manage a long list of people and institutions that matter to them and cultivate them assiduously. Look on the websites of Fortune 500 firms or in their annual reports; there will be something entitled a 'Public Affairs Report' or perhaps a 'Stakeholder Relations Report' transparently detailing what they've done to consult and engage with those that matter to them. Although it happens right across the board, this phenomenon is most visible in those industries that impinge upon public policy. So starting with aerospace, agriculture, automotive, banking, you can get a complete alphabet of business areas where it takes little nous to work out that industry players need a sound image. In short, CSR covers almost everything!

What you won't read in any published report is the vast amount of covert lobbying that individual companies and their trade associations undertake. In January 2009, a report by the House of Commons Public Administration Select Committee entitled *Lobbying: Access and Influence in Whitehall* gave the lobbying industry six months to put its house in order or face statutory regulation. But frankly, only some of this activity is susceptible to regulation, for the very act of dialogue that forms the 'consultation' between major companies and a range of stakeholders is itself a mechanism whereby each can influence the other.

Public institutions of all kinds, from quangos to councils, national charities and even regulatory bodies, have an image to safeguard. They worry about adverse headlines, and know from experience that a poor reputation can cost top jobs, prestige and budget. Local authorities face regular Audit Commission inspections, and among the indicators that are looked for are statistics on overall citizen satisfaction. Research has shown a correlation between high satisfaction ratings and expenditure on press and publicity; if we want to be generous we rephrase this to mean spending on keeping people informed.

This simply cannot be done without an extensive programme of consultation with local interest groups of all kind. Whether it's called consultation or not is beside the point. The fact is that image enhancement for a town hall, a housing association, an NHS trust or whatever is not possible unless an effort is made to engage with and hold dialogues with a wide range of those who matter.

The second characteristic of modern organisations is their internal and external interdependence. Large organisations are fiendishly complicated. Business systems, not just IT systems, have been built to take account of factors that simply could not be accommodated twenty years ago. Jobs that could be done in isolation from others have dwindled almost to zero; a fail-safe philosophy or a 'right-first-time' quality assurance culture means that checks and balances tend to be built into all processes. Simultaneously, we have reduced headcounts and eliminated support staff by letting business process tools take the strain.

The upshot of this is that change control has become a nightmare. Management textbooks teach us that before embarking on change, it is necessary to identify who might be impacted and then one should consult them to assess the implications etc. Fantastic theory! But it's getting jolly difficult, not least because the external dependencies mirror the complexities found internally, with the disadvantage that you have far less influence over what happens.

Smart organisations, therefore, find ways to institutionalise relationships between one function and another. So day-to-day, as well as more strategic, changes can benefit from at least some opportunities for dialogue. Some years ago Richard J. Schonberger wrote a book called *Building a Chain of Customers*. His idea was that every activity in business or administration was carried out for the benefit of one kind of customer or another. Even the most cerebral pen-pusher was crafting his or her prose for the benefit of some commissioning party. Indeed it is this which underpins the current public sector approach to many public services – witness Lord Darzi's review of the NHS and the idea of 'world-class commissioning'.

However, you cannot commission anything without a thorough understanding of what people want or what they need (not the same!) and the issues that influence such perceptions. That's where consultation comes in, for it is an integral part of the process. Ergo, if the relationships between departments and individuals in modern organisations make greater demands upon them, they will have to spend more time and devote more effort to those relationships.

There's a third factor – the pressure to perform. Way back there was an idea that private sector captains of industry might face serious questioning if their businesses under-achieved, but that public sector managers were in sinecure jobs which were totally secure unless you stole the silver or mistreated the office cat. Not any more.

Even if we quietly disregard the fate of failed bankers leaving their posts with their millions, the world has changed dramatically for most senior managers. You perform or you go. Yet success and failure is a variable measure and is not a straightforward financial equation. Many organisations expect a range of outcomes from their leaders; those who have got their MBAs will have been taught how to work with the cultural grain of their firms, not against it.

In practice this means harnessing resources in the right way. Get the most from your staff, incentivise your suppliers, motivate your distribution channels, and enthuse your customers. All of these can be cajoled to deliver, but it doesn't work if all it amounts to is a steady stream of top-down memos and exhortations. So the best leaders claim to 'walk the walk' as well as 'talk the talk', by which we think they mean that they roll up their sleeves and get into the shoes of their various stakeholders – so that they can empathise with them. Presumably that means that they will respond in a practical way by giving of their all. . . hence improved performance.

This is what, in our view, has led to these four consultation environments, or at least three of them. How organisations cultivate their reputations and image, which we discussed above, is accurately called **corporate consultation**. Even in tough times, this is a remarkable and innovative industry, employing thousands of well-paid consultants and supporting in-house teams from Tesco to Toyota. Less easily identifiable in the public and third sectors, it nevertheless exists there and has substantial influence. Invariably these people have the ear of the board chairman or authority chief executive; often they are seen as key deliverers of a corporate strategy. Talking to those who are important to your business is a skilled task and results matter.

**Customer consultation** is not nearly as central to a modern organisation as corporate consultation. It should be. But often it isn't. This is where best in class is streets ahead of the average and where far too many organisations pay only lip service to the concept.

Theoretically, every self-respecting firm and every publicly accountable board has this as a top priority – a no-brainer! In practice, however, a whole bagful of excuses are made to explain away the uncomfortable truth that they frequently ignore this group and somehow expect disappointed and disillusioned customers to continue to pay up. There used to be a popular poster that said 'Customers make paydays possible'. You wouldn't believe it from some of the products and services we've experienced.

In part this is the result of a half-hearted adoption of sensible customer management practices. Satisfaction surveys are everywhere, ranging from the rudimentary postcards you find in your hotel rooms through to sophisticated multi-layered surveys with data gathered face to face or maybe over the telephone. If, on all occasions, one could be confident that the resulting data was fully absorbed by the supplier, we would all be impressed. Sadly, too many firms go through the data-gathering motions and lose sight of what's meant to come after.

In fact there are lots of different sources of data that can be used to assess customer behaviour and the underlying sentiment. Just consider the immense power of the transactional data possessed by our supermarkets, or our banks, or indeed, the Government. Or think of the information gleaned by hundreds of call centres as they process tens of thousands of service or support requests. Then there are all the little bits of information gathered about us whenever we shop online or use our loyalty cards. Add to this what emerges through formal complaints processes – especially in high-volume services like the NHS. Frankly, suppliers have an excess of data; if the quality of what they produce reflected the amount of data, we'd all be living in a customer service nirvana. As it is, many fail due to an inability to complement this avalanche of information with the insights that can only be gained from actual dialogue with customers.

The best organisations have always understood this and their account-managers are schooled to develop the sort of relationships where both supplier and customer can talk constructively about the overall experience. Such a dialogue goes well beyond their views of today's product and extends to all aspects of the trading relationship. Ordering processes, product information, commercial terms and conditions, after-sales support and, of course, future product development are all of concern; a company that takes customer consultation seriously creates mechanisms for this to occur.

Customers aren't always labelled the same way. Some transport operators, not unreasonably, use the term 'passenger'; the NHS, of course, refers to 'patients'. The IT industry has 'users', hotels have 'guests' and housing associations have 'tenants'. Local authorities have council tax payers; in that capacity they are increasingly consulted on their views of the services provided for them.

When it comes to **employee consultation**, there is an equal amount of hypocrisy. For, if you believe the blurb, every large company is a model employer. They will sport the Investors in People logo; their recruitment pages bristle with confidence that theirs is a great organisation and that to join them would be the best career move you could ever make.

The public sector now follows suit, emphasising how it is either helping the environment, protecting the public, developing communities or working towards some similar desirable end. The voluntary sector adds the 'feel-good' factor and appeals to people's sense of mission.

Implicit in much of this is the idea that the employer is one that listens. More explicit is the suggestion that individuals will achieve a sense of fulfilment, that their skills will be properly used and of course that they will be rewarded. We don't expect to see many advertisements saying 'We take all the decisions here and you'll do as you're told'.

Smart bosses don't need to be told that to get the best from their people it is a good idea to consult them. Yet the management textbooks are strangely silent on the skills needed to take advice from your own staff. There is an abundance of guidance about the need to delegate and whole books on employee motivation. Still, too many managers cling to the authority model, whereby knowledge is power and asking for advice from subordinates is a sign of weakness.

True consultation is more than 'management by suggestion box' and the very best employers have always given it attention. They have regularly invested in attitude surveys, designed to aggregate individual opinions – a role once jealously guarded by the trades unions – and present to management a picture of staff concerns. Some consultative committees have been in existence for decades and now that the UK has, belatedly, signed up to the European Directive on Employee Information and Consultation 2004 there are legal means to enforce reluctant employers to set up such machinery.*

---

\* See http://www.cipd.co.uk/subjects/empreltns/comconslt/infocon.htm for more details.

Yet the very consultative culture that is evident in continental European or Far Eastern businesses goes somewhat against the grain of British industrial relations. Bosses in the Anglo-American model hold very dear their 'right to manage' and try their best to preserve their freedom of action. But there are inhibitions to consultations on business strategy from employees as well. In the UK the traditional stance of the unions was as adversarial opponents across a negotiating table and few officials wanted their positions compromised by having once sat on a committee or board that might have approved a particular business strategy. Genuine and meaningful business strategy consultations are therefore still a rarity.

These different environments are, of course, closely interlinked, and one organisation can easily be engaged simultaneously with all the different stakeholders we've discussed.

## PUBLIC POLICY – STARTING WITH PARLIAMENT

This is not the same as 'politics' – except that in so far as we have democratic accountability for public policy decisions, there will normally be, somewhere in the chain, an electoral or political element.

Public bodies of course take thousands of decisions every week and it is curious how custom and practice has led to some of them being routinely preceded by formal consultation while others are not.

Let's start with Parliament. In some ways this is the highest consultative body in the land. Our use of language confirms it. The House of Commons, especially when it gets on its high horse, demands to 'be consulted'. It freely offers its view, quite often when it lacks any meaningful influence on a situation. But, as the leading forum of public opinion, it has every right to claim for itself the role of reflecting that opinion. In times of crisis, or in matters of war and peace, parliamentarians take great pride in their ability to distil the 'mood of the nation'.

Much informal consultation takes place behind the scenes. Indeed, the conscientious backbench MP has always been something of an expert at consultation in such an informal way. Constituency surgeries have always been considered a uniquely valuable window on certain elements of public policy and most members learn very quickly about housing benefit, the inequities of council tax and the legalities of disputes between neighbours. However, lacking research budgets and, so far, only semi-equipped to exploit new technologies to gather the views of their constituents, few of them could be said to constitute organised formal consultations.

When MPs come together in select committees a different picture emerges. Select committee inquiries usually take the form of an announcement detailing a subject for investigation, usually with a topical rationale, and identifying a series of questions and issues as an open invitation for citizens or organisations to 'submit evidence'. What materialises is a set of papers usually prepared and submitted by policy staff working for the professional bodies most closely involved in the subject. They would regard themselves as key stakeholders. It is not uncommon for committees to receive hundreds of such submissions and, given the short timescales usually in force and the few hours which these committees devote to oral evidence, it must be a difficult task for the committee's staff to wade through the evidence and select appropriate witnesses to appear before MPs.

We suspect that the quality – or indeed, on occasion, the relevance – of the evidence does not always have much bearing on who is chosen to appear. MPs who are investigating aspects of local policing, for example, cannot avoid hauling the Home Office before the committee. MPs are acutely sensitive to charges of not doing their jobs properly and cannot be seen to fail to interrogate the minister and senior civil servants. Similarly, high-profile campaigners or critics of the *status quo* will also be more likely to receive a hearing, if only to forestall media criticism that their case was not being heard.

Whether witnesses enjoy the experience is another matter. Over the years, MPs have become better briefed and the traditional deference, particularly to ministers, is long gone. There has been spectacularly robust questioning, such as Andrew MacKinlay's much-criticised questions to Dr David Kelly,* prior to the latter's suicide. The occasion also provides a platform for some unusually forthright comments; Dr

---

\* Weapons expert Dr David Kelly was thrust into the spotlight after being identified in the media as the man the Government believed was the source for a BBC report on Iraq.

John Reid's complaint, shortly after becoming Home Secretary in May 2006, that parts of his new department 'were not fit for purpose' springs to mind.

Yet this process falls short of being a highly effective consultation because there are few incentives to systematic analysis and objective interpretations. There are regular and honourable attempts to abandon party loyalties and embark upon a search for truth, but everyone knows that when the chips are down this is difficult. Working in the Westminster goldfish bowl, select committees inevitably pursue an agenda of sorts and though they contribute to a debate on the issues, they reflect Parliament's party political balance and are therefore probably unlikely to be truly independent.

Undoubtedly the strength of the process lies in its ability to generate useful evidence. There is still kudos in making a submission to a select committee, even more if summoned to support it in person. Nowadays all submissions are published on the Parliament website and even if the committee makes little use of them, academics and policy-makers can do so.

The legislative process in the Westminster Parliament is badly lacking a formal consultative element. The assumption is that such dialogues as are necessary to establish policy have already been completed by the time a Bill is readied for its parliamentary journey. White Papers have usually been published and mulled over and where we once had Green Papers, there has probably been a formal consultation exercise.

The reality, of course, is that parliamentary draftsmen are seldom clever enough to anticipate all the nuances over which there will be legitimate debate and any lobbyist will confirm that the real fun only begins when the second reading is over. By this time, the principles of the legislation are pretty firmly established but, on the basis that the 'devil is in the detail', stakeholders have an enormous incentive to squeeze the maximum advantage from (or limit the damage caused by) the details of the Bill.

Count the number of corporate representatives or NGOs attracted like bees to a legislative honey-pot. We may not have the sheer numbers or money invested in the parallel process in Washington, DC, but lobbying is alive and well in the UK. This is possibly despite consultation, for in truth a wider public debate militates against some of the traditional added value offered by a lobbyist or 'parliamentary consultant'.

Over the years, these agencies have offered their clients an inside track to decision-makers and guided them around the corridors of Parliament, without always being totally frank about the limited influence MPs wield. Their money often came from knowing how to table a parliamentary question and who to approach in order to do so, how to secure an adjournment debate or signatures on an early day motion. The ultimate goal, however, was to influence a matter of policy where the essential requirement was access to a key individual. A minister, perhaps; but part of the lobbyist's trade is to know who really influences. It might be a senior civil servant, or a working party of officials, it might be a political advisor or even a think tank. But once the name is known, achieving privileged access, an opportunity to state the case, was the paramount deliverable.

Imagine therefore the impact on this august profession when the very officials whose names were once a closely guarded secret and to whom access was protected start running consultation exercises whereby anyone – not just the wealthy or wise that have employed a lobbyist – can offer them their advice. We are reminded of the famous Gilbertian truism from *The Gondoliers*: 'When everyone is somebody, then no one's anybody!'

Of course, consultation has not eradicated the lobbying trade; far from it. It has forced it to build added value in subtler ways. Some lobbyists help their clients participate in the formal consultation, but they recognise that they then compete on equal terms with opponents. Others will try to influence the process at an earlier stage before proposals are developed (always a good idea, but difficult to execute) and muscle in on the pre-consultation. Yet others will focus on the added value of briefing the MPs on the standing committee for the Bill in question or maybe members of the House of Lords, where, by current convention, many improvements are made to our legislation.

All this activity represents stakeholders taking the initiative. Parliament does not systematically go out of its way to seek the views of those its work is likely to impact. It absorbs representations rather than solicits advice. As such it is a set of passive processes relying on its members, briefed as best they can be, to argue out the dynamics of debate.

That debate is rarely particularly well organised. Except in standing committee, when in theory Bills are examined 'line by line', or at third reading, where attempts are made to group amendments together to generate a single discussion, parliamentary debates are singularly ineffective forms of dialogue. Compared with the cut and thrust of a television interview or panel discussion such as *Question Time*, too many parliamentary hours are taken up by MPs making set speeches to empty benches, with a minister able to avoid serious argument by reading from a completely pre-prepared Civil Service brief. This partly explains the media's gradual but very definite withdrawal from parliamentary coverage and the growing practice of ministers and opposition parties to address the nation on the *Today* programme rather than from the green benches.

It is for this reason that many consultations have become characterised as a 'parliamentary by-pass' – a way of undertaking a large-scale debate without much involvement from the Houses of Parliament. Consider some of the most visible public policy debates of recent years. The 2006 Energy Review attracted more than 5,000 contributions, raising issues and questions not considered on the floor of either House of Parliament. Indeed a minister announcing a consultation is not bound to come to the chamber and tell MPs of his or her intention. When Parliament is advised it is often in bulk as, for example, with the Budget or the annual Comprehensive Spending Review.

Few parliamentarians have come to terms with this sea change. They complain about reduced public interest in their activities and, *per* the Power Commission,* attribute these perceived ills to a reduced legitimacy stemming from a skewed electoral system, poor election turnouts or just apathy. In fact the reason for Parliament's diminished

---

\*    On 27 February 2006, the Power Commission, chaired by Helena Kennedy, Baroness
     Kennedy of the Shaws QC, published *Power to the People*, its final report, making thirty
     key recommendations designed to 'save British democracy from meltdown'.

role may be that the nation has found better ways to discuss serious issues than for 646 (in 2009) not-very-representative politicians to argue among themselves.

For what public policy consultation does is to broaden the debate, to invite a wide range of organisations and individuals to participate and to open up the process outside the artificial, cloistered environment of the Palace of Westminster. In many ways, this is good – not bad.

## CIVIL SERVANTS AND THE EXECUTIVE BUREAUCRACY

Whether Parliament consults the country adequately may, in the view of many, be irrelevant anyway. Senior civil servants would politely point out that most of the important policy-making is undertaken in their ministries, under the general direction of ministers, of course.

But even here there has been change. The reduction in Civil Service numbers and the proliferation of think tanks and other policy initiatives have effectively privatised much of this work. When the gurus talk about 'evidence-based policy making', the chances are that much of this evidence will either be supplied or compiled by someone outside the Civil Service; in other words, it has been outsourced. There may be howls of indignation from Civil Service diehards but in many ways this provides a better climate for new ideas and for objectivity. Ministries are prone to become inward-looking or beholden to particular interest or client groups. Relying on external advice can be very effective.

But this is not, of itself, consultation. External stakeholder organisations are frequently selected precisely because they are expected to conjure up a particular policy line. Only occasionally is a body or indeed an internal department told to go and consult extensively and, on the basis of what's said, develop a policy.

Much of the 'evidence' that is collected would struggle to merit the description in a court of law. Research data may be quantifiable and statistical but what passes as evidence is the opinions of experts or the perceptions of stakeholders. The big change has been that Government departments themselves have now started to integrate a period of consultation into their regular policy-making routines. There is a Government *Code of Practice on Consultation*, now in its third edition and, despite being softened in each revision, still a potent normative influence;* by and large ministries appear to adhere to its standards. The trouble with departments incorporating consultation into their routine work is that it is difficult to distinguish between those occasions where officials genuinely want to hear views and those where the decisions are all but taken so the consultation is unlikely to make any difference.

The same is true for some other public bodies. Executive agencies, one of the more lasting innovations of the 1980s, can affect people's lives to a significant extent. Some have appreciated the need for public consultation regarding their citizen-focused processes: for example the Driver & Vehicle Licensing Agency (DVLA), the Identity & Passport Service, the Highways Agency and the Environment Agency all frequently issue consultation papers.

HM Revenue & Customs (HMRC) has extensive consultative arrangements with trade bodies and professional associations as well as a track record of issuing consultation papers either on its own or in association with others. Then there are umpteen 'regulators' whose impact upon specific sectors is considerable and who have to choose on occasions between a highly technical dialogue with a small number of well-informed stakeholders or a 'high, wide and handsome' exercise involving the general public.†

In total there are nearly 800 so-called non-departmental public bodies (NDPBs),‡ many of which feel obliged these days to subject their plans or programmes to consultation. They do so in the main to garner sufficient support from stakeholders so as to ease the task of implementation. There is also probably a significant element of 'covering their backside'. Having gone to consultation is a good defence against critics. Such is the vast scale of central government public policy consultation, emanating as it does from hundreds of official bodies, the existence of which would be news to much of the general public.

---

\*     http://www.berr.gov.uk/files/file47158.pdf

†     A good example occurred in June 2008, when HMRC consulted on its new charter; see http://www.hmrc.gov.uk/consultations/index.htm.

‡     Quantity as at 31 March 2008. See *Public Bodies 2008* (Cabinet Office, 2009), p. 5; http://www.civilservice.gov.uk/Assets/PublicBodies2008_tcm6-6429.pdf.

## LOCAL GOVERNMENT AND LOCAL SERVICE PROVIDERS

What is more visible and often more relevant for the average citizen is local consultation, primarily from local authorities, the NHS or the police.

Local government is prolific as a source of public consultations and quite rightly too. If the principle underlying public dialogues is to ventilate the arguments on matters which affect people's daily lives, the truth is that locally delivered services play a more prominent part than any from central government. It has been estimated that 80 per cent of all transactions between the citizen and Government involve Local Authorities, each of which delivers hundreds of public services.

Almost any or every such service can give rise to a public consultation: a change in library opening hours, new traffic-calming speed humps on a housing estate, rationalisation of care homes by the adult care department, revised school transport arrangements and so on. Note that many of these happen at the micro-management level, where in a private company, decisions would be taken by competent managers and implemented with due speed. But this is public policy, involving public money and therefore also public accountability. Officials know that. Councils have acknowledged that stakeholder views should be taken into account before decisions are taken.

The consequence of this is that decisions of when, who and how to consult are taken at a relatively low level with the result that the standard varies enormously. There is also an inevitable lack of co-ordination, which we will discuss in detail later. Suffice to say, the average council undertakes so much consultation that it scarcely knows itself and has little insight into the total cost or likely benefits. And yet we suspect that much local consultation is far more effective than its central government counterpart. This would confound many Whitehall mandarins, but confirm council chiefs in their suspicions that they already do it better.

Part of this is down to the amount of practice they have had. The average civil servant moves up the career ranks and is involved in the occasional consultation along the way; local government is full of specialist professionals who will stay in a particular role for years, accumulating extensive and long-term practical experience. This will apply particularly to planning, highways and transport staff and to economic development units and housing and education departments.

Until the credit crunch, the whole regeneration agenda, combined with major changes in town planning, added an extra ingredient to the mix – money! Major programmes of urban investment often involving huge sums of private capital generated a consultation industry in its own right. This is not surprising. Everyone acknowledges that the post-war rebuilding of some of our towns and cities led to horrendous mistakes, largely because people were ignored and their views were not considered. Today's regeneration projects have sought to accommodate community views and even if, at times, developments appear to proceed in the face of great opposition, it is rare for consultation to be avoided or ignored altogether.

Another impetus for local consultation has been the Best Value concept. We think this programme is one of the less heralded success stories of the public sector in recent years, strangely and uncharacteristically devoid of spin. It has obliged local councils to systematically review their services against the four criteria of *comparison, challenge, competition* and *consultation*. This means that in the case, for example, of the household refuse collection service, Best Value requires the council

- to benchmark its preference against its neighbours' (comparison);
- to set 'stretching' year-on-year improvement targets (challenge);
- to examine alternative providers (competition); and
- to ask its customers for their views (consultation!).

Hey presto. At the stroke of a pen, the Government induced councils to monitor customer satisfaction. What many people don't realise is that this broke new ground, for most of the public sector had argued for years that private sector-style satisfaction measurement could not possibly work meaningfully in the public service. Most of this was utter nonsense, of course, but in their enthusiasm to escape the horrors of compulsory competitive tendering, local authorities happily embraced the new Best Value regime with scarcely a thought for the small print.

No doubt this does a great disservice to many local government officers, who will write to us detailing how customer focused they have been since 1980, and how they bought into the Citizen's Charter,* got the Charter Mark† and trained their staff in customer service skills. However, if we are all honest, it was not until Best Value took off that most local councils started to measure customer satisfaction at ground level. At the same time, Tony Blair's office began to capture this data through a nationwide survey, MORI started building Citizens' Panels all over the country and the word 'customer' started appearing in place of 'citizen' in thousands of official documents. But in our view, Best Value should take a lot of the credit.

The downside of this was that consultation, for a while, at least became synonymous with a survey. One can imagine the conversation. The Environmental Services director summons a subordinate. 'We need to do a consultation. Can you knock up a questionnaire?'

## HOW THE FOUR ENVIRONMENTS OVERLAP

Although our focus is on public policy, it is important to appreciate the way the different consultation environments interact.

Consider a major private sector oil company. It decides to mount a major consultation exercise on attitudes to newer, more environmentally friendly fuels. Here we have a piece of customer consultation with considerable implications for public policy (e.g. tax, road usage, pollution). The company would expect a positive spin-off in terms of image and positioning and would hope for participation from a range of stakeholders, one of which will be firm's own employees – probably an unusually well-informed group of people.

Here we have all four of our featured environments – customer, public policy, corporate, employee – in one task. That may be relatively unusual,

---

* The Citizen's Charter was a series of proposals aimed at improving public services in the UK, unveiled by Conservative Prime Minister John Major in 1991. It was particularly designed to help organisations focus on, and improve, their customer service and delivery to users.

† The Charter Mark was awarded to the most successful service-providers under the Citizen's Charter scheme.

but large-scale companies regularly involve themselves concurrently in exercises covering all four different scenarios. They could, of course, find themselves participating, not as a consultor, but as a consultee. They might, therefore, be responding to a Government consultation while simultaneously organising other stakeholder engagement exercises in respect of their customers or employees.

In the UK public sector the combination of all four is found more often. We recently spoke to a local authority which explained how a disproportionately large number of those who participated in consultation exercises were discovered to be its own employees.* Given the new emphasis on council brand image, the corporate consultation element, the impact of Best Value and customer consultation, there is clear evidence of consultation crossing all four environments.

What's interesting about this situation is that the different exercises are often conducted quite separately by different people and often in very different parts of an organisation. So policy staff initiate the public policy debates, HR specialists conduct employee consultation, the corporate PR department looks after CSR and the marketing unit sees to customers. It's all quite logical really, yet in aggregate amounts to something of a nonsense. This is because the stakeholders are frequently the same. From their perspective this is just one hand of the bureaucracy not knowing what the other is doing. Organisations such as those we've discussed in these chapters are not stupid, yet they contrive to talk to their key stakeholders in a pretty unco-ordinated way. This remains one of the big challenges of the consultation culture.

---

*    Interestingly, one of the explanations was the high propensity of teachers to respond.

# 5. THE THREE DRIVERS OF CONSULTATION

In all the consultation activity we have described in the early part of this book we can discern three separate forces at work: we call them the 'drivers of consultation'. They are not mutually exclusive, but they represent different strands of thought – all of which are present to some degree or other.

## DRIVER 1: PARTICIPATION-LED CONSULTATION

This is in vogue. It is best summarised as a sense that the more people become involved, or 'participate', the more satisfied they will be and the more they will identify with the organisation that involves them. Some of this stems from an analysis that attributes such signs of apathy as poor voter turnout, or low satisfaction with public services, to an inherent lack of involvement by citizens in the affairs of Government. If only, the argument goes, we could successfully engage more people, the quality, performance and responsiveness of public bodies would improve. Many a municipal leader, in these days of disappointing electoral turnouts, especially among young people, has lamented the failure to engage more with citizens. So the cry goes out: 'Consult more widely. Involve as many people as possible.'

This participation-led approach leads rapidly to 'consultation by numbers'. Success or failure becomes measured by the absolute numbers of questionnaires returned or people attending meetings or exhibitions. Targets are set, even bonuses paid!

We think this can be damaging. Too much emphasis on quantity at the expense of quality can undermine one of the basic principles of consultation: the understanding of who says what and why they are saying it. The numbers game can also easily become akin to a vote. When Transport for London sought views on a new tramline from west London to the centre of the city, the mass-questionnaire method they used resulted in more than 30,000 responses. High marks for participation then. The trouble, however, is that when combined with the yes/no style of the questions, the resulting statistics began to make the consultation look like a referendum – which it wasn't. Yet, it's a brave organisation that feels confident in overriding the purported 'will of the people'. Never mind that the overall number still constitutes a small percentage of all stakeholders, and that opponents of change have a greater pre-disposition to participate; the resulting answer acquires a status which is difficult to set aside. None of this is to deny the validity of this approach – under certain conditions.

Commercial firms with a low market share and little visibility have quite an incentive to involve as many as possible in their consultations. Being involved certainly makes people aware of the organisation but does not necessarily result in greater satisfaction with its products or services. In fact, we think that the equation *more participation = greater satisfaction* is flawed. Participating in a dialogue might make stakeholders more realistic about the constraints under which the consultor is operating. But it could equally work the other way. Stakeholders might as easily lose sympathy with the organisation. We know that repeatedly asking the same questions, with few discernible improvements since the last consultation, antagonises rather than satisfies stakeholders. True, a consultor that convinces them that it is seriously listening earns 'brownie points'. But it is equally possible that being involved frequently just raises expectations, thus making it even more difficult to fulfil them.

Participation-led consultation has a strong hold on many people, who see it as a cure for apathy. Well-meaning managers of relationships with 'hard-to-reach' groups or disadvantaged communities are often enthusiastic subscribers to this approach. But overall it needs a serious health warning.

## DRIVER 2: DECISION-LED CONSULTATION

This is different, in both style and motivation. It occurs when organisations realise that a significant decision needs to be taken and resolves to talk to those who are likely to be impacted, so that the decision is informed by as much understanding of the consequences as possible.

This has a long tradition. Town planning has always proceeded on the principle that before planning permission is considered those most likely to be affected are provided with the details and given the opportunity to object. Elsewhere the idea of Impact Assessments has taken hold and when legislation is now proposed, the relevant ministry has to prepare a comprehensive statement detailing its estimates of cost and the benefit accruing from what is proposed.

Today, the more organised local authorities publish a forward calendar of decisions to be taken by their Cabinet. On their website they may publish the paper to be tabled so that the decision can be taken, and this may include the results of consultations with key stakeholders. With this type of consultation, note that it is vital for the right stakeholders to be identified. If this doesn't happen, then decision-makers are likely to be proceeding on inadequate information. They also have to decide which decisions warrant this approach. It is neither practical nor desirable for every decision to be preceded by stakeholder consultation. And yet, someone somewhere is affected by almost every decision that is taken. This is where judgement has to be exercised. Knowing when a decision taken without consultation is likely to be better, or more defensible, and where a lack of consultation will lead to objections and complaints is often just a product of experience. But it can also be a highly 'political' judgement – and not always with a small 'p'.

Decision-led consultation can be a very small-scale affair. There might be very few individuals or organisations; sometimes they can be gathered together in a room and consulted *en masse* at one sitting. This means that, in comparison to the participation-led philosophy, there is less need for substantial budgets, big printing runs and high-wide-and-handsome publicity. This is a more focused approach and is often used when organisations favour a more modest consultation programme. 'Consult when we really need to' could be their motto.

## DRIVER 3: CHANGE MANAGEMENT-LED CONSULTATION

This kind of consultation is different again. It is conducted when the purpose of holding a debate is to assist in bringing about successful change. Almost every large organisation today faces enormous structural upheavals and, for this reason, probably sends its managers on expensive change management courses. These managers also read the appropriate books, of which there are dozens. We've read quite a few of these ourselves and have formed the conclusion that they all carry variants of the same rather simple message. It is this. If you impose change upon people, they will resist – but if you consult them meaningfully, change becomes much easier to manage.

Straightforward as this sounds, it is probably more difficult to implement than the previous two drivers. This is because stakeholders can be cynical and are quick to spot the use of consultation as a contrivance just to gain acceptance of something that would otherwise be unpalatable. Genuine change is always a question of pluses and minuses; the trick is to help all concerned see the advantages and to abandon too narrow a focus of 'what's in it for me?'. Approaching customers, employees or other stakeholders with a half-baked story and arousing suspicions that the real decisions have already been taken is hardly going to impress them – and will almost certainly give rise to even more hostility.

Maybe it's a question of timing. Initiating a genuine debate early enough, before managements or councils have formulated their plans, can give those likely to be affected a real sense of shared ownership in a problem. Facts may be unpalatable, the news may be bad, but there is evidence that a policy of candour and a sincerity of purpose can instil trust in stakeholder organisations.

Intelligent people can often work out answers for themselves and don't take kindly to a 'going through the motions' consultation that simply pretends to listen. If the debate commences too late, they will feel out-manoeuvred with little or no opportunity to offer suggestions that can make an iota of difference.

This type of consultation requires remarkable skill, particularly in defining the problem and in anticipating the knock-on effects of other organisations' plans and programmes. In many ways, of course, this is precisely the reason why such consultation is valuable. The chances are that some of your stakeholders will have a better insight into consequential changes than you have. We're talking here of the complexities that arise when several organisations which impinge upon each other all embark upon change at roughly the same time, but without a full appreciation of what each is intending. It often falls to the informed stakeholder to point out the synergies (if you're lucky) or the difficulties (if you are less fortunate) that are likely in consequence.

The public sector is full of such inter-relationships. Even in the private sector, proposed changes by one company may result in unintended consequences, because that company has only a partial view of the market and of what is intended by other players. In fact, it's often the customers that can best see the picture as a whole.

Undertaken carefully, consultation with change in mind carries strong 'educational' overtones and frequently appears with glossy overlays of PR and spin. No wonder it is vulnerable to a degree of cynicism. But it can also appear as an iterative sequence, as stakeholders are gradually exposed to the full extent of the challenges and the level of the response that may be required. Look at some of the more ambitious urban regeneration schemes and note how it is often impossible to consult over the full vision for these parts of our major cities – no-one has that clear a picture at the outset; it evolves over time. Hence the sequence of consultations. It is little wonder that groups opposing major change to their commitments feel 'bounced' by the process.

## CONCLUSIONS

These three drivers represent in a crude way three different philosophies of consultation and whereas elements of all three will often be found in one organisation, we find that, in most cases, one or another stands out. In our training courses we've invited hundreds of local government officers and other staff from public bodies to select which one of these predominates. The results have been fascinating and provide no correlation whatever with the type of public body from which they came. Instead, they seem to be more a function of the political leadership style of a chief executive.

There are municipal leaders or influential senior managers who believe strongly in the participation-led approach and who will sanction the promotional and publishing budgets necessary to succeed with this approach. But the alternatives require a different kind of investment. Decision-led consultation has an emphasis on process and needs excellent stakeholder information systems. The change management variant is demanding in terms of face-to-face meetings and partnership working, and it can last longer.

Leaving aside the different investments required, it is really a question of philosophy, and in our view organisations adopt consultation strategies with insufficient thought about the basic approach they wish to follow.

# 6. IMPLICATIONS OF THE CONSULTATION CULTURE

If the consultation culture is as we've described, so what? There may be a load of activity going on out there, but what does it accomplish? Does it make any difference?

As with many things in life, the answer is quite complicated. As we explain later, some consultations have more impact than others. But here we focus on the changes that have come about simply through the prevalence of the consultation culture itself. Below we examine five distinct consequences that have become visible to date.

## CONSULTATION SKILLS ARE BECOMING A CORE COMPETENCE

The world's top companies have always been pretty good at listening – unless of course they've invented the best-ever mousetrap and have enough of a monopoly to ignore everyone and just make money. If they are to survive over the longer term and re-invent themselves with new generations of products and services, they have to be adept at customer consultation. The question is whether this is something they can sub-contract or outsource, or whether they need to nurture the skills and knowledge themselves and retain them in house. Every company has this 'make-or-buy' equation and the answer obviously differs according to its size, its markets and its overall philosophy. Buying market research is, in principle, easy; a hundred consultancies will knock on your door claiming they can do it. Buying consultation skills is a bit more difficult – partly because most of those hundred will claim they can also do consultation. The case for doing most, if not all, of it yourself is that stakeholders are pretty savvy and will not be slow in telling you they're fed up with talking to the monkey when they really want a dialogue with the organ-grinder. . .

In the final analysis, companies have to reflect where future added value is to be found. It is quite possible that whereas having an efficient factory was the key in the nineteenth century, and having effective logistics and distribution operations was critical in the twentieth, the most important core competence of all in the coming years will be the ability to listen and to convert what they hear into business opportunities.

The public sector is also changing; nowhere is this better illustrated than in local government. Until recently, councils were first and foremost massive service delivery operations; various estimates put the number of separate services at up to 600. But this has changed. The Government's 'choice' agenda and the push towards using the voluntary and community sector mean that authorities are becoming 'commissioners' of services rather than the automatic and monopoly deliverers of them.

The new language is of 'community leadership' and 'place-shaping'. The new role for councils is to bring together all the requirements of a particular area and to co-ordinate the delivery of appropriate public services, regardless of who actually provides them. Using Local Strategic Partnerships and other mechanisms, the council of the future exercises a leadership role, working alongside the NHS, the police, the probation service and of course voluntary bodies.

If this vision of the future of local government holds, and not everyone agrees with it, then the implications are clear. What councils have to focus upon is an understanding of their citizen population and the stakeholder bodies that represent them. With the Audit Commission poised for a radical new approach, this cannot any longer be a superficial scan of generalised requirements. It needs to be comprehensive and precise. It needs the full range of consultation and public participation skills which this book describes. No longer can they be optional extras; they become an essential core competence. And exactly the same applies to central government departments and their agencies.

## THE DEMISE OF AUTHORITARIANISM

The consultation culture is just one aspect of a wider movement towards more inclusive decision-making. All three sectors have discovered from experience that it is easier to make progress when actions and proposals have a sufficient weight of agreement behind them.

Yet many organisations have traditionally relied upon strong, macho managers to establish what to do and to decide how to do it. In some cultures, including the USA, a domineering larger-than-life autocrat is still much admired. Equally, in some situations, such as in the armed forces, or in a crisis, most people accept the necessity for swift, decisive leadership. In most cases, however, such a style of leadership is seen to hold too many disadvantages. It relies for success upon a combination of carrots and sticks, with fear of punishment often more visible than the promise of rewards. Employees and stakeholders are expected to follow the leader without question and this stifles their own potential and personal growth. Denying them a say in key decisions that affect them and their work also cannot fail to undermine their commitment to the enterprise. In its favour, at least autocratic leadership can be said to be quick!

A more democratic style has to be slower. The leader who consults his or her colleagues somehow has to factor in the time required to gather this information and weigh it up and it won't necessarily always result in better decisions. Indeed, a consensual approach can militate against bold and imaginative actions and is quite likely to result in a 'lowest common denominator' position.

Clearly the trend is away from the autocratic approach, but which is cause and which is effect? Are we experiencing the rise of the consultation culture because pragmatic managers have found that it is best to consult widely before taking decisions? Or has the expectation of being consulted made the traditional autocrat less and less acceptable to people? Is it possible, perhaps, that we have arrived at a position where good people simply won't put up with being excluded from debate and just won't work for a manager who behaves in such a way? Will talent drain away from organisations that aren't consensual?

At a more detailed level, autocratic leadership styles survive in a form of knowing arrogance, whereby the decision-maker makes a choice and then retrospectively seeks to justify it through a sham consultation. 'You agree with me on this, don't you?' The bad news for such manipulators is that stakeholders, employees and, increasingly, the general public are becoming better at detecting these situations and will openly say so.

This trend transcends all sectors. The last bastions of autocratic leadership will probably be small and medium-sized private companies, answerable only to the main shareholder – who is the boss anyway; curiously, this also applies to some elements of the voluntary and community sector, where charismatic leader-campaigners can still be found. Elsewhere, the sheer complexity and inter-dependence of large corporates or public bodies makes top-down authoritarian management less and less viable. Public accountability in the government sector provides checks and balances against a dominant leader; in the wake of tighter governance in the commercial sector the same forces are now at work here too.

## CONSENSUS BECOMES THE HOLY GRAIL

Abandoning the authoritarian approach does not of itself create a benign democracy. There is a wide spectrum of models between the two extremes; in all discussion on this topic, the word 'consensus' appears over and over. It is based upon a fond belief that if this happy state exists, unpleasant controversy disappears, all becomes sweetness and light and problems evaporate. . .

This Elysian aspiration can be found in surprising places. It is mostly associated with the caricature of left-leaning trendies who are perceived as possessing a touching if naïve faith that every problem can be solved if only the parties get together and hammer out an amicable compromise – in other words the Churchillian dictum 'to jaw-jaw is always better than to war-war'.

Enthusiasts rightly point out that consensus is not the same as unanimity. With consensus, people can retain the integrity of a different viewpoint while agreeing with a majority, because they see the value of moving forward with a common position. A good chairman cultivates the skill of listening to a range of opinions, then distilling from them where there is sufficient common ground to build a general consensus.

Those with more extreme ideas are asked to elaborate upon their arguments, are politely challenged, and, in effect, given the opportunity to persuade their colleagues. Firm and skilful facilitation of such discussion is the stuff of consensus-building and is the hallmark of effective teams, whether in private industry, public service or the third sector.

It is now even enshrined in an Act of Parliament. The 2004 Planning and Compulsory Purchase Act obliges every council to prepare what is known as a Statement of Community Involvement, explaining how the public, statutory and other stakeholders should participate in planning matters. Quite rightly, the emphasis is on early involvement; it's an attempt to move away from the tradition of bureaucratic planners doing their homework behind closed doors and presenting hapless councillors with a range of equally unpalatable options. It's a determined effort to change the culture of planning departments and to seek consensus. Why did it happen?

Basically, what worried MPs was their immense postbag of complaints about the planning system. House-builders and industrialists complained about the delays in getting permission to build; householders and otherwise law-abiding citizens recounted their frustration getting planning permission; environmental lobby groups and conservation junkies protested at any encroachment of land they thought valuable. Planners themselves weren't happy. Some started to mutter under their breath about the 'BANANA' culture. We discovered that this stood for 'Build Absolutely Nothing Anywhere Near Anyone'! In practice, what happened was that almost everything went to appeal, with planning inspectors and Government departments far more likely to respond to the needs of the economy as a whole, overruling communities who quite liked their village as it was, thank you very much.

A bout of head-scratching in Whitehall culminated in a conclusion that up-front consensus would speed up this tortuous, expensive back end to the process. 'If only the parties could sit down together earlier', before plans became set in concrete, then there was a chance that mistakes would be fewer and that there wouldn't be as many us-and-them disputes. It was a bold move; it recognised that the old regime of 'DAD' (Decide, Announce, Defend) was a real weakness, and it had almost universal political and administrative support. The Royal Town Planning Institute and other professionals, having endured popular opprobrium for years, saw this as a way to reinvent planning as a more voter-friendly and modern art. The search for the Holy Grail – by legislation!

Unfortunately, in this story of noble endeavour, there were some party-poopers. Older town planners shook their experienced heads. They reflected that the use of land still stirred up the most primeval of human instincts and what they faced, had always faced and would always face were genuine conflicts of interest. Society has to find ways to determine between the interest of the out-of-town supermarket operator and the high-street grocer; between the mobile phone mast erector and the near neighbour worried about health risks; between young key workers needing affordable housing and the villagers who don't want further development. The old-school planners argue that no amount of new-age consensus-building will resolve such fundamental conflicts. Their more optimistic counterparts insist that there is ample scope for compromise – but only if stakeholders are engaged before positions have become entrenched.

Our view is that requiring a period of participation followed by a formal consultation period should ensure that new-style Local Development Plans have a greater chance of commanding general community support than their predecessors. But anyone who thinks that they will bring an end to the adversarial element of many planning issues is either a fool or cocooned in the cloisters of Westminster.

This digression into the world of town planners serves as an illustration of a wider truth – for we believe it has many parallels in other fields. The days of individualistic, idiosyncratic, opinionated mavericks have given way to those who reflect a more consensual approach. It has happened in politics and can also be seen in the arts, in medicine, the law and much else. Many will mourn their passing, for their activities make for an unpredictable and interesting life. Jeffrey Archer was always more newsworthy than Douglas Hurd! The media finds a safe pair of hands quite boring.

Despite this, consensus is now clearly the preferred model and arguably it only becomes possible in the context of the consultation culture. You can only reach for consensus if you listen and also if you respect and make an attempt to understand different viewpoints. The best dialogues will tease out of impenetrable complexities the most significant sticking points that reflect different stakeholders' fundamental values, beliefs and interests. In short, you can have consultation without achieving consensus; but if you reach consensus without consultation, you've had a happy accident.

## TENSION BETWEEN REPRESENTATIVE DEMOCRACY AND CONSULTATIVE DEMOCRACY

One consequence of the consultation culture has been to throw a particular issue into sharp focus. Although most visible in the political sphere, it has parallels wherever decision-makers with their own legitimacy are bemused and often wrongfooted by the current craze for consultation. So it can apply to the boardroom as well as to the council chamber.

Here we delve into the psychology of decision-making and especially the confidence and credibility which people need to demonstrate if others are to sustain and hold respect for their decisions. In the academic and scientific worlds, peer-group reviews, publication in reputable journals, participation in expert panels and an elaborate structure of recognition symbols all combine to support the credibility of those with significant powers. Political accountability is different. Members of Parliament or local councillors owe their power to an election; unlike the university professor whose reputation and knowledge is undiminished the day after her retirement, the defeated politician loses all legitimacy the morning after the poll. The nature of representative democracy concentrates on direct accountability and in our first-past-the-post system focuses on the relationship between the elected member and his or her constituency.

Imagine therefore the reaction of a councillor who has represented the 3,000-odd residents of her ward for a quarter of a century, when told by council officials that this time around, a decision upon which she has voted for years should now be deferred until a public consultation is first organised. Happily there are politicians who welcome the development. They will say to themselves that it is a jolly good thing to find out precisely what local people think about a particular issue – especially as only a third of them turned up to vote at the local elections and even among the civic minded the issue in question did not feature in the doorstep conversations during pre-election canvassing.

However, there will be others who see consultation as a monstrous restriction placed upon their decision-making. It is more than that – it is an affront to their legitimacy and implies that they cannot be trusted to represent the will of their constituents. A politician who has been repeatedly re-elected usually believes that that regular endorsement confirms that he or she is in tune with the mood of the area and most would claim that this extends beyond the majority will. They contend that a long-term association with any constituency brings them close to all sections of the community, regardless of whether they vote. Hence the convention that a Member of Parliament will work assiduously for local interests, even those most closely associated with political opponents – a characteristic of the British system which is seldom found elsewhere.

At first glance, therefore, consultation can appear to cut across the idea that, having been elected, representatives are there to take decisions on behalf of their constituents. We can see how defensive this can make some of them. Here they are, elected and legitimate, straining at the leash and wanting to get on and implement policies for which they believe they have a mandate and suddenly someone says: 'Hang on, first we have to go to consultation.' Damn it, it's a conspiracy!

On occasion that's quite an accurate view. When Parliament decreed that every local authority should consult its electorate before setting the annual council tax, the real agenda was to curb free-spending authorities alongside rate-capping. Likewise, the requirement to consult council tenants before their homes were transferred from municipal ownership is a Government-inspired move to stop over-enthusiastic councils from riding roughshod over the views of the principal stakeholders. Indeed, the recent practice of inserting into legislation the requirement to consult is a double-edged sword. On the one hand it circumscribes the discretion of decision-makers ('We may have been elected but we can't be trusted to decide without first listening to people. . .') but on the other hand it institutionalises the dialogue.

Or so it would seem. The danger, of course, is that the resentment which the elected or appointed feel at this constraint upon their power creates a 'tick the box' attitude. We think this becomes 'consultation because we've been told to do it' – instead of 'consultation because we need to know the answer to a question'. The result is often half-hearted and poorly executed dialogues, as we shall see in Part Two.

Right now, representative democracy faces many challenges; a cursory reading of the Power Commission report should convince anyone who doubts this. Consultation is, in fact, one of the few things that can be of real help. Taking difficult decisions, as, for example, in the field of town planning discussed above, becomes easier if an effective consultation has formed part of the process. Given the choice, consider which of these is easier for local councillor: 'We took the decision to site the waste incinerator at the bottom of your street, because, as elected politicians, we have to take tough decisions' or 'We've consulted all those who are going to be affected, and having considered all the interests and the arguments, on balance we've decided. . .'

Consultative democracy is rarely more palatable to those who suffer a decision they dislike than the representative variety! For the rest of the community it provides a benchmark for decisions and an admittedly imperfect reference point for awkward or difficult choices. Smart politicians, if they can overcome their initial scepticism about consultation, realise that the key to success is to be very selective as to when and when not to go down this route.

Every legislature, every parliament, every council has to resolve the tension in its own way; there is no universal template. Proportional representation can sometimes help, for the lack of (or weaker) constituency accountability might make it easier for elected members to take the role of objective seekers of evidence rather than supine lobby-fodder. On the other hand, in the additional member model used in Wales and Scotland, the allegiance of politicians to the party machine may induce them to rely on consultation primarily when party interests are best served.

If consultation is used as a tactical manoeuvre, it quickly loses credibility. In a contested council, for one party to seek consultation as a way of slowing down or preventing a policy they dislike (the phrase 'kicking into the long grass' springs to mind) is as damaging as for another to seek to stimulate populist support for something unpalatable by a PR campaign masquerading as a consultation. In both cases, it is a misuse of the process and quickly brings the idea of a genuine dialogue into disrepute.

This is why elected members need to resolve the tensions they experience in their role without further delay. As the consultation culture becomes even more entrenched, they will find that playing politics crudely will simply alienate the electorate and weaken their legitimacy even further. Having a sensible, balanced and strategic approach to the task of listening to the public and to stakeholder organisations will enhance their reputations; it may also make them humbler, but perhaps more successful, politicians.

## CONSULTATION FATIGUE

Finally, there is the phenomenon of consultation fatigue.

We've met some seasoned policy-makers whose attitude has a 'serves them right' flavour about it. Another way to describe it would be to reach for the well-known dictum 'Be careful what you wish for, in case it comes true'. In both cases the inference is that many of those who complain of consultation fatigue are among the loudest voices demanding to be consulted. When consultors experience difficulty persuading stakeholder organisations to participate in an exercise, it is remarkable how well they can remember, and how frequently they remind consultees that they were the ones who asked for the consultation in the first place.

'Fatigue' is perhaps not the best word to describe what is happening. It is not that people are too tired to respond, although that does probably happen on occasion. More likely, organisations are either fed up with too many requests for their time and contribution, or they may lack the resources to do justice to such requests.

As far as the general public is concerned, there is little evidence of fatigue. True, everyone we know has an anecdote or three about being rung up by anonymous call centres and invited to take part in a telephone survey – 'When did you last replace your windows, Mrs Jones?' But this is far from consultation; it's pretty far from market research as well and is quite close to the worst kind of high-pressure sales techniques. No doubt there is also a growing sense of exasperation with the endless stream of questionnaires that clutter our doormats. But the real thing – the kind of 'consultation fatigue' that turns otherwise sane managers into semi-coherent mumblers – is quite different. It's a combination of too much, too often and too likely to be ignored!

Let's break this down. Obviously the sheer number of exercises can cause problems for organisations with limited resources. The voluntary and community sector is particularly vulnerable here and is of course among the most vocal of those who demanded them. This also applies to statutory bodies, even those whose role in life is to advise others who need their inputs. Natural England (previously English Nature), for example, responds to hundreds of consultations per year; the Environment Agency to many thousands. The average town or community council is approached dozens of times every year and we estimate that a large English county council receives more than twenty consultations per month.

Larger bureaucracies of course have specialist staff on hand and can delegate at will. They still need to devote resources to chasing up and researching their responses and to co-ordinate their activities between departments or with partner organisations. As the number of consultations to which they respond rises, the job becomes harder, for overlaps and knock-on implications suddenly emerge. 'Hang on! If we say this to that Government department, we can't say that to the Environment Agency. . .'

In other words, it is not just an arithmetical formula, like twenty consultations each involving an average of six person-days of effort. The complexity involved probably doubles the effort required and makes it more like a logarithmic scale. Imagine twenty policy officers each writing their own responses, but having to check that they are not compromising one another's positions all the time. So when it comes to giving opinions on difficult issues, stakeholder organisations face a double whammy. One is the sheer weight of numbers; the second is that complexity drives them to spend more time on each one.

In reality, of course, there is only so much available resource. So people cut corners. You remember something you wrote in a previous, almost similar consultation two years ago and adapt it for your response this time round, adding that long passage from your annual report. To make it look even more comprehensive you can illustrate your point with that case study from the fund-raising pages of your website. With these short cuts you can offer a near-instant response. It's marvellous what you can do with 'cut and paste'!

Ironically, the consultor has been doing the same thing. The consultation paper itself was cobbled together from its antecedents; the questions were an amendment of someone else's and all the process pages are standard templates anyway.

The result is a not-too-sophisticated game of bluff. A major company or public body *pretends* to have gone to great trouble to organise a distinctive and original consultation and consultees *pretend* to have prepared an original and thought-provoking answer. Both sides of the dialogue know it. Football commentators complain that the standard of the game suffers because our best players are playing too often. Similarly the standard of public dialogue may be suffering because there is too much of it.

But fatigue is not just a question of scale; there is also an issue of relevance. For reasons we elaborate upon later, too many organisations maintain very crude, out-of-date lists of people they think might be interested in various subjects. They inevitably often get them wrong. So, if it is disheartening for a small charity to see yet another unexpected consultation arrive, it is even more irritating to find that it is not remotely relevant. Even worse, many organisations equate a propensity to consult with an unwillingness to listen. They see those who ask the loudest being least willing to act upon what they hear. After all, we all respond better to companies or bodies who, last time around, appeared genuinely eager to understand what we were saying. Nothing promotes consultation fatigue more than realising that the current batch of questions bear more than a passing resemblance to what was asked before, when our views went unheeded. If a dialogue is to succeed and if people are to be motivated to take part, there must be a sense that it is going somewhere.

A variant of consultation fatigue which we've come across is 'consultation sclerosis'. It was christened by Mark Durkan, leader of Northern Ireland's Social Democratic and Labour Party, who was exasperated with a long stream of endless Government consultations that gave the appearance of avoiding decisions, perpetuating a continuous dialogue without any discernible endgame. Durkan's image of the arteries of dialogue being increasingly congested – to the point of reducing the flow of blood to the rest of the body politic – is a powerful one.

Clearly one of the biggest implications of the consultation culture is the danger of having too much of a good thing and clogging up organisations' essential bloodstream with processes which consume resources. It has a debilitating effect; the resulting fatigue reflects the weight of such processes. This is one of the most urgent problems to fix if the undoubted benefits of improved public and stakeholder participation are not to be squandered.

# PART TWO
# WHAT GOES WRONG?

# 7. A MATTER OF HONOUR

## WELL-FOUNDED SCEPTICISM

The first thing to say is that things don't always go wrong! Patient readers will reach Part Three, which is entitled 'What Goes Right?'. But it has to be admitted that enough mistakes are made and the scepticism of many is so well founded that we have no choice but to confront the weaknesses of consultation head on.

We do so with positive intent. This is not a negative critique – it is intended to be constructive. The good news is that most of the problems are fixable, though some are, admittedly, easier than others.

In this chapter, we probe those aspects which touch upon the intentions of the consultors, and the way in which they approach their task. Later chapters will describe what goes awry in the operational side of consultations, but, strangely enough, it is easier to forgive technical failures than to excuse the more blatant abuses of process that we consider first.

In the British House of Commons, by long-standing tradition, everyone is either an 'Honourable Gentleman' or an 'Honourable Lady'. By analogy, everyone who organises a consultation is 'honourable' and it is not our intention to impugn the personal integrity of any politician, civil servant, chief executive or quango in the pages that follow. Indeed we doubt if on more than a handful of occasions a consultor has deliberately set out to run a bogus consultation. So dishonesty may be a strong allegation to make. It is a term we will avoid.

Yet thousands of stakeholders wouldn't think twice about using it. In fact their language would be much more colourful. So what is it that leads many otherwise reasonable, public-spirited consultees to see consultors as double-crossing rogues and scoundrels hell-bent on lying and cheating their way to a new policy? It is not just the pique of losing the case – for these sentiments are often shared by those who win the argument as well as those who are disappointed. What seems to be under fire is the integrity of the process. Personal abuse of the head honcho seems to be an optional extra, albeit a popular one.

We think that there are three things going on here. There is a confusion of objectives; there are suspicions that the decision has already been taken; and there is a lack of coherence in the consultation programme.

## CONFUSED OBJECTIVES

The versatility that makes consultation so popular is also the root cause of so many of its difficulties. One local authority we know listed fifteen reasons for undertaking a public consultation, all perfectly valid. Some are obvious, such as the need to find out what people think about a particular proposal; others are more obscure. The local authority talks about achieving a better-informed citizenry, no doubt in the hope of revitalising local democracy – a widely held aspiration.

We struggled a little more with this one, though: 'Promoting sustainability in improving existing services and introducing new ones'. At first glance we dismissed it as a bit of bureaucratic gobbledegook, probably entered into a competition to see how many in-words could be gathered together to secure brownie points from the Audit Commission. But when we read it through for perhaps the fifth time we realised that maybe the authority has a point. If you consult people well enough to find out what matters most to them, you may be able to reduce a lot of what's less important, thereby consuming fewer resources, eliminating waste, and bringing about a more sustainable community!

Now that's a rather subtle, even convoluted, train of thought. If, for the sake of argument, we accept it at face value it poses the consultor a communications problem. There are very few politicians or chief executives who are clever enough to say, in effect: 'We're going to consult you about your service needs in the hope we can identify things you no longer want.' That gives a negative message and every media advisor tells you to stress the positive. This example shows how easy it is to dream up a logical rationale for a consultation and yet find it necessary to 'spin' it somewhat differently. Combined with the proliferation of objectives, this causes confusion in the minds of both consultor and consultee.

In reality, the problem is even worse because of the use of loose language. It is not just that words such as 'involvement', 'engagement' and 'participation' are vague, but they have a natural tendency to mean something different to the speaker than the audience. When campaigning groups hear the words 'We're going to involve you fully in moving forward with this issue', what they think they're being told is 'We won't go ahead with something if you disagree'.

Classic confusions of expectation like this happen all the time. Friendly-sounding words used to promote greater participation often generate huge disillusionment later in the process.

## DECISION ALREADY TAKEN

Asking people their views when you've already decided what you're going to do is pointless. In the words of the cliché, you are shutting the stable door after the horse has bolted.

Had someone told the consultees the truth, their energies could have been directed elsewhere, but the deception was such that they were misled into undertaking an avoidable task. Afterwards, no doubt, the recriminations arrive. Was that particular horse worth it in the first place? Had the consultors known for certain that the horse was in the stable – were they really the most appropriate people to close that door? Should others have been asked? And so on.

This is a metaphor for all those occasions where consultees have woken up late to the reality that although they were asked their opinion, nothing they said could have had an impact – for the decision had already been taken. Imagine, therefore, how infuriating it must be if, half-way through the thankless task, you realise the consultation is actually a *fait accompli*. Your instinct is to down tools and leave the job. Then an emollient supervisor oozes forward with a mission to placate, saying how bad it would look if you didn't finish what you had started, how much it does for your 'credibility', and how you can be assured of preferential treatment the next round. . . honest!

Even more stakeholders will recognise that one. They enter into a dialogue in good faith, only to learn along the way that things aren't quite what they thought. Consider the company that enters into talks with trades unions denying fervently that it has decided to relocate to another country; then news filters though that it has already leased a new factory and started to fit it out with fixtures identical to the current plant. Or take the sales force that swears to its customer base that its products are 100 per cent safe, only later for it to be discovered that medical evidence in its possession indicates otherwise. The tobacco industry springs to mind.

Learning that decisions have already been taken half-way though a consultation exercise is something many consultees have experienced. Sometimes what happens is that events intervene. Because lead-times can sometimes be lengthy, it is perfectly possible for the decision to consult to have been taken many months earlier, with an intention to wait until the process was complete before taking the substantive decision. Then something happens. In the private sector it could be a major competitive announcement; in public policy-making it is more likely to be the interplay of party politics or the news agenda. When Harold Wilson said that 'a week is a long time in politics', he was rightly attesting to the unpredictability of his profession.

Policy-makers in public service realise that the inherent inter-dependence of one policy on another and the non-linear timescales for their evolution and implementation frequently disrupt the planned sequence of events. This can make Government departments look silly or, more generously, just unco-ordinated. A more culpable situation occurs when, in the enthusiasm of involving people at all costs, a consultation is framed so widely as to invite contributions on matters that were not intended. When the Labour Party launched its Big Conversation in November 2003 it did so by publishing a document so wide in scope that scarcely any aspect of public policy was omitted.[*] The

---

[*]    The Labour Party still speaks fondly of its Big Conversation; see http://www.labour.org.uk/
Improving_Partnership_in_Power.

result was predictable. Students, incensed by the policy of top-up fees, responded in their thousands.

Now in that particular case, purists could point to the distinction between the Labour Party and the Labour Government and in theory it can be argued that there was an opportunity to change party policy even if the Government's mind was made up. In practice, however, many thought it was a Government consultation anyway and relatively few young people could have expected that their voices would cut much ice with ministers.

What happened here is that a broadly defined consultation strayed into areas of limited or zero discretion. To the layman, it just looked as if the consultor was oblivious to or dismissive of the time and effort of the consultee, who could have justifiably commented: 'If you've already made up your mind, why bother to ask me?'

On occasions, there may be a defence to this charge. Ministers, councillors, or any other decision-makers can claim not to be beyond being influenced by the debate itself. They may become persuaded during the course of the consultation. It is singularly maladroit for decision-makers to express their views too early. While damage is limited if you are one of a large committee whose collective deliberation is yet to come, it sounds rather more conclusive when the boss speaks out.

When Jack McConnell, as First Minister of Scotland, came out in favour of banning smoking in public places while a public consultation was still in progress, the tobacco lobby and the landlords of smoker-friendly pubs all cried foul. Similar objections were raised when Tony Blair declared that civil nuclear power should be put back on the agenda. True, the 2006 Energy Review consultation had, on this occasion, closed, and civil servants were no doubt hard at work analysing the 5,338 written responses. But this premature statement was interpreted rightly or wrongly as an indication that Blair's opinion had been formed much earlier and had not emerged as a result of the debate itself. In short, the decision had already been taken.

The honourable thing to do, if decisions are taken mid-consultation, is to call off the exercise and stand everyone down. But public bodies find it difficult to take such seemingly obvious courses of action. For one thing, they will be greeted with cries of 'What's the hurry?' and 'Can't you wait a few more weeks?' For another, the usual pre-eminence of process means that, once embarked upon, there is usually neither precedent nor facility for a *volte-face*. It is much easier to proceed as if nothing had happened. A policy of candour would be much better.

A consultor who knows the answer to the question may be tempted to indulge in other forms of deception. A favourite one is to invent a whole range of plausible but ultimately unviable options and place them alongside the preferred policy. These make-weight options are often more trouble than they are worth.

Some years ago, the Government reopened the debate about the location of additional airport capacity in the south-east of England: out of the blue emerged a hitherto unconsidered option for Cliffe, in Kent. Such was the evident lack of homework that preceded its inclusion in the consultation that it needed the RSPB to point out that an airport there would have devastated not only Cliffe Pools, but four special protection areas in the Thames, Medway and Swale area affecting some 200,000 migrant and wintering water birds. A massive 'No Airport @ Cliffe' campaign brought conservation and communities into a powerful partnership and saw 150,000 protest postcards delivered to the UK Government; the airport plans were finally defeated in February 2005 and the option vanished from the agenda.

Stakeholders waste a lot of time pursuing red herrings like this. Seasoned lobbyists and professional interest groups can instantly detect when there is a front-runner option. Provided that minds are not closed, that other alternatives are truly viable and will be considered on their merits, there is no great difficulty in having a 'preferred option'. The trouble is that organisations rarely come clean. Instead they bias the consultation narrative towards their favoured outcome. Selective choice of statistics, a partial account of the background context or a misleading Impact Assessment are but some of the methods that can be used by an unscrupulous consultor.

Of course they're not always unscrupulous. Public bodies often find themselves bound by statute to consult when they think there is no real alternative to their chosen course of action. They must tick the box called 'consultation'. So they go ahead. They're not really listening and in such cases, Parliament's intention of forcing managements to respond to public pressure is frustrated. No wonder we hear cries of a sham consultation, for the mind has been made up, and the exercise has no influence on the outcome.

## COHERENCE

Accusations of dishonour come about for a third reason. Some organisations acquire a reputation for honesty and transparency. Their policy-making process appears open; their willingness to listen is well proven and they have a track record of previous participative exercises that have generally satisfied those involved. But others fail to achieve this status. They are viewed with suspicion by those who are affected by their decisions. When those bodies utter the word 'consultation', the first reaction is to ask: 'Where's the catch?'

Here we discuss the way in which a consultor determines when and whether to consult. Is it a matter of expediency – or of consistent policy?

Consultors define themselves according to the coherence of their public participation strategies. Some have clearly determined where they will and where they will not seek stakeholder opinions. In the absence of such thinking consultations appear as if by random. One of the most frequent signs of such behaviour is when a consultation is confused with information-giving. The scenario goes something like this. The consultor determines a new policy, or a new initiative, and is hell-bent on telling all those who may be interested. This information-giving is then embellished with issues upon which views are welcome. Yet the main thrust of the exercise is decidedly one way. No-one admits that the consultation is cosmetic; if anyone did, the consultor would have a reasonable enough case. On one or two occasions, it will get away with it. When there is a pattern of such exercises, however, questions are asked and the stakeholder community starts to mutter phrases like 'going through the motions'.

To convince the sceptics, consultor organisations these days need to deliver up front a programme of public involvement that makes sense overall. When they don't, it stands out a mile, looking like a sequence of largely unrelated consultations. A coherent programme makes sense as a whole. So when a standards body such as the Health & Safety Executive embarks upon a long-term commitment to update a large number of regulations and systematically implements a consistent process to collate and consider the views of specialist industry experts, its consultations acquire credibility by virtue of their context.

In consultation, context is everything. What goes wrong too often is that the wider background fails to support the participative initiative in question. Consultors frequently forget that the stakeholder memory is often superior. If a trade body visits a Government department, for example, it is something of a special occasion and one can be sure that the delegation will remember the meeting well. Every word spoken by the minister or senior civil servants will be etched in the consultees' memory. Yet officials hold hundreds of such meetings and therefore rely upon their notes to recall who said what to whom. Note also that staff frequently move posts in our bureaucracies – the voluntary and community sector, on the other hand, is full of single-employer 'believers' who have made their cause their life's work. The context in which civil servants often come to grief is a failure to appreciate what happened last time. New faces in key positions rarely check the history, yet the stakeholder base knows the past without recourse to files.

Consultation that is obviously piecemeal can lead to absurd results and is akin to asking people to pass comment on a tiny fragment of an incomplete jigsaw. At its worst, it can include simplistic questions about money and resources. Should we invest more in preventative healthcare? Do we buy more snow-ploughs? Of course, there are techniques for finding out where people think the extra funds should be taken from. When taken out of context, though, many questions yield a different answer from that which would be forthcoming if they were presented in a wider picture.

Nowhere is this better illustrated than in the evident troubles of the National Health Service as it seeks to implement changes to long-standing ways of delivering services. By law* it is bound to consult local

---

\*    Section 242 of the 2006 NHS Act.

people on significant service changes – an onerous obligation which private companies would avoid like the plague.

Three things make this a difficult task. The first is the intense loyalty of NHS 'customers' to their local institutions. Buried somewhere deep in the psyche of a nation that created the NHS in the post-war rebuilding process, and based upon even earlier allegiances to local hospitals and clinics, is a reverence for old bricks and mortar – almost irrespective of the quality of care being delivered. Any threat to long-established facilities arouses considerable opposition and past weak managements may have persevered with unsustainable sites just for a quiet life – adding to the problem that now needs to be addressed.

The second difficulty is that 'services reconfiguration' (as the jargon has christened the latest rounds of modernisation) is itself controversial. Clinicians disagree and critics of the medical professions are quick to point out that medical politics frequently cloud the issues. 'Are these doctors opposing change because of its potential disruption to their own working lives or because of the advantages or disadvantages to their patients?'

Thirdly, a succession of administrative revamps has completely confused the public and made day-to-day management of an already problematic public service much worse. When a management team is still on the learning curve from being appointed and cannot see beyond the next already looming reorganisation, it is really challenging to focus on the medium and long term, where careful decisions informed by consultation have to be taken. Community opinion-leaders, the very people whose help is needed to carry local opinion with significant change, are unsure who is really calling the shots. Is it the primary care trust? Is it the strategic health authority? Is it the Department of Health? One thing has become clear, though. If an NHS trust convenes a public meeting to consult on service changes, those running the meeting are rarely in a position to take the key decisions. No wonder people have become upset.

The trouble here – and in many other public services – goes beyond these issues and is to do with the overall coherence of forward planning. Few NHS services can be looked at in isolation. Primary care and hospital services are inextricably linked; local services have a dependency on core centralised facilities, or on out-of-area support services. Then there is the linkage with local authority-delivered social care provision. So if a consultation is attempted on one facet of a complicated scenario, it can easily be dumbed down into a crude yes/no question, for example 'Should the heart (or stroke or kidney) unit at Bottlesham-on-Sea be closed, or should it remain open?'

This is not just a health service problem. We recently came across a vigorous campaign to 'Save Our Fire Station'. There are innumerable protest movements to save post offices, bus services, libraries, swimming pools and so on. Then, as we noted earlier, there will be equally organised attempts to stop the erection of locally unpopular facilities or infrastructure.

Let's not blame residents for 'nimbyism'; we know that there has to be a threshold of relevance before the great British public stirs itself. The point being made here is that if you approach people in a piecemeal way and ask them to form a view on single projects or single initiatives, rather than on the totality of the plan, they will naturally respond instinctively and routinely reject progressive change.

At this point, consultors will naturally claim that there may have been a consultation on the wider picture, but no-one took a blind bit of notice. Look at such consultations, however, and they emerge as dense, bureaucratic tomes rightly avoided by all but those whose job it was to respond. No doubt it is a challenge to present complicated long-term plans so that everyone can understand them and feel a desire to contribute to a dialogue. But, make no mistake, a failure to engage people in this wider picture can make it look as if the whole process is piecemeal. Hence the reality that lack of coherence in a consultation programme damages its perceived integrity.

# 8. READY. . . AIM. . . MISS!

## THE WEAKEST LINK

It goes without saying that for a consultation to achieve its proper purpose, it should engage with its target audience. Sadly this does not always happen. To understand what's happening here, we need to spend time on another voguish concept – that of the stakeholder.

Most people realise that this isn't a new 21st-century term. Its origins go back to the sixteenth century, when those who gambled appointed a trusted 'stakeholder' to hold the money, and tales of gold-diggers staking their claim in the American Wild West are familiar to many. Yet the term 'stakeholder' is an increasingly popular way to describe someone or some body that is affected by decisions taken by someone else. By extension, it can also be used more loosely to refer to any representative group with whom the consultor has a relationship. We are even seeing the first wave of stakeholder-managers – those whose jobs it is to manage such relationships.

There is much that is positive about the adoption of the stakeholder concept, but it is yet to make sufficient impact upon some consultors. The truth is that what goes wrong with many consultations is that they do not succeed in engaging with the right people. Whether by accident or design, whatever dialogue takes place fails to include some of those who most need to be involved.

This highlights one of our most important assertions – that stakeholder management is the weakest link in the chain of activities which form part of the consultative process. Public bodies and their private counterparts can be brilliant at organising the mechanics of dialogues. They can design excellent surveys, mount high-quality focus groups or build the finest possible website. But unless these methods are directed at the most appropriate audience, it is a waste of time. Truly, identifying and engaging with the right people is pivotal.

No-one sets out to miss the target. At least we assume not. Obviously, it is possible that where advocates of a particular outcome are obliged by statute or expectation to consult, there may be a temptation to focus attention on those that are likely to say 'Yes'. And there are suspicious scenarios. For example, if a supermarket wants to build out of town, it knows from experience that shoppers with cars are more likely to favour its plans than non-drivers, who maybe rely upon their local shops. Hopefully, not many planning applicants will cheat in this way, but there are subtle ways of holding consultations in such a way as to favour a particular result.

So, let's assume that the consultor harbours no such agenda and that there is to be a genuine attempt at an honest and meaningful exercise. What goes wrong? In the following sections we consider some common pitfalls.

### Relying upon inherited lists of consultees

In virtually every department of every public body in the UK, there are lists of consultees – stakeholders. These lists exist in a wide range of formats and, in keeping with the technology of the age, are as likely to be electronic as handwritten. Some are label-runs from a word processor; some can be quite sophisticated databases. Some are well cared for and constantly updated by those who understand the department's stakeholder base really well. Others are completely neglected.

This culture of departmental lists is well known to specialists in knowledge management. They explain that for many employees, knowledge is power and possession of a particular list or key information not only proves an individual's value to the organisation, it also enables them to accomplish tasks which others cannot, by virtue of not having the data.

In stakeholder management, there is clear evidence that departmental teams have, on occasion, hoarded lists of names and addresses of those who probably took part in previous consultations – or who have declared an interest in a specific topic. Holding stakeholder data close to the front line has many advantages. After all, where better to test the validity of the information? This is where mistakes are most likely to cause difficulties and where the advantages of accuracy and being up to date are most evident. However, there are downsides; chief among these is that gathering and maintaining data becomes a part-time task for those whose main activities are something else. It leads to variable standards, as lists become highly idiosyncratic and reflect their author rather than the requirements of the job. Indeed, some are so fond of their own data and so proprietorial in their approach to the information that they spend unjustifiably large amounts of time on their lists and woe betide anyone who asks them to part with this knowledge!

Such a picture is not unique to the British public sector. Tom Davenport, in his seminal book *Working Knowledge,*[*] comments that data-owners frequently neglect more important parts of their jobs in order to concentrate on building and refining ever more impressive datasets that will enhance their own self-worth.

It is against this background that we must view the proliferation of stakeholder data lists that appear all over any large organisation. They generally arise in a totally unplanned way. Through serendipity and the happenstance of who was asked to do what and when, someone says: 'Let's compile a list of those likely to be interested in. . ' Every time this occurs, a sequence of processes kicks off that is almost impossible to reverse. The lists take on a life of their own. Ownership can transfer from individual to individual; lists go into stasis; nothing is ever heard of them for years. Then, *eureka*, they come to light, are given a quick respray plus a nominal safety-check and are wheeled back into service.

Later in the book, we recommend that these be subsumed into a single comprehensive stakeholder database. But for now, the argument is that too many public participation exercises are based upon highly variable,

---

\*    Thomas H. Davenport and Laurence Prusak, *Working Knowledge: How Organizations Manage What They Know* (Harvard Business School Press, 1998). 'Knowledge is neither data nor information, though it is related to both, and the differences between these terms are often a matter of degree.'

seldom accurate, probably obsolete lists of those who are thought to be interested. As a consequence, there are omissions, overlaps, duplications, addresses that are no longer current and consultees that are no longer there – or even alive!

### *The usual suspects*

It's probably a politically incorrect phrase, but anyone with experience of organising a public consultation will confirm that there is always a tendency to engage with the same people – or the same organisations. These are the civic minded or congenitally curious types who always turn up at a public meeting, or who constantly write to the local press. It is a shame to denigrate such individuals, for we surely need to champion their enthusiasm for participation and use them as role-models. Unfortunately, however, among their number are a motley selection of cranks and eccentrics and a fair sprinkling of those whose attendance positively deters others from taking part. Honouring their right to participate without putting others off is quite an art and we have great respect for community leaders and consultation organisers who have to do this on a regular basis.

Collectively, certain organisations have over the years demonstrated their willingness to engage in dialogue and therefore naturally gravitate towards the top of every list. There is little wrong in this – it is the natural way of influence, for bodies with a mission or a message to impart quite sensibly organise themselves to express it in the most effective ways. Historically, in most towns, the chamber of commerce has had little difficulty being heard – certainly as regards business or commercial matters. In traditional northern cities, with long-standing Labour municipal administrations, the local trades council – representing many of the trades unions – could similarly rely upon a good hearing. One might speculate that in Tory shire counties, the local country landowners' organisation would have held equivalent status. Often a local pressure group's credibility relies heavily upon the individual clout of those who run it. If the local civic trust is run by the ex-chief executive of the council, one might expect it to wield a certain degree of influence; if that person was chairman of the angling club, or even the rugby club, the same might be true.

Once upon a time, to recite the list of such usual suspects in a particular locality would have been tantamount to a picture of the Establishment. We have a number of phrases that express similar ideas, such as 'the great and the good' and 'movers and shakers'. In practice, these people are opinion-leaders and many feel that they have earned the right to be at the top of the lists by virtue of civic contribution, or the extent to which they represent a particular community of interest.

The same thing happens at national level, except of course that there are far more bodies who claim to be indispensable for the consideration of particular subjects. Government ministries faced with hundreds of representative bodies, all claiming special insight or positioning, inevitably resort to talking with a favoured few. Often this is completely logical, and probably reflects the balance of inherited influence. There may be fewer lists *per se*, but the idea that there are a fixed number of representative bodies whose views will be important for the Government to consider holds fast.

The downside of all this is that the wider stakeholder base is naturally suspicious of the favoured status of those who are close to the top of the lists. In any contentious issue, there is immense distrust from the protagonists that the decision-makers are too close to the other side – and that the debate can be distorted as a result. A more serious objection is that the presence of the usual suspects deters others from participating. 'Oh, if they're involved, we may as well not bother!'

### Assumed representativeness
It's a shame that we can't devise a better word for what is a really important concept, namely how sure can we be that an organisation truly speaks for its members.

Modern society consists of hundreds of thousands – indeed millions – of voluntary or formally constituted organisations whose role includes an element of representing the views of individuals or interests. These are almost always stakeholders in that they are affected by the decisions of public or private bodies. Many of these take part in consultation or other types of dialogue and will normally hold themselves out to be speaking 'on behalf of' those who belong to or support their organisation.

The trouble is that there is a wide range of representativeness. Take, for example, a well-established chamber of commerce in a big city. It has hundreds of member companies; those who belong are often the true movers and shakers of the local business community. They take their roles seriously; they thrash out their approach to key issues through working groups, sub-committees or some other process. When this chamber pronounces upon a subject, one has a degree of confidence that its members' views have been considered and people speaking on its behalf have the credibility that their processes generate.

Contrast this with a small-town chamber that is effectively run by one person. Okay, he or she may be a larger-than-life, charismatic character and no doubt he or she is great at obtaining good publicity. Beneath the headline and the photo in the local paper, this organisation is somewhat less impressive; there are few active members and no real debate. Our leader takes all the decisions and makes his or her mind up when the chamber needs to express an opinion on matters of importance.

These are, no doubt, two extreme examples – but they exist. Now, at a local level, there will be a reasonable understanding of which model a particular organisation follows. Elsewhere, there is a tendency to take consultees at face value. If the Department for Transport receives two submissions from our two mythical chambers of commerce, it will almost certainly give them equal weight. Both will be assumed to be equally representative of its members.

In practice, many organisations inevitably contain a wide range of views; it by no means follows that what is expressed is representative of the debate within. Pressure groups and representative bodies, in terms of their own governance, have their own version of the same debates as we have in western democracies – do we take decisions on the first-past-the-post principle or try to reflect the balance of opinion in a more proportional way?

A good illustration of the problem is to cast our minds back to the last time when the decision whether the UK should join the euro was high on the agenda. An eminently respectable consultee was the Confederation of British Industry (CBI). Opinion among its members was divided for years. Yet at some point in time, broad support for joining changed, the policy changed and it started to oppose entry.

Now imagine if there had been a consultation on the subject, but before its policy *volte-face*. The CBI would have said: 'Join the euro-zone.' And the consultor would have assumed this to be representative. In reality, the majority view would have been marginal at the time and a relatively small shift in opinion led to the change of policy. Few organisations come clean about the differences in their own ranks – and unless consultors are truly on the ball, a misleading impression of the support for certain policies is inevitable.

We are not arguing that consultees deliberately conceal the truth or obfuscate in any way – though that may well happen from time to time. But we are keen to highlight the drawbacks of making the assumption that legitimacy equals representativeness. Quite rightly, consultors will try to ensure that submissions received from an organisation are from those with legitimate authority to act on its behalf. This may be taken for granted in the realm of the written word, but can be much more dubious where the consultation is predominantly verbal.

Legitimacy is different from representativeness. The same issue of turnout affects the ability of a body to speak on behalf its members. In the same way that central government questions the validity of listening to local councillors who may have been elected by fewer than 30 per cent of the relevant electorate, public bodies may raise similar doubts if they know that very few of an organisation's members take an interest in the elections of its officers. Legitimacy may not be in doubt – but questions are raised as to whether a body's spokespersons reflect the whole movement or just a small proportion of activists.

Nowhere does this matter more than in the sensitive world of racial or ethnic tensions in our big cities. We know that municipal authorities worry that community leaders with whom they have painstakingly built good relations over many years may not, after all, be as representative of their communities as they previously thought. In an age where many young people consciously opt out of conventional politics, those who hold dialogues with community leaders may well fail to appreciate the depth of disaffection that truly exists.

Assumed representativeness is a serious concern. Although there are ways to minimise its impact, many organisations that organise consultations and participation exercises are prone to fall into the trap.

### Over-use of umbrella bodies

They are everywhere – and rightly so, for they represent the natural coming together of groups with common interests. Some are umbrella bodies of umbrella bodies. Others are permanent fixtures, necessarily created so that an otherwise disparate collection of voluntary or community groups can express a view with one voice or organise an initiative without getting in each other's way. From the perspective of the consultor, the existence of such umbrella bodies is supremely useful, enabling you to talk to one organisation instead of fifty.

When they work well, umbrella bodies do indeed save time and complexity; they are able to distil a common position from disparate strands of opinion within a single community of interest. So there is nothing wrong in these conglomerations as such. However, beneath the surface lie many problems inherent in these types of organisation.

Many suffer from the 'lowest common denominator' syndrome, which occurs when a consensus can be reached only by relying upon an unambitious set of opinions that is shared by the vast majority. Those with progressive or subtler views, or often those who have invested time to master a more detailed level of response, cannot convince enough colleagues so have to settle for a modest submission. In time, this leaves the more forward-thinking members of an umbrella body dissatisfied with it. They often leave, only to return a few years later when isolation from the rest of the group becomes a noticeable disadvantage.

Another problem frequently suffered by umbrella organisations is infighting. It comes with the territory and is especially virulent where there is much at stake. In the early days of Scottish devolution, there was considerable debate about the allocation of resources within local government. Councils were represented by the Convention of Scottish Local Authorities (COSLA). As with its English and Welsh counterparts, this body has the uncomfortable role of representing authorities both large and small; therefore its members end up in competition with one another for the limited funds available. Disagreement culminated in the largest Council in Scotland, Glasgow City, resigning from COSLA and seeking to negotiate separately with the Scottish Executive.

The trouble with umbrella bodies is that stories like the Glasgow one are all too common. Because there are often leaders and followers, big fish and little ones, those who see themselves at one end of the spectrum find it difficult to empathise with those at the opposite end. The bigger members feel the umbrella body under-plays their strengths and contribution; the minnows grumble that their association is dictated to by the bigger members. But whereas the larger members may be emboldened to go it alone, and seek to be heard on their own, the great majority within an umbrella body has no such choice; opting out is tantamount to losing what little voice they have.

Those who run trade associations or other umbrella groups are acutely aware of the delicate balancing act required of them. Lean too much to accommodate the bigger members and the majority complain; pay them insufficient attention and they threaten to leave! No wonder it's a tough job, and it makes them very concerned to avoid initiatives that exacerbate the differences between their own members. They therefore become gatekeepers – people who effectively stand guard outside a particular group or community of interest. The term accurately describes their stance when facing a request to seek the views of those they represent. If you want to consult an umbrella group of some kind, be prepared for some predictable questions: 'Why are you asking? Upon whose authority? What do you intend to do with the answers?' It's a little like the doorman who looks you over before letting you into the banquet. 'Who are you? Are you properly dressed?' The subtext is always about control: 'We're in charge here; if you want to find out something, tell us and we'll decide how to handle it.'

Now some gatekeepers will object to this characterisation. In the voluntary and community sector, they are almost always decent, hard-working, committed individuals who face this balancing act and have no desire to be obstructive. But the dynamics of the situation force them towards a restrictive view of their role – particularly in a climate of abundant participation and consultation fatigue. They become a fixture in the dialogue process, filtering requests for involvement and smoothing out the rough edges of responses to ensure they will command general support and won't highlight differences within the organisation. No wonder therefore that gatekeepers are likely to form better relationships with some consultors than others. Life is easier if the filtering process can be eased by virtue of previous experience and mutual respect.

So many organisations who consult stakeholder groups try hard to cultivate and build relationships with those who run key umbrella bodies. Getting them onside is half the battle – if only to neutralise the gatekeepers and the delays and distortions they can cause. It can be beneficial for both sides. The consultor can have confidence that an important set of stakeholder interests will join the dialogue. The umbrella body is seen to be doing its job in getting closer to those it seeks to influence and, superficially at least, strengthens its credibility with its members. But sweetheart arrangements like this can come unstuck and the reason why we discuss this under the overall heading of 'Why Things Go Wrong' is that over-reliance upon a smallish number of umbrella groups may reduce the range of views being heard and smother or marginalise minority opinions.

A really effective consultation process ensures that there are multiple channels of communication; if an organisation does not feel that the umbrella body to which it belongs is effectively transmitting a particular message, it can express its thoughts in some other way. When the dialogue process relies heavily upon the umbrella body and is light on alternative channels, it can restrict the debate and exclude important voices.

### FAILURE TO FIND

With the proliferation of lists, the ready willingness of the 'usual suspects' and the likely existence of many umbrella bodies, there really should be no difficulty in making contact with all stakeholders likely to be affected by the actions of a public body. So how come so many individuals and groups claim they didn't know about a consultation? How on earth do competent bureaucrats miss so many? The answer is much influenced by two emerging rules of stakeholder management.

The first rule is that there are far more stakeholders than anyone realises; their numbers can be mind-numbing. Civic society has spawned many forms of association whereby people combine to share and enjoy their individual preferences. A small district council covering maybe a population of 100,000 can easily have 1,000 to 1,500 representative bodies. Consider a county council made up of six such districts. Can you imagine what a list of 6,000 organisations looks like? With a massive turnover of activity as new campaigning groups start and older ones wither on the vine, this dynamic picture challenges the best-organised councils.

The second rule is that no matter how meticulous you are in maintaining information about stakeholders, you will never anticipate all who may have an interest. There will always be someone who has been overlooked. Sometimes it is not because you don't know that they exist; it is because you never imagined that they would have an interest in this particular issue. This rule is about serendipity. Odd things happen. The redevelopment of the east side of town, while of some interest to businesses in the west, would not normally be of paramount significance to the rest of the business community in the west. How could a pen-pusher in the town hall possibly know that one small company had intended to move to a new site right in the middle of the site for proposed demolition?

So if you can never be certain of who will and who will not have an interest, you have to rely upon excellent publicity. Word must get around. The consultation has to be visible; its purport must be comprehensible in language that the stakeholders will understand. When this doesn't happen and when the local media doesn't pick up the story, we have these silent debates when really important issues are on the table, but substantial slices of the community don't find it in time.

One source of difficulty is the existence of out-of-area stakeholders. These are organisations which have an interest in the subject, but are not based in the immediate locality. They may include the regional office of an environmental charity, or residents of a neighbouring council who commute to or shop in the town under consideration. They can also be much further afield. When the Londonderry Port and Harbour Commissioners invited ideas on what should be done with a 14-acre site being relinquished by the military following the Northern Ireland peace process, it was amazed to find interest from expatriates in the Antipodes, in California, the Mediterranean. . . as well as in Dublin. Some of these had grown up in Northern Ireland, had left the country during its troubles and genuinely wanted to give something back to their home town. No-one predicted their interest. It's a classic example of the second rule.

These are local examples. A national consultation is even more challenging. Just suppose you are a Whitehall Government department and you want to solicit views about policies affecting secondary schools. How many schools are there? And how many branches of the relevant teaching unions? How many parent–teacher associations? How many school governors? How many education authorities? And so on. Oh, and there are probably about three million pupils. . . and their parents. Then don't forget the private sector. So let's add all the independent schools, their pupils, and their parents!

What do you do? Do you write to all of these separately? Surely not! So do you select umbrella or representative bodies? But if you approach them, there may be some who will willingly co-operate and others who cordially hate each other.

Such mind-blowing complexity is good reason to exonerate most consultors of missing some stakeholders. To their rescue comes the internet. When pressed, consultors can now always claim that their request for responses has been published and that anyone with enough interest in what they were up to as an organisation would surely find it. Of course, this is mostly rubbish, as people generally have better things to do than aimlessly surf the web just in case there is a nice juicy consultation exercise to which they can respond.

For national or large regional consultations, therefore, failure to find is, to an extent, inevitable. It is not the same as the hard-to-reach issue (or preferably the seldom-heard), for, as we argue in Part Three, that is a problem approaching resolution. This is just the result of an inherent inability to locate everyone who has a stake.

## INADEQUATE PUBLICITY

Finally, even when all the stakeholders have been properly identified, it is still possible to fail to engage them on account of insufficient publicity.

It has taken a long time for some public bodies to recognise that their message can easily get lost in the traffic noise that characterises modern society. Many policy staff organising consultations have little experience of public relations and are not always close to such specialists as may inhabit the corporate communications departments. Tell-tale signs of inadequate publicity include amateurish leaflets or poor web pages; just as common is a failure to have promotional material ready in time. Many a consultee can tell tales of the press release that comes to hand two-thirds the way through the consultation period.

Ironically, over-egging the PR pudding can also cause problems. Give an enthusiastic 'communications professional' a brief to produce attractive collateral with a compelling message that would appeal to thousands of citizens and you run the risk of glossy leaflets more suitable for the local travel agent than the average town hall. Striking the right balance is not easy and consultation organisers constantly need to be sensitive to the theme of the public dialogue. Using glossy images on high-quality paper may be fine for ambitious urban regeneration projects where there is a case for stirring young imaginations on what's possible with currently run-down or neglected areas. Similar treatment of a consultation exercise on the rationalisation of hospital services would ignite a furious public response.

Yet without publicity, public consultation can easily miss its targets. There are just too many rival claims on the attention of the average citizen and the message 'we want to know what you think' is more complicated than the enticements to buy which we mostly hear. Done properly, effective consultation publicity explains who is asking, why and what will be done with the results.

At local level, the most effective publicity of all is word of mouth. Here the elected councillor can come into his or her own. If an issue stirs hearts and minds in a particular community; if part of its resolution may involve a consultation or another type of participation exercise, it can often be 'spun' to reflect well on the elected member. The script writes itself: 'This is an important issue and we need to hear all shades of opinion; come to the public meeting I've organised. . .'

If, on the other hand, the exercise is a national or large-scale consultation, the trick may be to alert enough of those likely to be interested so that *they* find *you*, rather than the other way around. A high-profile interview with John Humphrys on the *Today* programme helps, but equally important these days is to secure coverage in the most relevant online newsletters subscribed to by so many who follow particular subjects. This is because of the bond created by the use of language. So many communities of interest come together at least in part through the shared use of a particular vocabulary. Belonging to the group is often a question of being able to use its own lexicon convincingly, and the fraudulent impostor can frequently be found out by his or her failure to do so.

Successful promotion of specialist consultations is, therefore, a matter of penetrating the culture of target audiences and addressing them in language and using methods with which they identify. IT geeks rely on online newsletters; university departments use academic journals; general practitioners read *The Lancet*, and so on. Suffice to say, such modes of promotion will rarely be activated unless the consultor has a pretty good understanding of the target audience. As with advertising, the key to success is detailed knowledge of the market; what's clear from so many of the consultations we've studied is that what advertisers describe as the 'call to action' betrays little true empathy for the consultees they wish to attract.

# 9. CONFUSING THE ISSUE

## THE EASIEST PART

You might not think so, but asking people their view is by far the easiest part of organising a consultation. Compared to the traumas of figuring out why and with what objectives and the agonies of the aftermath, the mechanical tasks of applying the dialogue methods themselves should be child's play. After all, there are a lot of experienced people out there. And you can always buy in the expertise. So why do so many exercises in public participation generate more heat than light? How do we make so many mistakes?

Part of the problem is the tendency towards back-to-front thinking. Instead of logically thinking about what the consultor is seeking to accomplish, senior managers, by far the most common culprits, jump immediately to the methodology. It's a case of 'Jane, come here, I need you to organise a questionnaire for us', or 'Please can you run some public meetings for us, Bill?'

The irony is that only too often, the specified action is the last thing the situation requires. Indeed, it may well be that a consultation is not at all the right form of participation. Where there are two sides to an argument and everyone understands that one party wants one thing and another something else, there is no need for a consultation – just get on with a negotiation. And if that doesn't work, try some mediation. Using consultation techniques under such circumstances just confuses the issue.

Assume, however, that consultation is indeed what's required. Whatever the predisposition of managers towards particular methods of seeking consultee views, what goes wrong with the dialogue phase?

## USING THE WRONG DIALOGUE METHODS

The problem here is one of too much choice.

At the last count, the Consultation Institute reckoned that there are well over fifty documented methods and some enterprising consultant somewhere will have invented another last week. No-one has experience of all of them, but the temptation, especially in some of the stuffier-seeming public sector organisations, is to use a sexy-sounding method – say, Unfacilitated Bolivian Innovation Circles – in an attempt to appear up to date and trendy. Now, we've made this one up – but only to illustrate the point! It would be far better if enthusiastic consultants learnt how to implement more established methods better. There is no shortage.

Part of the difficulty is that so many of the traditional methods are regarded as passé. They have been done to death and the novelty has worn off. Questionnaires are a case in point. Experienced consultants know that there is far more to consultation than surveys and recognise that quantitative data is frequently less useful than the qualitative variety. But they have also realised that more often than not, when putting together a dialogue plan, there is usually a case for surveys somewhere in the mix.

That's when the trouble starts, for the skills required to design and implement an effective survey are less widely available than people think. In the same way that few motorists will admit to being poor or indifferent drivers, we've yet to meet many experienced consultants who acknowledge that they are not very good at questionnaire design! The reason why good-quality market research companies thrive is that eventually their clients discover that the home-made variety don't work so well and it is best to call in the professionals.

We have witnessed a fascinating range of survey howlers: questions that are incomprehensible, layouts that prevent respondents from answering properly, the use of eccentric scales or numerical scales that lack or have inappropriate 'semantic anchors' (the words associated with different numbers on scales) and, very frequently, inadequate demographic questions. This last issue is a classic example of unthinking amateurism. In his or her enthusiasm to focus on the issues upon which people's views are to be sought, the questioner asks few, if any, questions about the individual respondent. Yet the data that is produced in the answers to the substantive questions is only of real value if you can analyse it according to the different types of respondents who have taken part in the survey. So while it may be useful to know that 66 per cent of the population favour the town centre redevelopment scheme, what's really valuable is to understand that, say, 87 per cent of young people, but only 43 per cent of the older generation, share this view. Now, questions on age, sex and even income levels may increasingly be found in the better town hall surveys, but only recently have we started to see more contentious questions that enable analysts to distinguish between disabled people and their able-bodied counterparts, or to discover the views of ethnic, religious or linguistic minorities.

Over-reliance on surveys is only part of the issue. A well-designed dialogue mix will balance such methods with other techniques in a way that covers all the angles and targets those stakeholders with whom the consultor wishes to engage. An unbalanced mix can easily distort the output of a consultation, or can lead to a skewed sample, which might require the use of weightings to correct.

Occasionally, over-enthusiasm for a particular methodology leads consultors to build their plans exclusively around one particular dialogue method, and this can open them for criticism. In Chapter 7 we mentioned the Labour Party's Big Conversation. This was indeed an impressive exercise. Its centrepiece was a policy document of thirteen chapters in eighty-three pages covering virtually every subject of political interest in the spectrum. Participants were invited to comment on any of these issues, or respond to pre-prepared questions found in every chapter. It worked, too. More than 10,000 contributions were made to the debate, and although we have other criticisms of the exercise (such as its inevitably straying into areas of zero discretion), there is no denying its effectiveness in attracting thousands who might not otherwise have become involved in the party's policy-making process.

However, you couldn't buy the policy document in your local bookshop, or even order it from them. In fact it was only available on the internet and although you could travel to meet senior Labour

Party figures at special meetings held up and down the country, the Big Conversation was 90 per cent a web-based consultation. It fitted the image of New Labour nicely, but one wonders what more traditional or older members made of it all. Increasingly Government consultations are becoming online only.

Take another example. Mobile phone companies seeking to erect radio masts, often in the teeth of community opposition, deliberately choose methods whereby they avoid meeting residents in numbers. Instead they organise drop-in centres, where individuals and their families are encouraged to come for informal conversations with company representatives who will, no doubt, provide such reassurance as they can alongside the tea and sympathy.

These illustrations show how the chosen forms of dialogue can reflect the values and ethos of an organisation and how many public bodies and private companies inadvertently send out the wrong signals by their selection of methods.

## INSUFFICIENT TIME

We've noticed something about the calendar used by consultors. It follows the school year, taking three longish breaks over Christmas, Easter and the summer. It's the only way we can explain the proven phenomenon of consultation launches peaking in November and July.

The practice of 'consult in July and then go away' is in many ways quite rational. For governments, it accommodates the parliamentary timetable. Do your research in the first half of the year, get to a position where you can offer options for consultation before the summer break, be in a position to analyse the results in the autumn, equip your minister to make a statement to the House and be well prepared for the Queen's Speech to announce legislation sometime in November. All perfectly logical.

Except that this is all in the supplier's mindset. From the perspective of the consultee, things look somewhat different. Few of them are in a position where one policy wonk knows enough about the subject and is trusted sufficiently to respond on an organisation's behalf. Far more will need to go through various internal discussions in order to agree their position; some will need to go through a formal process of consulting their own membership – a mirror-image of the process being undertaken by the principal consultor.

This secondary consultation can be a complex exercise. At its simplest, it means convening special technical committees or groups of interested specialists. In local government, it may mean waiting for the next appropriate sub-committee either to provide a steer to the officers preparing a response, or maybe to rubber-stamp the work that officers have already undertaken. But for mass-membership bodies, there could be far more to do. Many have regional forums or committees which would expect to have a say in the response. In some cases, survey forms might be sent to hundreds of thousands of members.

Not every organisation faces such challenges, of course – but many do, and the principle of secondary consultation most certainly applies to many stakeholders. Imagine therefore the difficulties that arise when consultations land on their desks at the wrong time of year. As a rule of thumb, Christmas can effectively lose consultees three or four weeks of time, Easter up to three weeks and summer holidays a minimum of five weeks.

In the light of this, it is perhaps fortunate that there is a twelve-week time frame for Government consultations and that over the years Whitehall ministries have become better at adhering to this rule. Having a recognisable fixed period has much to commend it from the point of view of consultee expectations. They can generally rely upon this being the period they will have to formulate their response. In other ways, however, the standard is a bit of a nonsense. Twelve weeks seems about right for the traditional written or documentary process, but is probably too long for an eConsultation exercise. In truth, the period specified should relate to the methods being used, plus an additional allowance for the required publicity and time for stakeholders to get to know about the consultation.

In practice, however, letting each and every consultor fix a separate timetable would be a recipe for chaos; before long complaints would start coming in that some were terribly tight while others were loose. Stakeholders at least know where they stand at present, and although there are departures from the twelve-week standard (planning legislation inexplicably prescribed just six weeks for the consultation phase of local development frameworks), most people believe that the benefits of certainty outweigh the disadvantages of inflexibility. Sadly this means that for a number of important consultations, there really isn't enough time for those who are affected to seriously consider what's up for discussion.

There is another aspect to timescales which causes even more difficulty. This relates to the whole end-to-end timetable.

Managers in the public sector, to their credit, appear to have taken the twelve-week standard on board. But this only concerns the dialogue period itself, and the periods before and after are every bit as important – maybe even more so. The lead-in time or planning window clearly has to vary according to the nature and complexity of the consultation. We know of major reconfigurations of the NHS where the gestation period for the options put to the public lasted about three years. In other cases it can be significantly shorter. But it can't be zero! Even the simplest form of consultation requires a minimum period of planning time. In our training courses, we advise trainees to watch for the boss who says: 'Jenny, we need to do a consultation quickly. But don't worry; you've got your twelve weeks.'

One of the reasons why this is unsustainable is that you need to add a third element – what we call the 'decision window'. This is the time needed to analyse the data, interpret it and consider it properly as part of the decision-making process. Enthusiastic consultors who think they can finesse this part of the process and break speed records to truncate it should beware. In an important court judgment on a helter-skelter consultation about water charges in Northern Ireland, the judge ruled that there was no realistic possibility that the minister in question could have properly considered the output of the consultation in the period the ministry claimed had been available.*

Time is at the heart of many things that go wrong in consultations. Even if the dialogue phase is sufficiently provided for in terms of time,

---

* See http://www.consumercouncil.org.uk/newsroom/360/
  judicial-health-warning-on-water-legislation.

there are plenty of examples where aspects of planning have been skimped on. The consultation document has been ill prepared, options not fully thought through, dialogue methods selected for their ease and speed of implementation rather than their suitability for the task of communicating with the stakeholders.

## DUPLICATION

We once visited a London borough where they told us the story of a local branch of an older citizens' charity. One Monday it received a consultation from a firm acting on behalf of something called the East London Multi-modal Transport Study. From what we heard, this seemed a professional piece of work and, in predictable fashion, its consultants had segmented the users of transport on a logical basis, including children, young people, shoppers, parents and businesspeople. Also in this list were retired people and in common with the other segments, their reasons for travel had been identified, one of them being attendance at day centres. That's how this particular consultation came to ask questions about older people travelling to day centres.

On the Thursday, another consultation arrived. This time it was from the social services department of the relevant London borough council. They were conducting a review of services for older residents, and among these, naturally, was the provision of day centres. In this consultation, the borough sought the views of relevant voluntary and community sector organisations regarding many aspects of this provision. One of the aspects covered was transport – and that's how this other consultation also came to ask questions about older people travelling to day centres!

This is maybe an extreme case and it was bad luck that both consultations arrived the same week. But talking to consultees for many years has convinced us that this is far from atypical; of course, stories like this spread like wildfire by word of mouth, becoming the kind of urban legend whereby community activists can *prove* that the bureaucratic right hand does not know what the left hand is doing.

But let's analyse this story a little further. It has three different messages which tell us a lot about the nature of this problem and the difficulties involved.

Firstly, both requests were reasonable and could be supposed to result in better decision-making if an effort were made to understand these particular transport users' needs, preferences and constraints. Secondly, the consultors, while also clearly legitimate, represented very different organisations. The first, we assume, was a one-off project, designed for a single purpose, and duty bound to ensure value for money in a single expenditure commitment. The second, the borough council, has a continuous relationship with its older people and was seeking to ensure more effective stewardship of its ongoing financial commitment to this population. In other words, the same question came from opposite ends of the causation spectrum.

The third point, arising from the second, is that there probably would have been no mechanism for integrating the two exercises. Of course, in theory, the Transport Study people could have approached the social services staff and sought their view, and, yes, in theory, they might have exclaimed with delight that, as luck would have it, they were about to ask the same question themselves. But the reality is that connections between busy departments are seldom that good and it is hard to envisage a procedural mechanism that can stop embarrassments like this from occurring. Later on, we will have much to say about joined-up government and about joined-up consultations in particular. But at this point, it is sufficient to demonstrate how difficult it is to solve this problem and how, at times, it is virtually impossible to convince consultees that there is method in consultors' apparent madness.

In the case we illustrate, what might have helped is a degree of advance warning and effective pre-consultation. There is no reason why the borough council, given the longer-term nature of its inquiry, could not have planned the consultation with time to spare, and it should, ideally, have discussed the forthcoming exercise with the relevant Council for Voluntary Services or its equivalent. Then, at least, one of the two consultations would have been expected.

The wider point is that every community organisation we know can point to a tale of this kind. Indeed, we have heard far more candid stories of far less defensible duplication from within local authorities themselves. There is usually a logical explanation. Every department has its own imperative for going ahead. The questions may be slightly different; the target audiences are marginally different; the timescales aren't in synch; the output needs to be presented differently, and to different people. Failing that, departmental politics can insist that it is too painful to subsume one's own pet consultation into an exercise run by somebody else.

Unfortunately, no matter what the excuses, it makes public bodies look careless or wasteful, or both. They will have to fix this problem, for serious stakeholders will not tolerate such duplication of effort and resources for long. The Government has recognised the problem and the 2006 White Paper on local government* called for each council to have a 'comprehensive engagement strategy'. We think this was intended to address the problem of duplication, but, as we show in Part Four of this book, far more will be needed for significant improvements.

## POOR CO-ORDINATION

Duplication is probably the most visible manifestation of a wider malaise whose root cause is a lack of co-ordination both within and between public agencies. This causes far more problems than duplication alone and goes well beyond that obvious symptom.

At heart, few managers have yet recognised the need to co-ordinate public participation. After all, they can argue that many exercises consist of service delivery agencies talking to their own users; often these are unique. So libraries consult library users; trading standards staff consult some of their customers or clients; the highways department might have a dialogue with motorists or cyclists; environmental services staff can run a focus group of residents to talk about refuse disposal. Best-value consultation has successfully been undertaken in this way and it works fine when people and services can be so compartmentalised.

But life is more complicated than this. The really challenging issues are described as 'cross-cutting' in that they straddle the boundaries between one agency and another. Consider recent findings from a

---

\*    *Strong and Prosperous Communities,* Cm 6939; see http://www.communities.gov.uk/
publications/localgovernment/strongprosperous.

consultation in a fairly average southern English town. High on the list of problems citizens wanted solved was the habit of teenagers loitering around the town centre while playing truant from school. To make matters worse, they occasionally injected themselves with drugs and left used needles and other rubbish as a dangerous and unsightly reminder of their presence. This not atypical situation illustrates the complex inter-relationships between public services. Responsibility for dealing with kids playing truant rests with the education authority – in this case, the county council. Drug prevention programmes are often shared between the county council's adult services department and the local NHS trust. The police are naturally concerned about anti-social or criminal behaviour and it's the lot of the district council to clear up the mess!

The balance that has to be struck in public participation is between encouraging good managers to seek the views of affected people before initiating significant change and presenting citizens with more coherent policy choices – which might involve far more departments or agencies.

We have identified five other consequences of poor co-ordination (and there may well be more):

- Organisations running consultations on their own will tend to use their own *stakeholder lists* and suffer all the disadvantages we earlier discussed.
- Consultors pursuing their own *timetable*, while remaining largely ignorant of other parallel exercises, can lead to a congestion of fixtures (the 'London bus' syndrome), a direct cause of consultation fatigue in the voluntary and community sector.
- A do-it-yourself approach leads to a wider variation in *standards*; some agencies will have trained, experienced staff, while others won't.
- Where skilled people exist, or special facilities (e.g. public participation technology) have been acquired, they tend to be under-exploited if every organisation insists on *doing its own thing*.
- The inability to take advantage of *cost-sharing* opportunities means that the total spent on listening to consultees is greater than it needs to be.

Worst of all is that public bodies are just too unwilling to reveal their thinking. Sharing thoughts about future policy options is seen by many to be politically risky. After all, by encouraging separate agencies to co-operate in public consultation, what we are in effect asking is that they should pool their forward planning. Imagine the issues that arise; will one agency seek more powers? Another less? What happens to their budgets? Or their staff? The shape of the future inevitably raises the spectre of winners and losers and subjecting future options to public consultation can, therefore, hold many risks for vulnerable organisations. They will seek to minimise this by ensuring that they retain absolute control over the process.

Such are the institutional pressures on organisations that limit their ability to co-operate more fully. In many ways, it is surprising and quite impressive that they work together to the extent that they do. Overall, though, this is a weakness of the current consultation scenario; a real culture change towards greater transparency and a licence to think about the future, with fewer recriminations, are prerequisites for greater co-ordination in the future.

# 10. TOO LITTLE. . . TOO LATE

## OUTPUTS AND OUTCOMES

If you asked experienced consultees to name the single most unsatisfactory aspect of their experience of public sector consultations, they would reply in one word – 'feedback'. We suspect that private sector exercises would suffer a similar fate.

Quite why this should be is a mystery. Most people organising a consultation have every intention of providing adequate feedback; indeed, many of them have enough experience of being on the receiving end to know how important this is. Somehow, between planning and executing, something goes wrong here; we need to explore the issue in more detail to disentangle what is really happening.

The most important thing to recognise is that different people mean very different things when they use the term 'feedback'. There is a difference between sharing with others what's been learnt from the exercise and being told what the ultimate decision has been. The former is *feedback of output*; the latter is *feedback of outcome*. Either by accident or design, many consultors contrive to get these two mixed up.

If you want a transparent consultation – where everyone can see how dialogue with groups of stakeholders has actually influenced decisions or policies – you need to make the output as visible as possible. This is so that others can see what's been said and can weigh up the balance of the argument. It can be done in several ways. One option is to publish everything. Some Government departments do this now as a matter of routine. In fact, Parliament has traditionally published written evidence submitted to its select committees, so in principle there is nothing new here. The form of publication has changed, so whereas select committee evidence is in hard copy, most consultation responses that are published now just appear on the relevant website. How valuable this is, on its own, is questionable. It helps you answer the question 'What did this trade association have to say about that subject?' But you may have to plough through a huge number of published submissions before you can form an accurate picture of the debate as a whole.

This explains the popularity of submission abstracts, where someone in the consultor's organisation (or a third party paid by the consultor) has tried to summarise the key points of each respondent's submission. This is a pretty thankless task, for it is highly unlikely that your précis of a consultee's lovingly drafted prose will do justice to the subtlety of his or her handiwork. In theory, you could send your proposed summary to the respondent and ask if it is a fair representation of what they are saying, but in practice, you may be inviting a time-consuming exchange with people who may be very pedantic and probably incapable of finding anything shorter than their original submission acceptable. When abstracts of this kind are prepared, therefore, they seem to be more useful as briefings for the decision-makers themselves rather than as feedback material.

A third option is to publish an analysis of the responses. Whatever dialogue method is used, the raw data will need to be analysed. In principle, this is easier for quantitative methods such as surveys and questionnaires than for more qualitative options. But in all cases, there is still the need to analyse what's been said and to understand who says it – and maybe why. You may have prepared such an analysis as part of informing decision-makers anyway, so the issue here is whether or not to publish that same analysis as part of feedback.

All these practices are alive and well and are used in one form or another, or in combination. Unfortunately, they can also be used to present a different picture – not a faithful representation of what has been said, but a somewhat coloured version that reflects some of the consultor's own prejudices or beliefs.

We once came across a hilarious example from a Government department that at first glance seemed to be getting it right. The document was called *Analysis of Consultation* and it was organised into five chapters, each dealing with one of the five options that had been published in the original consultation paper. Each chapter started with a section headed 'Introduction', which explained what the option was. The next section was called 'What you said' and contained between ten and twenty extended quotations from those who responded. Fair enough, we thought; here is a pretty representative selection of views. The final section in each chapter was called 'Conclusions' and, from what we could see, there seemed to be a reasonable correlation between what came before and what was stated in those final paragraphs.

It was only later, when we examined the document in greater detail, that we noticed that an extra section had magically crept into one of the option chapters. After 'What you said' but before 'Conclusions' there appeared a new section under the heading 'However. . .'. The title says it all, doesn't it? The consultors might as easily have written 'This is why you've got it wrong. . .' and left it to the readers to work it out for themselves!

Few feedback documents are as blatant as that, but the hidden message is often the same. Even when it isn't, there is always the danger that disappointed consultees interpret it as if it were so intended.

This is the trouble with outcome feedback. Waiting until you're ready to announce to the world what you've decided to do makes any feedback you publish look as if it's been doctored for the purpose. This may be grossly unfair, but that's the way it appears and it is difficult for policy-makers to refute charges that they have selectively used consultation responses to support conclusions they had already determined upon.

There are other objections to outcome feedback. One is delay. Stakeholders who have contributed to a debate are naturally keen to see something – anything – quite quickly. Delay only suggests that everything has disappeared into a big, deep hole never to appear again. If the consultor can be persuaded to publish the output of the consultation, or an analysis of that output, in reasonably short order, there is at least, to the visibility of those who took part, the impression of continuing movement and of progress towards an outcome. Failure to publish the output leaves everybody wondering what happened. Did other respondents agree with us? Were they vehemently opposed to our views? What was the overall balance of the debate? Did anyone come up with anything radical or new? There are times when silence may be golden, but this is categorically not one of them. Silence at this time just builds anxiety or reinforces conspiracy theories of one description or another. For full transparency, the best policy is candour, or full disclosure of what took place during the consultation. The quicker this can happen, the better. Instead, reliance on outcome feedback encourages the very delay that adds to the problem.

A further disadvantage is that the causal connection between the consultation and the decision is further weakened. Now we all know that a consultation is usually just one input among many into a complex decision; sometimes there are lots of other factors, but equally there are times when stakeholder views can be expected to have a dominant influence. An effective exercise of listening to these people will explain clearly what role their views are likely to have in the decision-making process. Too often this opportunity is missed and the first that consultees hear of the relative importance placed upon their contribution to the exercise is when the outcome feedback basically says: 'This is what you told us, but frankly, this was outweighed by all these other factors . . . and therefore we have decided as follows. . .' In other words, outcome feedback allows unscrupulous consultors to decide, after the event, how much weight to give a consultation!

## FEEDBACK FOR WHOM?

Regardless of the kind of feedback being published, there is the question of who exactly should be the intended audience. Should it be those who participated, or the relevant community as a whole? Should each and every submission receive an individualised response?

Seasoned consultees would claim that consultors have an uncanny knack of choosing the wrong option as often as not. Different consultations tend towards different practices. Planners, for example, are accustomed to acknowledging every submission (or 'objection' as they pre-judgingly call them!) and drafting a separately argued response to each one. More typically, the range and quantity of submissions precludes this possibility.

But the fundamental question remains. Who exactly is the intended audience? If the feedback is written primarily for those who took part, one can suppose a depth of knowledge that broadly assumes that the original paper was read and absorbed. In a world where written consultation is becoming a back-stop to other more participative techniques, it is a little more difficult to pitch the response at a level that is suitable for all those who participated. Some would have answered questionnaires; others might have attended a public meeting; yet others might have become involved in focus groups or other discussion modes that might have concentrated on only a part of the overall consultation's agenda. How does one design a feedback format that speaks equally to all these various participants?

The trouble is, of course, that too many don't even try. It is just too difficult and the chances are that by the time the feedback is due for publication, the project team has been disbanded, the budget over-spent and management attention already switched to something else. Feedback has become an afterthought – and consultees, not being stupid, see this clearly. What has become the second-best standby is a hastily prepared all-purpose report cobbled together and posted on the internet in the hope that anyone who is interested will persevere and find it. These reports are deeply unsatisfying documents, particularly for contributors, who regularly get the feeling that their time was probably wasted!

Feeble feedback positively encourages mistrust of consultors by adding to suspicions that they are not really listening. In the same way that teaching theory (at one time, at any rate) held that writing something down was a positive aid to learning, the very act of compiling and analysing what consultees have said is an important therapeutic task in the overall process of hearing stakeholder views.

We would argue that this task should actively involve the most senior people who commission the consultation in the first place – it obliges them to familiarise themselves thoroughly with the content of the dialogue. Too often, though, it is delegated to junior staff who may well be competent to perform the technical demands of the job, but who are rarely the people most likely to be making the ultimate decisions, or who may need to be influenced by what is said. It is true that they learn quickly the arguments in favour and against any issue, but the art of preparing sound feedback is not only to report factually what's been heard, but also to convey a serious concern both about the subject and for those who have bothered to participate.

Feedback that disappoints contaminates stakeholders' expectations of the decision itself. If, they argue, the consultor cannot organise itself to publish a decent and balanced account of what happened, what hope is there that it can do justice to the same content when it comes to influencing the eventual decision? Feedback, in short, becomes a signpost to the 'influencing' phase. Professional feedback augurs well for stakeholder opinions to be properly considered; sloppy feedback spells less rigorous standards.

## NEVER-ENDING DEBATE

So how well do we all do in the feedback stakes? Even if stakeholder views are dismissed as jaundiced, many consultors we know accept that this is an area of weakness. They admit to inadequate preparation, lacklustre presentation and inconsistent publication. They accept that putting feedback on the organisation's website is not enough and, if pressed, admit that one of the key reasons for these failures is that they are afraid that providing excellent feedback only prolongs the debate.

And there, we think, is the nub of the problem. Those who organise consultations have either persuaded themselves consciously or have assumed unconsciously that if they publish the kind of feedback that makes sense, that everyone will restart the dialogue that they thought they had effectively ended. Remember how important is the consultor's timescale and how critical it may be to know that a given moment means 'game over' and that no new evidence comes to light after that point.

This desire to move on and to tackle the next stage of a policy-making or decision-making process is understandable but leaves consultation respondents deeply dissatisfied. Admittedly some of this reflects their eagerness to continue arguing and their reluctance to call time on a debate that matters to them. After all, many stakeholders do not see a consultation as a one-off exercise. For them it is but one episode in a permanent campaign to win hearts and minds for whatever cause they espouse. The moment we understand this about consultees, we begin to see the problem with feedback. The consultor who diligently produces meaningful feedback, first of the output and later of the outcome, is merely feeding the campaigning stakeholder with more opportunities to publicise its cause and push its case further.

There is no easy way to reconcile these different approaches. Neglecting to provide feedback at all is clearly not the answer, for all the reasons we have adduced. But equally, one can sympathise with consultors who realise that they have to avoid never-ending debates and move on. The best we can recommend is for the consultation to be well timetabled – for each stakeholder to hear at first hand and preferably buy into an unwritten agreement that excellent output feedback will be followed by a period of purdah, during which the consultor will wish to consider the consultation submissions alongside other inputs, in order to make a timely decision.

But that takes us to the most critical failure of all.

# 11. BUT NOTHING CHANGED!

## AN URBAN MYTH?

We've highlighted the weaknesses of consultation in this part of the book, but nothing we've covered so far does justice to the most abiding criticism of all that can be levelled at these processes. In brief, too many people think they are a colossal con trick because, in the last analysis, *nothing changed.*

Some of this is an urban myth. Those who organise consultations will point out that on this occasion or on that, significant changes occurred, but across the whole spectrum of public and stakeholder opinion, most informed people just don't believe it.

When we set up the Institute some years ago, we launched a search to find the most relevant academic studies which would show how public consultation and participation had led to better decisions. To our astonishment, we couldn't find any. Worse still, we struggled to find any academic work being done on the subject. There are many excellent departments of politics in the UK, yet we could find none that had looked in any depth at the practice of public consultations. True, there is a respectable literature on the concepts of public involvement and public participation, but little original research and very little data from which one could infer that the process actually helps. So, in one sense, the popular perception of those who have been consulted – that consultation doesn't make much difference – is supported by the lack of academic evidence that it does!

We think there are three or four scenarios at work here, each with subtly different effects.

## A HIGHLY PREDICTABLE DECISION

The first, and most obvious, scenario relates to the discussion about the integrity of the consultation exercise in the first place. Clearly when a decision has in effect already been taken, the stakeholders' complaint that their views made no difference comes second to their grievance that there should not have been a consultation at all.

But the situation isn't always as clear cut. In summer 2006, the Northern Ireland Department of Social Development launched a consultation on whether or not the province should separate its water charges from the council rates. The General Consumer Council for Northern Ireland (GCCNI), representing an outraged population, dropped everything to contribute its views, only to find that other key stakeholders were already being briefed by civil servants that the decision had, in reality, already been taken. Their suspicions were further aroused when the minister managed to announce his decision to proceed with the new charges only three days after the closing date of the consultation. The GCCNI won its case. The judge declared that it was not possible for the minister to have considered all the views submitted in such a short period of time!

Four months later, an even more dramatic case hit the headlines. In 2003, Tony Blair's government had promised the fullest possible consultation before any resumption of a civil nuclear power programme for the UK. It then appeared to change its mind but still went ahead with its glossy Energy Review, through which it intended this consultation exercise to take place. In February 2007, months after the closing date, and following the Prime Minister's decision to go ahead with new-generation nuclear power stations, Greenpeace took the Government to court and also won.

This time, the judge was scathing. Not only had the Government failed to consult properly, but something had 'clearly and radically' gone wrong. All kinds of mistakes had been made. The consultation paper posed no options and was therefore more of an 'issues paper'; significant information germane to the debate had not been available to the public during the consultation period and only became available later; the twelve-week period, he said, was only a minimum and scarcely amounted to the 'fullest consultation' promised by the Government. But he also stated that the Aarhus Convention applied,* with the result that in matters of environmental policy, the Government would henceforward be bound by a duty to consult.

The Greenpeace case is without doubt a landmark event and probably one which Whitehall's lawyers will wish to have distinguished from the general rule as quickly as they can. But it could just restore faith in the process among stakeholder communities who, to date at least, have worried that whatever they say or do makes no difference. What it means is that if, in future, a consultor tries to explain a consultation away as making little impact upon a decision, it had better have good grounds for doing so.

## DECISIONS THAT DISAPPEAR

This is not a joke. It really happens. Public (or, for that matter, private) bodies have a good idea – but think better of it. Some of these are nine days' wonders, barely destined for more than a brief moment in the sun. Others have been laboriously developed over a long time but still fall at one of the final hurdles. In both cases, it is becoming increasingly popular to subject new ideas to consultation as part of the process of validating them.

The trouble is that those who dream up these new ideas and have maybe been unwise enough to trumpet their innovation to everyone who would listen are curiously reluctant to advertise their change of mind with quite the same enthusiasm. We came across a perfect illustration of this in the months following the Labour Party conference of 2002 – and we're still not sure how best to interpret the story.

In his speech to the party faithful, the Prime Minister announced that anti-social tenants in Britain's housing estates would in future lose housing benefits: 'Anti-social tenants and their anti-social landlords who make money out of abusing housing benefit, while making life hell for the community, should lose their right to it.' Consultation followed. Residents of one housing association signed a petition in favour of the policy, but that was just about the only support it received.

---

*     The Aarhus Convention grants the public rights regarding access to information, public participation and access to justice, in governmental decision-making processes on matters concerning the local, national and cross-boundary environment. It focuses on interactions between the public and public authorities and was signed on 25 June 1998 in the Danish city of Aarhus. It entered into force on 30 October 2001.

A total of 400 local authorities submitted their views and these were universally hostile, as were those from other concerned bodies. The Child Poverty Action Group responded:

> *In our view for the reasons set out above, these proposals do not meet any of the consultation document's own 'key principles for success' . . . In brief these are: deterrent effect, speed and decisiveness, fairness, practicality, reduction of social exclusion, compatibility with the ECHR. On the contrary they are likely to be ineffective, uncertain, arbitrary, unfair, impractical, and will have the effect of increasing social exclusion. We would urge the Department to abandon them.*

Housing benefit staff hardly relished the task of telling their least favourite clients that their benefit was to be suspended, and hundreds of housing managers queued up to explain why this would probably make each situation worse rather than better. The Government listened and in a balanced statement at the end of the process, the junior minister at the Department for Work and Pensions, Chris Pond MP, quietly buried the idea. 'I accept the strength of feeling among local authorities and others. We will seek alternatives', he said.

Much can be gleaned from this far-from-unique episode. At one level it is an archetypal justification of consultation. Here was an idea, subjected to classic kite-flying in front of an audience which could be expected to appreciate its good intentions, which eventually foundered on the rocks of practicable administration and the opposition of the delivery channel without whose co-operation it could never work.

At another level, however, one can argue that this was a colossal waste of money. Just consider what took place in the local authorities that responded. Very few would have mandated their officials to prepare and submit a response on behalf of the council without any elected member involvement. Quite a lot would have convened committees to consider the proposal; some may have consulted a range of voluntary and community sector bodies or discussed the matter at length with relevant staff. Some probably even commissioned research. How much did all this cost?

The lion's share of the cost of consultation always falls upon consultees, but in this example, we think the consultation could easily have cost £10 million. All to achieve what? For the fact is that many people suspect that 10 Downing Street knew full well that this policy was most unlikely to fly. Critics of the Blair administration insist that gimmicks of this kind were regularly dreamt up solely for the purpose of securing a populist headline in the next morning's *Sun* or *Daily Mirror*. They would argue that this initiative never stood a snowball's chance in hell of happening and that consultation was merely a convenient device to justify its burial.

But we're not sure. Those who argued against what they saw as Blair gimmickry also opposed virtually everything else his administration did. Sorting out what can work from what can't is an invaluable task, even if in this case it did cost millions; generally, it is probably cheaper than launching into a new policy that then fails to work.

The story highlights one factor, however, that's not in dispute. The retreat of an army is seldom as visible as its advance, and the same applies in consultation; the likelihood is that relatively few of those who contributed, and even fewer of the public at large, noticed the quiet abandonment of this idea.

For this is what happens to lots of consultations. The town centre redevelopment that some liked and others didn't but which was eventually dropped; the new qualification that an institute proposed to its members, ultimately dropped because it was too expensive; closure of the cottage hospital ward, which will surely go ahead some day, but which has been indefinitely postponed for the time being; all these announcements tend to be tucked away on page 37 of the local paper, or subject to a press release on a day when there's lots of other news. Instead of trumpeting such decisions as a triumph of consultation, their advocates squirm and are ashamed to admit what they see as failure. In other words, the success of consultation can look like a failure of policy!

## UNFORESEEN EVENTS

A more frequent cause of the prevailing view that nothing changed as a result of consultation is that, frankly, nothing did and that some intervening event prevented the consultor from proceeding.

Quintin Oliver, the Northern Ireland-based chair of the Consultation Institute, tells the story of a consultation he organised in the city of

Londonderry in the wake of the Good Friday Agreement. One of the happier consequences of the peace process was a reduction in the British Army's requirement for facilities in the city, and it decided to relinquish a potentially valuable 14-acre riverside site on the outskirts of the city. This was Fort George and in a commendable spirit of community involvement, the Londonderry Port and Harbour Commissioners, which owned the land, launched a very professional, award-winning consultation in 2001. The trouble was that, after Quintin's firm concluded the exercise with a responsible and useful report, nothing seemed to happen.

The story unfolds that after the consultation exercise finished, the authorities realised that the peace process was releasing far more land than anyone had predicted and felt it inappropriate to proceed to consult on each and every site individually. It is almost possible to see in the mind's eye a clever young consultant advising them that the obvious thing to do would be to conduct a complete and comprehensive review of all the surplus land. That is indeed what happened, but only after eight long years.

Quintin regularly visits Londonderry and frequently meets those who took part in that consultation. 'What happened?' they ask. Even if he tells it as it is, he has to admit to a feeling of shame. These people gave their time and effort to express their views and yet, for bureaucratic reasons, barely understandable to civil servants and certainly incomprehensible to the people of the city, the whole thing has become embroiled in an administrative nightmare that reflects badly on everyone.

We think that unforeseen events are the single most common cause of consultations failing to live up to their expected influence. In the public sector, the amazing overlaps between organisations and their being driven by incompatible or downright contradictory objectives leads to a situation where very few are totally in control of their entire destinies. It only takes a new ministerial announcement or a new partnership initiative to change what was once within the effective control of the consultor into something which requires others' involvement.

Much of this is manageable provided there is a policy of complete candour with consultees. It is perfectly possible, even if embarrassing, to tell respondents that suddenly the situation has changed and the recent consultation will now have to be set aside, or, preferably, wrapped into a broader policy review. There may be some irritation but, on balance, they will give a respected consultor the benefit of the doubt. What will not be acceptable is a sudden abandonment of what was promised. One has to treat respondents just as we now have learnt to treat customers, and just because something unexpected arises, we can't expect the latter to accept it as an excuse for failing to match their expectations.

## STAYING THE COURSE

Those expectations are critical. These days, consultees expect their views to be properly considered and will be deeply offended if it looks as if relevant decisions have been taken or policies determined without reference to what a previous consultation produced.

Consultees accept that this may not be an overnight process. They also understand that there may have to be a degree of consolidating – and that if fifty respondents have come up with a similar viewpoint, it may be necessary to pull the many variations together into a single coherent argument; they also accept that views other than their own will similarly need to be expressed. They will even concede that the individual or organisation collating the consultation output may have a role in making recommendations.

But what they will not easily tolerate is allowing their arguments to go by default. Even if they are in a small minority advocating an unpopular course of action, it will not be acceptable for the decision-maker to be unaware that their view was expressed. Whatever the process that takes consultation output and puts it in a form for the eventual decision-makers to consider, consultees will expect their opinions to be expressed.

It may be hard to imagine that such an obviously reasonable expectation cannot be uniformly met. Sadly, however, life is not that simple. Too many consultations are run by those who have a shrewd idea of what their bosses want and are skilled at picking those elements that are helpful from respondents' contributions. There are many ways of fudging the issue and incorporating selected quotes from a consultation in a wider paper submitted to those who decide.

Tracking the course of various views along a sometimes tortuous path through committees and boards through to individual or collective decision-makers would try the patience of the most seasoned bureaucracy-watcher, but it can be done. The Freedom of Information Act can, in theory, assist the really persistent to follow the precise audit trail from receipt of a submission through to its eventual communication to the decision-making body at the end of the chain.

In practice, of course, that audit trail remains hidden. No-one publicises any of the steps taken on this journey and consultees have to take the consultor at its word that all will be done fairly and above board. Ultimately, they will conclude that the proof of the pudding is in the eating and the acid test will have to be whether or not the consultation appears to have made a difference.

Evaluating whether or not something has changed is a challenge and to an extent this is a subjective, not an objective, test. If the housing development proceeds but with a lower housing density than originally proposed, that is an objective fact. But whether the change can be attributed to an overwhelming consensus among stakeholders who responded to a consultation, or whether it happened because the chief planning officer had never been happy with the original plan, can be difficult to discern. If a Government scheme to alter the scope of an education grant for local authorities is altered, how can one tell if the change of policy stems from the consultation?

What goes wrong for consultation is that even when it produces results, little effort is made to communicate the fact. Indeed, on occasions, there is no-one there to explain the situation, Project teams, appointed for the purpose of planning and undertaking a consultation, have a habit of being disbanded long before the influencing stage takes full effect. This partly explains the paltry pickings found on websites for anyone eager enough to look into what happened as a result of seeking the views of consultees.

The Consultation Institute has devised a simple but effective test that can be applied to any public consultation. We call it the 'twelve-month test'. It consists of waiting till the anniversary of the closing date for a consultation and examining the public documentation to seek clear evidence of what happened as a result. Too often it is impossible to trace cause and effect.

This can be explained in lots of ways. There was a really significant impact, but somehow no-one had documented it well. If there was such a record, no-one had bothered to publish it on the internet. Maybe it was there, but our experienced researcher hadn't managed to find it. Or maybe there wasn't any significant impact anyway.

In which case, was your consultation really necessary?

# PART THREE
# WHAT GOES RIGHT?

# 12. HERE'S THE EVIDENCE, MY LORD

## EVIDENCE-BASED POLICY-MAKING

We live in an age where there is huge demand for evidence. We don't take much on trust any longer and the days of doctrinaire decision-making seem to be over. Indeed, the most compelling argument for consultation is that it provides decision-makers with a wider basis of evidence upon which to make their judgements. In this respect, today's policy-makers are much better informed than their predecessors.

There is a strong body of literature now that supports the notion of evidence-based policy-making, but we don't think the idea of gathering such supporting data should be confined to policy-making. Operational decisions are often more far-reaching than more abstract policies and the two domains merge together often enough.

By now, there are only a few zealots who might occasionally argue that too much evidence is a disadvantage and that decisions should be based upon good old-fashioned gut principles. In some ways, Margaret Thatcher was the last of the conviction politicians, which might possibly lend weight to the idea that it is still possible to take major decisions without the evidence to support them (unless the Blair Cabinet's decision to go to war in Iraq is cited). But in general, the world has accepted the proposition that it is wise to collect the evidence, even if it is not always reasonably interpreted or acted upon.

In many ways, this is an antidote to a very British phenomenon – the culture of the expert. Evidence becomes less important if you can find a suitable authority figure who can claim to know the answer. We have all been famously in thrall to medical experts. Until relatively recently, we dared not question our GP and as for hospital consultants, we hold our breath lest the act of inhaling disturb their concentration. They are not the only specialists who have cultivated the art of being beyond criticism. The highway engineer knows exactly where the bypass should go; the architect looks at the critic who deigns to question a new design by patiently pointing out that we will all learn to love concrete and glass in the end!

Experts don't like being questioned. It undermines their sense of professional superiority; it fails to recognise their sacrifice in undergoing so much learning. 'My dear Mrs Smith, how can you possibly understand what's happening to your liver? You're only the patient; I'm the one that's been to medical school.' For years, they were used to explain decisions that were often indefensible and the gradual erosion of their mystique causes many of them to mourn the passing of the good old days. Many will blame the internet and the growing tendency of the Mrs Smiths of this world to come to a clinic armed with the latest medical research on diseased livers! But actually, it's the popularity of seeking evidence that's really to blame. It goes hand in hand with new freedom of information legislation and together they change the balance of power between the decision-maker or policy-maker and the public. The latter won't now automatically accept what the expert says. They seek corroboration; they look for evidence.

A good example of this trend in action is the whole idea of Impact Assessments. These were devised in part to help politicians escape the dreaded law of unintended consequences, whose application invariably left ministers wringing their hands in exasperation when well-intended policy initiatives failed to deliver their anticipated benefits, or cost ten times as much, or both. What they really wanted to do, of course, was to wring the necks of those civil servants that had advised them in the first place and had curiously failed to draw some of the subsequent downsides to their attention.

So Impact Assessments are attempts to anticipate what will occur as and when such initiatives take place – a bureaucrat's 'what-if' document, if you like. Parliament certainly liked the idea, so when new Bills are presented they are today accompanied by a formal statement that purports to describe the costs and benefits of the new legislation. A more recent refinement is the advent of environmental Impact Assessments, where an attempt is made to guess the consequences of various policies or activities on our increasingly fragile planet. The planning profession is not to be outdone in this area and has now given us 'sustainability appraisals', which place an emphasis on the longer-term perspective.

Our intention is not to pour scorn on these well-meaning processes. Indeed if we just wanted to be critical, we could point to the anodyne way some of them have been written and the relative failure to revisit what was originally stated once experience has been gained. On the contrary, we wish to celebrate such tools, for, in our eyes, they are clearly complementary to the consultation culture. Both are manifestations of a more evidence-based approach to taking decisions. Where they differ is that whereas Impact Assessments can be the product of one specialist analyst or expert, consultation widens the dialogue and necessitates listening to a variety of different voices.

## DEFINING CONSULTATION ACCURATELY

To think of public or stakeholder consultation as an evidence-gathering exercise helps understand much about its definition. One of the weaknesses of some consultations is that the process is often half baked and has very imprecise objectives. However, the great strength of high-quality consultation is that it sticks firmly to the best definition we've ever encountered. We gave that definition in Chapter 1, but we repeat it here as it is worth looking at in detail.

*Consultation is the dynamic process of dialogue between individuals or groups, based upon a genuine exchange of views, with the clear objective of influencing decisions, policies or programmes of action.*

Because the key to getting it right is to understand the nuances of this definition, there are aspects that deserve detailed comment.

### 'Consultation is [a] dialogue'

This is what distinguishes it from so much data-gathering and market research and makes consultation more of an art than a science. It needs to be a two-way process and that is why many surveys struggle to justify being termed consultation. If someone stops us in the street and asks us which team we think will win the Premiership, and if we answer, there has been two-way communication, but it is a pretty lowly form of dialogue.

### 'Dynamic process'

Consultation cannot be a static conversation – it needs to go somewhere, preferably towards better, if not closer, understanding. To take the Premiership analogy, if that initial question-and-answer leads to a discussion as to why a particular team can be expected to win, then there has been something approaching a viable consultation.

### 'Genuine exchange of views'

From all that we discussed in Part Two, it should by now be clear that we see the lack of honest intent as a significant issue and consequently the need for dialogue to be genuine. If a consultee replies 'Hull City', just to be provocative (an interpretation many might share), then it probably isn't for real!

### 'Influencing decisions, policies or programmes of action'

This is the *raison d'être* of the exercise. At one time, the definition hedged this around with the qualification 'normally with the objective of influencing. . .' until we realised that we couldn't any longer think of any scenarios where this important requirement wouldn't apply. Presumably, when one indulges in blue-skies market research or exploratory dialogues with nothing specific in mind, then this could be relevant. But then those would not be consultations – and that is why this becomes the defining characteristic of the process. There has to be something pretty concrete in mind.

When experienced organisers are asked to identify what other attributes make for a meaningful consultation, they mention such factors as timeliness, fairness, inclusivity and accountability. These are clearly important, but do not form part of the definition itself.

## UPDATING THE LADDER OF PARTICIPATION

Successful consultors have learnt to stick to this tried-and-tested formula and to be wary of trying out esoteric variations, although there are many temptations. It is quite fashionable to look down one's nose at consultation and to bemoan its limitations. After all, it does not exactly empower people very much and holds a pretty lowly position in Sherry Arnstein's famous ladder of participation.

**The ladder of participation**

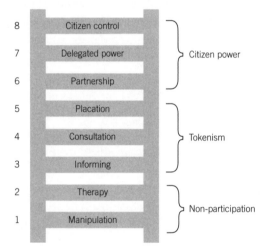

Originally published in Sherry R. Arnstein, 'A Ladder of Citizen Participation', *Journal of the American Institute of Planners*, vol. 35, no. 4, July 1969.

This analytical construct is now showing its age, but is still quoted far too often and at times in quite unhelpful ways. It is rather over-engineered and inclined to identify variations of participation which are difficult to recognise in practice; it also proceeds from an assumption that those who organise different forms of involvement do so from the worst, rather than the best, of motives. Most likely it reflects its origin, having emerged from a post-war American environment where recognition of the manipulative tendency of organisations was still relatively new and many in their universities delighted in their new-found discovery.

On one level, to equate consultation with tokenism may be fair enough. No-one denies that a consultor's ability to ignore everything it hears can leave consultees feeling pretty dissatisfied. But to pretend that all consultation exercises are like that is equally mistaken.

If we want to find a handy reference model that helps understand the different varieties of public participation, we would do better to follow David Wilcox (*Guide to Effective Participation*, 1995), who produced a simplified version. In his model, 'Consultation' occupies the second rung up, above 'Information', but below 'Deciding together'. He defines consultation as follows: 'You encourage others to provide some additional ideas and options, and join in deciding the best way forward.'

### The Wilcox ladder

The really interesting parts of the ladder, however, are the two top rungs. Wilcox calls the fourth rung 'Acting together', where participation takes the form of sitting down and jointly organising things – a kind of shared sovereignty if you like, where the parties are equal in status, even if governance arrangements might allow one party to out-vote another. His top rung is called 'Supporting', and describes the situation when activities have been hived off and given to the participants to run autonomously. The activities become their 'thing' and while other bodies can provide support, in funding or in kind, those who run the organisations are effectively in charge.

The most striking feature of this ladder is that different participants, when asked to spot which rung is the relevant one, can come to entirely different conclusions. Much of this is consultee wishful thinking. Given the choice, of course they would love to be acting together; in truth they would like to wield a veto over any proposals they dislike. Consultation cannot provide that, so Rung 2 is hardly attractive.

It is not just the consultee community that sees many attractions in moving as far up the ladder as possible. Politicians think it makes for a good soundbite and it can resonate with both right and left. The latter love its link to greater democratisation and collective management of community assets. Right-wingers find it chimes with ideas of self-sufficiency, individual responsibility and escape from bureaucratic interference.

It's quite possible that the tide of history is with them. Certainly in the UK, the last decade has seen myriad attempts to devise structures that lock in various interests and give them the incentive of real power. They may be called partnerships, trusts or arm's-length management organisations (ALMOs), but they are all variations on a similar theme, based upon the premise that the greater the extent of involvement, the better the likely outcome, if only because key stakeholder interests will be accommodated.

For all these reasons, the cry goes out: 'Let's go beyond consultation – and let's have *true* public involvement.'

Now we don't wish to be kill-joys, but someone needs to sound a few notes of caution. Here are six reasons why a helter-skelter surge up the ladder of participation may not necessarily deliver all that its advocates claim.

1. Many of the 'acting together' and 'supporting' models are ways of sub-contracting the difficult 'doing' bits for governments or other public bodies who ultimately fund their projects. They are hoping to take the credit for improved outcomes, but want to distance themselves sufficiently to avoid taking the flak if their 'independent' participation-based satellites fail or become unpopular. It's an *unstable relationship* that can easily come unstuck.

2. True accountability is difficult to pin down. Just as with many existing NDPBs, whose success depends not just upon their own efforts but

upon the way they are set up and overseen, real accountability is highly opaque. Those who think they are independent, or are acting together round the table, are often disillusioned when they realise the *constraints* under which they find themselves operating in practice.

3.  There is a limit to the number of people who genuinely want to absorb the responsibility for acting together or running supported ventures. Research has repeatedly shown that while about 70 per cent of the public are in favour of greater participation in principle, *far fewer are willing to participate themselves!* It may explain the modern difficulty of attracting people to stand for their local council, or the problems experienced some years ago in recruiting citizens to join public–patient involvement forums, or even become school governors. Civic involvement is far from dead, but they aren't exactly queuing in the aisles for a seat on the newer bodies we have recently invented.

4.  They all suffer from appalling *expectation management*. Both participants themselves and their sponsors can't resist the urge to talk up these new governance models. So strong is the belief that greater participation is bound to make for better outcomes that the more challenging tasks of working through disagreements and building consensus is taken for granted; when these delay or destroy progress towards the hoped-for outcome, a credibility gap can open between expectation and reality; watch out!

5.  Being involved in more participative activities further up the ladder does nothing to lessen the problems of *representativeness* that can impact the value of stakeholder contributions in the consultation model. The time commitments required alone restrict the pool of available talent, particularly from the voluntary and community sectors, and recalling the earlier discussion of the role of gatekeepers, it is easy to see how these models might offer them particular leverage.

6.  Neither are more participative structures necessarily more *inclusive*. In theory, communities that are 'empowered' to do their own thing might be expected to reflect all shades of opinion, but, in practice,

the loudest voices may dominate; indeed, the more sophisticated the form of participation, the more likely it is that the usual suspects predominate!

None of this is to disparage the many advantages of greater participation – just to temper the enthusiasm with which it is touted as the inevitable and superior form of engaging with people. It also serves to demonstrate that consultation may not be quite such an inadequate mechanism. Its role as a form of evidence-gathering supports other aspects of decision-making which may or may not be strong on legitimacy. Consultation, for example, can be used both alongside totally autocratic or even corrupt decision-making as well as the most transparent, morally upright democratic structures. In both these extremes, what consultation does is to help gather the evidence so that those with authority can then make their minds up.

This is why the outcomes to consultation are no better and no worse than the decision-making processes they support. But the consultation processes themselves have to be judged for their ability to provide the evidence effectively.

# 13. ROLL UP, ROLL UP; EVERYONE WELCOME

## A MORE INCLUSIVE WORLD

Good quality consultation is all about widening the range of people involved in the debate. Frankly speaking, inclusivity has rarely been a hallmark of policy-making processes in the past. Whether one looks at formal democratic structures such as Parliament and local authorities, or the vast number of quangos or other public bodies, the traditional picture is of a small elite, with a historically slow trend towards including a few representatives from the more obvious minority interests.

Public appointments are a case in point. Only in recent years has there been progress towards greater transparency in the nomination and appointment of individuals to the thousands of public bodies to whom official patronage applies. In recent decades, we have seen the token woman, then the token ethnic minority person and more recently the token disabled person. . . and that word 'token' really hurts. It undermines the individual's legitimacy and compromises the contribution he or she can make to the body to which they have been appointed.

Slowly but surely, however, these people have fought to overcome the prejudice that weakened their positions. In many organisations, this will have taken years, and possibly several generations of appointments.

But here's the interesting issue. Consultation processes may well do more to make decisions responsive to a wider range of interests than placing token representatives on the decision-making bodies themselves. Clearly, more representative boards, trusts and councils improve the chances of sensitive decisions being taken, but what really matters is the information gathered and the recommendations placed before these bodies. So we believe that one of the principal strengths of consultation, when undertaken properly, is that it is likely to be a far more inclusive process than most other elements in the participatory mix.

To discover how this has happened, it is useful to look to Northern Ireland. Quintin Oliver thinks this is the most heavily consulted area of Europe and he is probably right. The years leading up to the peace process saw the British Government strain every sinew in the cause of being seen to take account of different opinions when developing its administrative policies. When negotiations started to become serious, the province's political parties were all determined to safeguard their rights to be consulted on a regular basis and wished the same for their many client groups.

What became part of the Good Friday Agreement eventually found its way into the 1998 Northern Ireland Act and, as Section 75, became its best-known and most often quoted provision. It stated in essence that before a public body could take any significant decision, it had to show that it had not discriminated against any of nine groups or criteria: age, gender, marital status, religion, racial group, disability, dependants, political opinions and sexual orientation.*

A blanket, all-embracing anti-discrimination provision might have sufficed in England, Wales or Scotland, but given the peculiar history of the six counties, more was needed. The result was an over-prescriptive provision that had the effect of obliging everyone to consult everybody about everything! It led to a veritable industry of list-broking as everyone sought details of groups and communities of interest who could be regarded as representative of those they needed to consult. The result may have been to convert some consultations into a meaningless paper-chase.

But its other consequence – and probably the one intended by the provision's authors all along – was to change the climate of bureaucratic opinion, and make consulting these groups part of a routine process. In

---

\*    See http://www.ofmdfmni.gov.uk/section_75.

other words, it 'mainstreamed' the inclusivity dimension of consultation dialogues. This came at a price. A voluntary sector thought by many to be bloated and over-elaborate on the back of EU 'peace money' found it could scarcely cope with the avalanche of consultation papers that descended upon it in consequence of Section 75, and it was not long before complaints of consultation fatigue echoed throughout the province.

Now compare the approach to the same issue the other side of the Irish Sea. Separate initiatives had historically been taken to address the different sources of perceived inequality. First came race discrimination, with the Race Relations (Amendment) Act 2000, followed by the Sex Discrimination Act 1975 (Amendment) Regulations 2003 and later still, the Disability Discrimination Act 2005. None of these of course specifically referred to public bodies' behaviour in relation to policy-making or consultation – but they did provide a remedy in law for people who felt badly treated.

To our knowledge, no-one ever brought a court case alleging that they had not been consulted and had therefore been discriminated against. That does not mean to say that no-one would have a *prima facie* case. The disabled in particular had a reasonably well-articulated case. There are hundreds of NHS or social care services specifically designed for disabled people and over which they had seldom, if ever, been effectively consulted. But the thrust of the legislation was not about policy-making, it was about policy application, and the agencies set up in respect of the major causes of discrimination were focused towards mediation for individual cases. Prosecution was very much held back as a last resort and directed towards particularly recalcitrant employers or traders.

New Labour came in with an agenda to strengthen community cohesion and further remove barriers that made it difficult for minority groups to participate fully in public life. It suddenly became *de rigueur* to take positive steps to bring these minority groups into the full range of involvement. Again, no-one mentioned consultation as such, but public bodies were in general exhorted to consider the 'hard to reach'. This took some time, for in its initial phase, it was assumed that this was just another tightening up of codes of practice and guidelines which had no doubt existed for some time. Some public bodies did nothing new.

But then the 2000 Act required them to produce a Race Equality Scheme and suddenly they lost the option of doing nothing. Public bodies and councils had to state unambiguously what they were going to do to meet the Government's agenda and of course the relevant stakeholder groups were starting to watch.

Later, the Disability Equality Duty was introduced. This time, as part of the Disability Discrimination Act 2005, it was specifically provided that disability groups had to be fully engaged and consulted in the process leading up to its adoption. Local authorities, many of which had developed units to tackle social inclusion and who had specialist officers whose full-time role was working with disadvantaged or minority groups, found this relatively straightforward. But other public bodies, lacking the scale or the community focus of local councils, found this very challenging; for some it was their first ever encounter with hard-to-reach groups.

There were some curious idiosyncrasies. Health trusts, for example had (or should have had) a reasonable insight into a wide range of disabled groups, but had little contact with ethnic minority groups. Government departments, well informed and aware of the stakeholder organisations relevant to their own fields, were suddenly required to develop relationships with communities that were entirely new to them.

The Gender Equality Duty came into force in April 2007 and a new regulatory framework replaced separate agencies for gender, disability and racial equality. The new, multi-functional Equality and Human Rights Commission takes a more holistic approach to the whole problem. It comes at a time when other developments in the field of consultation and participation have meant that very few public bodies are clueless. Even those for whom the inclusivity agenda was new have now gone past the first faltering steps to engage with those who can speak on behalf of groups that were traditionally excluded.

To illustrate how this works, it may be useful to look in turn at some of the main groups whom we now engage more successfully.

## CHILDREN AND YOUNG PEOPLE
Historically, children and young people had been pretty low in the pecking order. No-one said it out loud, and there was no shortage of

platitudes to the effect that these people are our future and of course we should take their views into account. We never did, though!

It was only in this millennium that things began to change, as a result of a mixture of external political gestures and some grassroots stirrings. Although the Government had ratified the UN Convention on the Rights of the Child back in 1991,* it was only in 2002 that the UN committee that monitors progress published its observations on the UK. It didn't exactly give a ringing endorsement! One of the committee's recommendations was that the Government 'should take further steps to promote, facilitate and monitor children's effective participation, including in schools, like school councils'.

Schools councils have proliferated and provide a mechanism for young people's views to be articulated – in the main to local authorities, the police or other bodies. No doubt they are excellent vehicles to promote the whole idea of public involvement among a generation that is rarely motivated to do so and complements the recent move to teach 'citizenship' as a curriculum subject in schools. The trouble with schools councils, however, is that they are likely to mobilise the very same children or young people as might have found ways to express themselves anyway. We have been more impressed when teachers have used these councils to provide outlets for children from less favoured backgrounds and where they have little domestic background of civic involvement.

A more specific form of participation within schools is an idea known as 'pupil voice'. It takes the principle of user involvement or customer involvement and promotes pupils' rights to be consulted about aspects of their own schooling. This may be anathema to many a traditional schoolteacher but is gaining support steadily. In so far as it provides a more relevant focus for their views, it is likely to be a more compelling form of participation. Rather like employee consultation or customer consultation, it is likely to engage individuals over matters upon which they feel strongly. Forward-looking headteachers will see pupil voice mechanisms as ways to respond to student grievances and to

---

\*    See http://www.unicef.org/crc.

ensure better dialogue on contentious policies. Better still, they should strengthen the sense of school community. In the words of a 2006 study by the Carnegie Trust, 'better teacher–student relationships emerged, as students felt they were listened to, and teachers felt students understood their role'.*

What form does this participation take? A student council is one model; another is to appoint student governors who can have a voice in the decisions taken by that body. More ambitiously, some schools are involving pupils in discussions about such parts of the curriculum as are discretionary. A few brave schools have even experimented with having pupils sit in on appointment interviews.

Organisational structures such as schools and colleges present a favourable environment for consultation and participation. It is far more difficult to manage a dialogue with young people in other contexts. Yet it is in relation to other services that children often need to be heard. In 2004 the Government launched a nationwide consultation called Every Child Matters and obliged every local authority to enter into discussion with appropriate stakeholders in their areas. The aim was to redesign children's services and make them more responsive to the needs of the children themselves. A huge amount of activity followed; most councils would claim that this informed the decisions they took as to how to organise themselves. The trouble is that an average county council covers 100,000 or more children and young people; how could they canvass a sufficiently representative range of views without having to rely heavily on professional youth workers, young people's organisations and of course, schools? Some did better than others.

There are practical and ethical issues involved in consulting young people. Those who organise focus groups or other dialogues need to fulfil legislative requirements, of course, but great care is needed with the information obtained in such exercises. Some of the most meaningful consultations held with young people have revolved around sensitive issues such as drug-taking, domestic violence or even sexual orientation. Unfortunately, we've heard disturbing stories of views

---

\* See http://www.phoenixeducation.co.uk.

expressed by youngsters being repeated inappropriately, so, in contrast with the default position for adult consultations, exercises involving young people often have to be handled in confidence.

Engaging with young people can, in many ways, be among the most rewarding of all forms of public participation. It can start surprisingly early in life. Barnardo's, the UK children's charity, described to us how they take tiny three-year-olds on 'sensory walks' on the streets of London – just to watch and assess their reactions to the sights and sounds of this busy and dangerous environment. Such moderated forms of dialogue can be replicated up the age groups, and skilful teachers have long been able to elicit from their pupils a rare honesty of contribution that adults frequently fail to emulate.

## RACIAL AND ETHNIC MINORITIES

The rise of multiculturalism in the UK has without doubt led to a much more committed programme of consultation with those who represent what has become known as the BME (black and minority ethnic) community. But as the ethnic distribution varies so much, local models of dialogue are bound to vary widely, as many of these communities observe their own procedures and values in the way they approach such participation. In some towns, ethnic champions have made it to the council chamber and have status and standing, sufficient to play a prominent part in discussions and debates over key issues. In others, they still fall outside the mainstream political process and are treated as hard-to-reach groups, which, frankly, they mostly are not.

The one constant about BME groups is that an effort has to be made to engage with them professionally. Sitting back and waiting for them to make representations works only where a consultative framework has already been established. Fortunately, a useful infrastructure of bodies already exists, notably race equality councils, many of which are funded by local authorities and the Equality and Human Rights Commission. Although the main focus of such organisations is on dealing with individual issues, they also have a role to play in brokering wider dialogues between groups and various public bodies. This might be on a one-off basis, when a particular issue needs informed input from such a group. Or it could be a more permanent mechanism – designed as a reference point for consultors to access regularly.

Such forums or councils bear all the hallmarks of umbrella bodies in that they are not always truly representative – and frequently suffer from problems with gatekeepers. But for the BME community they have, in addition, the complication that they often reflect very different cultures. Some are comfortable with written language and abstract ideas; others are intensely colloquial and practical. Some reflect very diverse social structures, and within this the most commonly recognised difficulty is the reluctance of many Muslim communities to allow women to participate in formal or public dialogues.

Sometimes the more cosmopolitan areas of the UK find themselves with so many different ethnic communities that it becomes difficult to know when to start – and when to stop. The London Borough of Southwark, for example, finds it necessary to consult sixteen separate ethnic groupings;* such cultural diversity requires the council to offer interpreters and translators in more than seventy languages. This presumably arises from a conscious policy regarding equality and diversity which seeks to redress the balance in favour of minority groups that may struggle with conventional civic participation and public services.

But that issue of language illustrates in microcosm some of the challenges that lie in this field. Translating public information leaflets, notices or even consultation papers into foreign languages arouses conflicting views. Many professionals insist that this is an important signal to those with little or poor English, that they are welcome in the community and that their participation is sought. Others argue that it is a waste of resources which could be better spent on direct face-to-face dialogue. It is a classic case of the argument between principle and pragmatism. Those in the former camp claim that any contribution to a consultation debate offered by a minority ethnic group may be open to criticism if it can be suggested that they had an imperfect understanding of the issues. Their opponents counter-claim that the only people able to advise upon whether written translation is warranted are community

---

\*   2001 Census.

leaders themselves. Translation at meetings is quite another matter, but that in turn raises the question of whether meetings should be held with specific groups on their own, or whether it works to conduct general public meetings with a translation facility for those who may need it.

Some groups coalesce around identifiable focal points – a community leader, a community newspaper, a social centre or a church. Others are more diffuse. In 2006, we heard a fascinating account by Westminster City Council of their attempts to initiate a dialogue with newly arrived economic migrants from eastern Europe. It appears that they effectively link into informal networks of fellow-travellers and, if successful in obtaining employment and accommodation, integrate into the Polish, Czech, Hungarian or whatever national community is relevant. The council's effort to understand their views and requirements meant tapping into these networks – but this proved very difficult if individuals failed to integrate economically and disappeared below the official radar.

In this case, and in some of the more intractable situations for dialogues with officialdom, the problem stems from the status of the people concerned. Asylum-seekers and refugees are often hard to reach, particularly if they are in fear of repatriation or other administrative disadvantage. Seeking their views has almost always involved skilled specialists working largely informally.

Far more typically, the BME viewpoint is expressed locally through forums or the vast number of self-help groups. The Council for Ethnic Minority Voluntary Organisations represents some 9,500 organisations and is able to support individual groups with skills and resources when required. It also acts as a voice for this hugely disparate community on a national stage, where it takes its place alongside dozens of other pressure groups which represent them. These groups will be on ministerial lists of stakeholders and will have developed links with Members of Parliament and the media. In this respect they are not significantly different from other NGOs that represent important communities of interest.

## PEOPLE WITH DISABILITIES
Disabled people are by common consent the classic hard-to-reach group. Most consultors understand the hurdles that they face in engaging in

dialogue with public bodies. The trouble is, however, that most of us have a narrow view of what is meant by 'disabled'. It has been remarked that one of the biggest mistakes made by the disability lobby was to adopt the wheelchair symbol as the representational logo for disability. It is estimated that there are about 9.8 million people in the UK with some form of disability – one in seven of the population. Some years ago there were 750,000 wheelchair users in the UK – less than 10 per cent of the higher number.

In fact, the new, wider definition of disability means that one in five of us will be considered disabled at one time or another. The 2003 Disability Discrimination Act uses this definition: 'A physical or mental impairment which has a substantial and long-term effect on (a person's) ability to carry out normal day-to-day activities.'* Applying this criterion, as public bodies were required to do to implement their disability equality schemes, resulted in most local authorities discovering that there are far more disabled people than was previously acknowledged.

The reasons why disabled people find it difficult to engage in proper dialogues have been well documented and are part of a wider picture of disadvantage. Some of the facts still come as an unpleasant surprise to those of us who have not previously examined the subject. Disabled people leave school with fewer qualifications, their life expectancy is seriously reduced and they are more vulnerable to a whole range of life's more distressing experiences. For example, they are four times more likely to have property stolen from them under the threat of violence and twice as likely to be burgled.

It is in this context that we need to see the obstacles disabled people face in public participation. Restricted movement is one obvious problem; those that are housebound or under constant care, or who cannot drive or use public transport, will clearly be less able to attend public (or private) meetings, exhibitions or other participatory events. Even if they can, too many venues are unsuitable for too many disabled people. A ramp is not enough.

---

* Full details of the provisions of the relevant legislation are available from the EHRC. See http://www.equalityhumanrights.com/your-rights/disability.

A couple of years ago, we spoke at a large conference of officers from London borough councils to which representatives of the voluntary sector had also been invited. No sooner than the Mayor had finished his welcoming speech than a lady rose from the body of the hall to harangue the organisers for not having a working induction loop system, which she needed as she was hard of hearing. An explanation that a loop had been provided but failed to work cut little ice. With 19 per cent of men and 13 per cent of women reported as having hearing difficulties,* deaf people now expect public events always to be held in well-equipped locations with this basic, but effective, technology fully functional. The provision of sign language is more negotiable – with a degree of latitude reasonably afforded to consultors to make informed judgements about the likely requirement. A parallel requirement these days is for deaf people to be accompanied by a palantypist – someone who accompanies them to prepare an instant transcript of what is said.

It is claimed that new technology offers many solutions to the problems that some – not all – disabled people have; we strongly support this notion, provided it does not become a panacea. Access to a personal computer has indeed revolutionised the opportunity to contribute to public debate for people who were previously struggling to be heard, and the ability of software to support innovative protocols never ceases to amaze. Text-to-speech enables blind people to use the internet and speech-to-text is similarly useful for deaf people. Web designers are themselves urged to meet demanding new accessibility standards to ensure that disabled people can take advantage of these latest forms of communications.

However, the real experts on disability claim that the most pernicious disincentive to participation is that so many disabled people live on reduced incomes. What's the point of having new whiz-bang tools, they argue, if you can't afford them? People with learning difficulties, it is claimed, have a particularly raw deal. What they often need, apparently, is time: time to absorb and to digest what other people are saying. They are especially affected by over-use of jargon and 'bureaucratese', so they

---

\*     2002/3 figures.

may need special events and special presentation techniques to ensure they are properly included in debates. The good news is that almost all these issues have been recognised; even if we are still some distance from addressing them, we are at least on the way, although the journey can't go fast enough for some.

As in many other communities, there are two distinct views about the direction of improvement. There are several nationally respected major charities that represent the mainstream disability 'establishment'. The Big Five are RNIB, RNID, Scope, MENCAP and Sane,* and their pressure upon Parliament and the then Disability Rights Commission persuaded many that the way forward was to require public bodies to publish their approach – and then, presumably, to be held accountable for fulfilling their promises. Leverage would be applied by obliging these organisations to consult disabled people themselves on the preparation of these documents. The theory is that if the disabled community in a particular area express a clear view that they need improvements to their village hall, say, so that it would accommodate their needs better, then local service providers such as the council will most probably accede to this view and write it into their disability equality scheme. Thus, over time, practical improvements would be made and participation in civic life be enhanced for disabled people.

But there is another analysis. There are disabled people who resent the leading role of the Big Five and who worry that administrators and officials working for these charities cannot possibly empathise with people who are themselves disabled. This is exacerbated by what they see as a trend towards more and more Government expenditure on services for the disabled being channelled through the voluntary sector and these bodies in particular. It can compromise their positions *vis-à-vis* the Government, claim the critics – and of course it applies in exactly the same way to local groups who similarly receive operational funding from local public service providers. Indeed, there is much soul-searching about this issue all round. The alternative vision of better participation

---

\* These organisations respectively represent blind people, deaf people, people with cerebral palsy, people with learning disabilities and people with mental illnesses.

is to seek to involve more disabled people directly in dialogues – and the track record of most public bodies is slowly improving to this end. Often it is the simple solutions that work best – like providing financial recompense or expenses for attending consultation events, or employing interviewers with direct knowledge of the conditions which affected those whose views they are seeking.

No-one in the business will argue that the ability of disabled people to be active in public consultation has not improved greatly in the past decade. But few will be able yet to attest to the impact it may have had.

## OTHER SELDOM-HEARD GROUPS

As has been noted many times already, there is a lot of confusion about what exactly constitutes such groups and we've come to the conclusion that often one person's hard-to-reach is another's routine stakeholder base – it's really down to perception, experience and track record.

There are pockets of people whom it is a challenge to engage under all kinds of circumstances. We have heard vociferous claims that women are inadequately represented in important consultations and that far more should be done to make this easier for them. There is some force of argument in the idea that where childcare responsibilities or cultural traditions create barriers, attempts should be made to circumvent them. But we are largely unconvinced by the suggestion that special means must be found to encourage more women to participate in each and every consultation.

Somewhat more persuasive is the need to help older people to be heard more effectively. On the basis of numbers alone, we're not sure that they are under-represented in many consultation exercises. If you attend most public meetings, chances are that older people are in a majority. Middle-class older people certainly show a greater propensity to participate in a wide range of voluntary and community bodies and are particularly well represented in areas such as health, where of course they often have a direct interest as disproportionate consumers of NHS services.

Beneath this reassuring picture, however, lies a more complex picture. When old age is combined with disability, or with membership of some BME groups, there are serious gaps in participation. Then, as people age, and become more dependent upon carers or support services, their voices naturally become weaker and their networking with fellow-consultees less productive. Major charities such as Age Concern and Help the Aged create frameworks whereby older people's views can be compiled through local groups with regional co-ordination, similar to the models already discussed regarding BME and disability groups.

Far more convincing as hard-to-reach groups are those involving sexual preference. The accepted terminology is LGBT, standing for lesbian, gay, bisexual, transgender, and their emergence on stakeholder lists has caused much head-scratching among more traditional councillors, local government officers and civil servants. Around 10 per cent of the population falls into these categories, and without doubt there have not been adequate mechanisms to enable their views to be properly heard. Once again, the gravest examples of failures in public involvement arise where this condition is compounded by one or more other hard-to-reach factors. Notorious cases of young people agonising over their emerging sexual preference and having their views inappropriately reported to third parties are, alas, too common.

Among the most problematic of communities with whom UK public bodies struggle to engage are gypsies and travellers. Long-standing issues including the provision of official sites, unofficial squatting on inappropriate sites, health, welfare, education and alleged criminality mean that many different public service departments have reason to deal with them, and from time to time need to consult with them. Conventional techniques just don't work and an inheritance of mistrust and antipathy colours the dialogue. Most local authorities make an attempt to build relationships with leaders of these groups, but their transient nature often makes this a difficult task. We have heard accounts of good practice, including a heartening consultation in Ireland (where the traveller community is much larger and there's a greater inherited commitment to interface with them) whereby a wide range of opinions were gathered on the best design for new permanent accommodation.

Sadly, good news stories are still few and far between; here is a hard-to-reach group that truly merits the label.

There are many other groups which are particularly relevant for specific services, and whose views are needed for one reason or another. Ex-offenders constitute one such group, and as with many others, there are usually specialist voluntary bodies who can act as a conduit for such consultations, such as in this case the Apex Trust.* Even within these groups there are sub-categories that have been subject to considerable research.

Drug-users and many who are believed to engage in anti-social behaviour are hard to reach almost by definition, but are also hard to help, often because they are hard to hear. Respectable pillars of the community sometimes find it distasteful to get involved with marginal groups that live on the fringes of legality and prefer that they remain out of sight and out of mind. Yet for many in the public and the voluntary and community sectors, it is becoming part of the job to consider whether groups like this need to be contacted so that a better understanding of their needs and perceptions can be found.

Not all such groups pose such challenges. Dealing with some can sound positively idyllic. If you fancy a job driving round the west coast of Scotland you may be delighted to hear that rural dwellers have been identified as needing special input on account of unique problems that affect the provision of services in isolated areas or in the remoter parts of the country.

Finally, and on a somewhat thought-provoking note, it is ironic but true that among some of the more difficult to engage are businessmen. Go-getting, work-obsessed, self-employed entrepreneurs are among the least likely to respond to public sector consultation exercises. They see their time as too valuable to spend attending public meetings; they would sooner plough through a 200-page contract than open the pages of a consultation document; and unless they are rich enough to use their wealth to impress and influence politicians, they generally can't

---

*    The Apex Trust helps more than 10,000 ex-offenders every year. See http://www.apextrust.com/apexhome.asp.

abide the thought of meetings with civil servants and bureaucrats. The Federation of Small Businesses and other umbrella organisations try to provide a reasonable conduit of their collective views, but a large number of public bodies are finding that the voice of small businesses is pretty hard to discern and only by treating them as hard to reach, and making special efforts to engage them, can their voices be heard.

## A SEA CHANGE

We have witnessed an astonishing sea change in the emphasis placed by public bodies on reaching out to the community as a whole.

There are some who think it's gone too far. In a town near us, the council closed two car parks as the land was being redeveloped, so worshippers at two local churches had nowhere to park their cars on a Sunday morning. In fact there was a massive multi-storey car park within 100 yards. The trouble was that the council refused to open it on a Sunday. They were happy to open it on Sundays before Christmas as quite a lot of shoppers needed to park their cars, and on the same principle they opened it on bank holidays. Church members started to argue that had the places of worship not been Christian, and had they belonged to a more recognisably minority religion, the council would have been more responsive. They quoted other recent cases of perceived discrimination against Christians, in an echo of British Airways' attempt to prevent their staff wearing a crucifix and the regular stories each winter of libraries banning the advertisement of carol concerts.

Right or wrong, what these tales reflect is the extent to which some – clearly not all – public bodies have become programmed to listen out for minority voices. They may not always make the right judgements based upon what they hear, and we suspect there is fair amount of posturing and special pleading around. There is also uncertainty as to whether it is worse to be over-zealous and be pilloried by the *Daily Mail*, or over-cautious and face criticism in *The Guardian*.

What is undeniable, however, is that the process of consultation is now a significant tool of wider dialogue, that an increasing number of previously excluded groups and communities take part in it, and that consultors are hearing voices that were once seldom heard.

# 14. BETTER OUTCOMES, HAPPIER STAKEHOLDERS

## OUTCOMES. . . AND OUTCOMES

We are not about to argue that we are at that utopian point where in every consultation the organisers cry 'Eureka!' because they have found the obvious solution to problems that had baffled them for years. As always, there is a real mixture of experiences, and as we have acknowledged, there are far too many forays into public participation that are little more than tokenistic exercises, where neither party holds any expectation that anything meaningful will emerge.

There is also the problem of defining what we mean by 'better outcomes'. Better for whom? We recently heard a distinguished but magnificently controversial Scottish broadcaster and sometime talk show host criticise the long-standing debate they have north of the border on the contentious issue of wind farms. There was no mistake as to where she stood. In a wonderfully crafted phrase, she characterised Scotland as 'the Saudi Arabia of renewable energy', which we suspect she felt more appropriate than boasting that the Scots experience more wind than anyone else. Why on earth, she demanded, were they pussyfooting around and endlessly debating whether to build these massive on-shore and off-shore generators and the transmission lines needed to exploit this natural bonanza? She blamed it on consultation. By letting every crofter and village community have their say over and over, it was preventing the country from making its pre-destined contribution to saving the planet.

But then, we thought, what if some of the objectors to these schemes were also present in the room? Might they be saying 'thank goodness we have a culture of consultation' that has stopped the powers that be from railroading through a 40-mile-long string of windmills 300 feet high, like a procession of demonic robots, traversing some of the most scenic parts of the Outer Hebrides? For them, the very process of dialogue which the journalist found unacceptable was a godsend. You don't have to take sides on a contentious issue like this to recognise that there may be little agreement on what exactly constitutes a better outcome.

For years, infrastructure planners in Britain have bemoaned the fact that, compared with the French, we seem incapable of building roads, airports, nuclear power stations and other major projects when faced with community opposition. The French TGV is envied and the same people argue that we could never have built Charles de Gaulle airport. (But then the French had several square miles of flat agricultural land just outside their capital, and we didn't.) The *Barker Review of Land Use Planning* (2006) was specifically aimed at finding ways to reduce what the Treasury perceived as being an economic disadvantage;* this was allegedly because the British are too eager to give every objector an opportunity to be consulted. Supermarkets and other businesses had successfully lobbied to the effect that their operations were being hampered by environmentalists and other Luddites who didn't understand the harm they were doing the country.

We see such moves as a backhanded compliment to the consultation culture. Clearly the process has an effect. Now whether that produces a better outcome or not depends upon your point of view. In the example we quoted about Scottish wind farms, the battle-lines appear pretty clearly drawn, but in other cases, the picture is more complex with shades of opinion and room for compromise and consensus.

What a good consultation does is to accomplish a transparent review of the facts and the opinions (very different concepts) surrounding an

---

* The review had considerable influence on professional opinion and subsequent legislation. See http://www.communities.gov.uk/planningandbuilding/planning/planningpolicyimplementation/reformplanningsystem/barkerreviewplanning.

issue and place them in the public domain so that decisions become better informed. It does not, of itself, make the decisions better; indeed, it is almost impossible on occasion to know what is a good or a bad decision. There is no objective way of telling; one person's opinion can differ from another according to their values, experience, upbringing or culture.

Take a decision such as the allocation of funding to new projects in the health service – something managers have to decide on a daily basis. Every consultant will argue for his or her speciality. The paediatrician wants more money to treat sick children; the geriatrician wants it for the other end of the age spectrum. The drug abuse treatment unit cries out for new facilities and the poor over-used accident and emergency facility is bursting at the seams. How do they decide?

Despite public perceptions to the contrary, most well-run parts of the health service have sophisticated ways to evaluate cost and benefit for competing projects, but in all likelihood the focus will be on return on investment and on the project's contribution to meeting managerial or Government targets. A 'wrong' answer presumably would be to spend precious money on a project which bore little relevance to any target placed upon the organisation and which would result in no savings elsewhere.

But what the consultation culture has started to do is to widen the context of the debate. We now have the means to place on the agenda an item called public or stakeholder opinions. Now the public may not be as technically informed as the expert consultant who is fighting for a particular speciality, but they are informed from another perspective, namely how the service looks to an end user.

There are problems to overcome. People who are asked about their priorities and preferences naturally draw upon their own experiences. If you've had a difficult time at childbirth, you are more likely to be conscious of the need for better maternity services; if you have an elderly relative needing nursing care, you are more attuned to the need for those facilities. There is also the difficulty that people who have never experienced a particular disease or condition or who think it can never happen to them have little or no idea that certain services are either needed or available. So one can argue that listening to patients is no more valuable than listening to the specialists; all one gets is a mirror-image of self-interest, but without as much detailed knowledge.

But a public service is ultimately held to account by the public. So politicians are acutely conscious of the need to strike a balance between the concerns of citizens, either individually or collectively, and the interests of the provider community – back to the culture of the expert if you like. What is better about decision-making that has been preceded by a properly conducted consultation is that there should be a more transparent audit trail that can link various strands of the issues together in some way.

So in our NHS example, managers conducting a wide-ranging debate might find predictable support for competing specialisms but also some undercurrents of overall preference. By carefully listening to these, responsive leaders are often able to adjust the projects in subtle ways that can go some distance towards meeting citizen aspirations. Maybe what emerges from dialogue is a feeling that whatever new facilities are built, people don't think they are properly maintained and that they become tacky and tired-looking far too soon. It may not help managers decide which project to favour, but it helps them produce a better scheme if they heed the messages they hear.

All this is to explain that better outcomes aren't always a simple matter of a decision being right or wrong, better or worse. It's more subtle than that and much of the most valuable benefit is therapeutic. A willingness to listen is a favourite image which organisations increasingly pursue. It resonates with all the various stakeholder types.

## CULTURE CHANGE

Many of the best examples of improved relationships with stakeholders are found in the commercial world. Many firms have sought to stimulate a 'culture change' – usually as a means to respond to changing market conditions. Success seems to depend upon inculcating and promoting a sense of shared values through dialogue.

Now the clever thing about processes of this kind is that they help the top and the bottom of an organisation to understand one another better. There is not necessarily a neat and tidy outcome in the shape of a document detailing a new company culture, or a new staff manual; few firms now go in for that kind of collateral. But, over a period of time, behaviour changes as acceptable norms of conduct become absorbed into daily routine. If the focus group ended up talking about the inordinate amount of time staff spent wrestling with a badly designed expense claim form, chances are that someone will take an initiative and improve it.

This bread-and-butter micro-change management process is hardly in the same league as major Government policy consultations, yet the principles are strikingly similar. Better outcomes result from organising dialogues with the right people at the right time to make a difference.

Public sector managers also talk blithely about culture change, often with limited understanding of what it entails. If they persist and seek to bring about genuine behaviour change, they will find this only happens if they institute such dialogues – and if the ambient environment is conducive. The most propitious time for radical change is often when there are major threats, external market or economic convulsions. On this basis, the recent banking failures and the consequent recession may prove to be a stimulus for far-reaching change.

## BETTER RELATIONSHIPS WITH STAKEHOLDERS
A public body or company that secures improved performance through the process described above is basically reaping the harvest of better relationships with its own staff. It also works in other scenarios.

An increasingly popular form of consultation is called 'programme approval'. This describes when organisations set out their strategies and plans and ask stakeholders to comment. Our verdict on such exercises is that, by and large, they succeed – not because the responses lead to better decisions necessarily, but because they should lead to better relationships. This is because coming clean about your intentions is generally welcomed by those likely to be affected by your actions. They are glad to know where they stand and normally find it useful to figure out where they disagree and may need to take action.

We think that the major part of 'better outcomes' flows from today's practice of publishing such statements of intent up front. It may not always be called a consultation but, when properly planned, that is what it is. Note the issue of timing once again. This is something one does when that trigger moment happens. It does not work when inserted in the annual report or the monthly staff newsletter. The act of publishing has to attract proper attention and lead to a genuine debate; acquiescence does not count.

If we take different kinds of stakeholders and try to guess what they make of all these attempts to involve them, we believe that, on balance, they see that the advantages outweigh the inevitable frustrations. True, they have every right to complain about the shortcomings we have tried to capture earlier in the book, but if we take them one by one, are they happier?

### Customers

Customers, it is recognised, have an ambivalent attitude to suppliers, with huge differences from one industry to another. When buying a car from the local garage, we may not blame the dealer for design faults or manufacturing blemishes, but we will be very hard on him if he falls down on a maintenance job. This is because we readily understand who is responsible for what. But if you buy a new computer over the internet and find you have wrongly configured it, you may feel uncertain as to whether to blame yourself, the website-designer or the supplier for designing the options in a particular way.

Such is the revolution now happening to consumers as buying habits change and we lose some of the relationships we once had in the commercial process. What they call disintermediation takes away a whole layer of people with whom we used to have relationships. This has already happened with travel agents, financial services and even music retailing. But it means that suppliers have lost one of their traditional forms of customer consultation. The holiday company that wanted an insight into what customers thought of this year's brochure used to phone up travel agents and discuss the issue. Increasingly, this won't work as there are fewer travel agents and the new direct channels have – in this industry at least – eclipsed the older ones. So when it comes to consultation, they have to go directly to the end consumer – hence the avalanche of questionnaires. Do customers mind? Very rarely, for when this is done well, suppliers place the whole thing in the context of the overall service or product experience. Being asked about it becomes part of the holiday!

Customers of public services are also becoming accustomed to the built-in feedback. Best Value analysis obliges many service providers to enquire but it probably lacks the credibility of private sector equivalents – if only because so many public services are delivered from monopolies and sceptical customers have less confidence that criticism will be acted upon.

In general, however, customers like being approached, provided it is done without causing them inconvenience and at a frequency that makes sense in relation to the frequency of the service and the respondent's expectations for action.

### Pressure groups

Specialist pressure groups have their complaints both about political adversaries and about the process of consultations of which they disapprove. But they now inhabit a world where they have so many more opportunities to engage than previously that it becomes increasingly difficult to raise objections. Freedom of Information legislation, a sensationalist press, 24-hour news and its voracious appetite for stories all help to give them tools to force their views upon consultors and the public at large. They are more concerned about the volume of requests for responses and their inability to do justice to them all. A veteran civil servant once remarked privately that he thought that voluntary bodies in his part of the UK had been the victims of 'the curse of the answered prayer'. What he meant was that for years, some of the organisations that were now complaining of consultation fatigue had in fact been knocking on his door pleading to be involved in the decision-making process.

This should not obscure the fact that few pressure groups would willingly return to the dark days when they could scarcely discover the name of the official dealing with a question that mattered to them. In theory they prefer the new system. In practice they find it a strain. Few will admit it, lest they lose the audience rights so assiduously campaigned for.

Even fewer will admit to having little influence. No matter how frequently we hear organisations express their frustrations that their wise words are being ignored, they have difficulty saying so in public. This is because they need to boast to their members. To motivate membership and support their claims to be taken seriously, they have every reason to exaggerate their victories and minimise any failures. It means that stakeholder organisations are frequently portrayed as being happier with consultation arrangements than in fact they are.

### Public bodies

Looking a little wider, what of public bodies themselves? We sometimes forget that they too are consultees; in fact many of them spend more time and resources responding to each other's consultations and to Government requests than they do enquiring of their own customers or clients. This dual role can be uncomfortable, in that the skills of asking and the skills of answering have much in common, but the tasks are rarely organised alongside each other. Local authorities, for example, often place the responsibility for preparing the council's response to a consultation in a central unit usually answerable to the chief executive. The routine task of consulting the public is distributed all over the place, however, and conducted to variable standards. This means in practice that councils and other public bodies are often more satisfied with their performance as consultees than as consultors. As consultees, they employ staff to do it properly, take steps to be selective and mostly believe that they are listened to. Intra-agency tensions still surface but overall, public bodies are learning how consultation can help them do their jobs better. Gradually we are inching our way towards joined-up government.

In fact, embedded consultation can be a major factor in forcing different agencies to work together. By 'embedded' we mean consultation – whether required by statute or just adopted as a modus operandi by management – that is built into the administrative processes of various services. Planning permission is a perfect example. The law requires planning authorities to consult those who are affected by changes of use or new buildings, so the process has been designed in such a way that obtaining their views is part and parcel of the process; that's when we can say that consultation has been truly embedded within a service.

To make joined-up government work, pressure has mounted for slick, rapid-response consultation, one department with another. As an example, take the 2003 Licensing Act. One of its provisions is that when the local Olde Tyme dancing troupe wants to serve alcohol at an event at the village hall, they now have to apply for an expensive licence. The cost is high because embedded within the process is a requirement that the council consult the police – presumably to ensure that the dancers and their guests are not likely to be binge drinkers and cause aggravated damage to the adjacent duck pond. The serious point, though, is that as consultation is often a daily mechanism that involves more than one agency in various forms of dialogue with others, we need to distinguish between sensible applications and some that are somewhat less so.

## BETTER CO-OPERATION IN THE PUBLIC SECTOR
Sensible or not, the last decade has seen an upsurge in partnership working, though the barriers – institutional as well as psychological – are great. So great are they in fact that in the Local Government and Public Involvement in Health Act 2007, Parliament felt obliged to introduce a new 'duty to co-operate', specifying a whole range of public agencies that need to play ball. Apparently in some two-tier local government areas, there are districts and counties that are barely on speaking terms, despite the recent introduction of Local Area Agreements,* the idea of which is that they all work together to pursue specified target outcomes.

Public bodies consulting each other better may be a strange conclusion for a chapter we have entitled 'Better Outcomes, Happier Stakeholders', but in a sense it is a natural result of the public participation boom. The weight of expectation has forced the very organisations that face the biggest obstacles to collaboration to tackle this difficult agenda and become better at it. No-one who understands Whitehall or the public

---

\* For details of Local Area Agreements see http://www.communities.gov.uk/localgovernment/performanceframeworkpartnerships/localareaagreements.

services in general will under-estimate the organisational and cultural barriers to joined-up working. Those who think it is easy just do not appreciate the complexities.

Every agency has been set up with its own legal obligations and these have been overlaid with departmental guidance or, in cases, independent regulators. Then those with democratic governance have to perform to the tune of elected members whose priorities may be different again. It results in hundreds of quite autonomous organisations, all of which march to a slightly different beat. Getting them to modulate to the key of their neighbour or to dance to a different rhythm is very difficult.

Advocates of better local government have adopted the phrase 'place-shapers' as a more meaningful label than 'community leadership', which was previously favoured. There is not a lot of difference, but we suspect people may identify better with the idea that the quality and characteristics of the services provided in a locality profoundly affect its identity, its culture and the day-to-day experience of its residents, visitors and workers. That the mixture of service providers has hitherto operated largely independently is thought, by many, to account for the chaotic state of so many of our towns and cities. Having them all work to an agreed programme should, it is argued, help produce the kind of places we want.

Lest this sound just like motherhood and apple pie, there are seasoned realists who accept that without better partnership working, things will get worse, not better. Some of this is the simple arithmetic of resources. Civil servants in both central and local government are already acutely aware of the Gershon agenda,* which is all about making savings in public expenditure. They have scarcely seen anything yet. The credit crunch, and the demographics of an ageing population and the pressure it will place on health and social care budgets, will see to it that commitments will be chasing funding for years to come.

Public bodies will have no option but to share any tasks that can possibly be undertaken jointly. In the next chapter, we suggest some. For

---

*    See Sir Peter Gershon, *Releasing Resources for the Frontline: An Independent Review of Public Sector Efficiency* (HM Treasury, 2004).

now, what's important to note is that part of the steep learning curve that 21st-century public bodies have to ascend is the value of consultation, so that they listen to voices other than their own. To the extent that this is becoming the norm, it represents real progress and a promising good news story.

# 15. CREATIVE INNOVATION

One of the most interesting aspects of public participation and consultation is that there is no one standard methodology. There are dozens.

## IN THE BEGINNING

In the field of public policy consultation, the traditional method involved the production of a big fat document designed primarily as a B2B process, only this time the abbreviation stands for 'bureaucrat to bureaucrat'. This is classic written consultation and is still the mainstay of Government departments and many executive agencies. We don't want to knock it, for it has many advantages. If there is a need to explain complicated options, possibly of a technical nature, and to invite responses to tough questions, it is not possible to summarise them all in a simple leaflet. An authoritative account of the consultation narrative is essential.

Its principal drawback has always been accessibility. Not necessarily people being able to get their hands on the document, more being able to understand what's on the pages. The Plain English Campaign took a long time to reach the authors of these papers and still hasn't found some of them. Part of the problem is that they tend to be written by policy specialists rather than by communications professionals. And so they should be. When PR people get their hands on a consultation document, watch out; accuracy and precision are ultimately more important than spin.*

---

\* In March 2009 the Local Government Association published a list of 200 terms that public bodies should not use when communicating with the public. It attracted much criticism. . . but made its point. See: http://www.lga.gov.uk/lga/core/page.do?pageId=1716341.

Fortunately, recent years have seen an explosion of creativity, with imaginative people seeking, and finding, new ways of engaging with stakeholders. In general, consultation techniques can be summarised as being mainly quantitative, mainly qualitative or mainly participative, and it is in the last of these three categories that much of the most innovative work has been done.

But there are other drivers as well and among these the role of new technology is the most evident. Indeed, public engagement mirrors what has happened in society at large – namely a massive proliferation of the channels of communication. If shopping has moved on from the time when we had to travel to the high street and physically enter the emporium to today's choice of direct mail, telephone call centre or internet ordering, so also has the toolbox of interaction methods open to the consultor.

## QUANTITATIVE DATA-GATHERING

This is the most established of the methods in common use and has been with us since the universal adoption of market research. It is highly dependent upon the skill of scientific sampling and it can still go wrong. Only a few years ago pollsters got the result of the 1992 UK general election badly adrift and were sent back to the drawing board to look again at their techniques. Recent advances in this science have been slow and not particularly spectacular, centring around speed of data analysis and the ability to predict from a small number of bellwether data points. In the meantime, we have all become far more accustomed to finding the ubiquitous questionnaire in an increasing number of life experiences.

To use a terrible pun, questionnaires come in many forms! When you stay in a hotel you are likely to find a satisfaction survey to be completed at the end of your visit and for this type of application, maybe the simpler the better. At the other end of the spectrum, we recently looked at a lifestyle survey from a leading supermarket that would in our view have taken an hour to complete – and longer if you really thought about it. We have previously listed some of the errors and mistakes which are commonly found, but thanks to good survey techniques, we believe the overall standard is pretty good.

Gathering this data is a substantial industry in its own right. Leading companies have ultra-sophisticated methodologies with good quality assurance processes that should, all other things being equal, generate reliable data. They are highly experienced in the black arts of sampling and also in survey design. Like others, they have discovered that the best quantitative data-gathering stems from good qualitative research.

The process goes something like this. First run a thematic workshop with the client, to establish what they think the issues might be. Then, organise focus groups of those whose opinions are to be sought and in so doing, try to elicit from them a range of opinions from which you can derive certain hypotheses. Then, and only then, should you go out and undertake the fieldwork.

Let's take a simple example. If the task is to consult people as to their views on recycling household rubbish, you might gather the thoughts of the local authority and its waste collection sub-contractor. Then you assemble focus groups from different parts of the town, which might suggest conclusions. One might be that retired people appear to be more willing to recycle and visit the local bottle bank, whereas younger working people say they don't have the time.

If we stop right there, just at the point where the discussion appears to point towards such a conclusion, we have to acknowledge how flaky is the basis upon which we have arrived at that observation. After all, who exactly came to the focus group? How were they selected? Were they representative? And did all voices get an equal hearing? (In other words, were you any good as a facilitator?) In short, what you have is a suggestion that maybe there is a valid conclusion here. But we cannot be sure. That is why we prefer to call it a hypothesis.

It is the role of surveys in a consultation to test a hypothesis and discover the extent to which a systematic sample might support it. Without them, there is a danger of anecdotally hearing something we really want to hear, and basing decisions upon it without validating its currency. This is the case for using third parties. Even more, this situation cries out for a quantitative survey to measure support for particular views. Calibrating well-considered hypotheses is certainly more likely to produce answers that are useful for policy-makers or indeed for decision-makers generally.

In pursuit of this, we have seen the growing popularity of panels. These have enormous advantages. Firstly, they represent the willing – a not inconsiderable advantage and a cost- and inconvenience-saver for pollsters and researchers. Secondly, panels can help overcome one of the perennial weaknesses of surveys, which is the changing sample from one exercise to another. Raw numbers are seldom as meaningful as the direction in which they move. But if your main interest lies in such a movement or, to use the jargon, a tracking survey, then you need confidence that the sample is sufficiently similar. A panel cannot altogether fix this problem, but it can help. A third advantage is that panels can help secure a more balanced true sample, reducing the need to use weighting in order to correct an initially unrepresentative respondent profile.

They also have drawbacks, however. Critics point out that once people have belonged to a panel for some time and participated in many surveys, they soon stop being typical or representative of the community from whence they are drawn. They become better informed and even more survey-wise. To accommodate this bias, rotational refreshing of panels has become best practice, though this is not universal. At least it makes the data more reliable.

Arguably, the other improvement-driver has been the creative use of better data-gathering techniques, such as telephone interviewing. This is vastly superior to postal surveys, whose low and probably unrepresentative response rates reduce their credibility, if not their popularity! Public bodies persist in the cheap-and-cheerful option of a mail survey, despite growing evidence that data collected in this way is highly suspect unless one has the luxury of a very large sample.

It is far better to use one's budget on a more limited but methodologically sounder exercise – maybe using the telephone. Modern CATI software (computer-assisted telephone interviewing) can help specialist agencies assemble a true structured sample, but it is a job for professionals and seasoned commissioners of such consultations recognise this. The economics are quite interesting too. The operational cost of quality telephone interviewing is relatively modest; much of the cost is in the up-front design, set-up and piloting. For a small project, this can make up a disproportional percentage of the overall budget and drives the cost per interview up. But for bigger exercises, the up-front costs are absorbed across a larger respondent base and the cost per interview can drop dramatically. It makes this a good choice for the quantitative part of more extensive consultations.

Where in-depth data is required, there are few effective alternatives to the old-fashioned face-to-face interview. Trained researchers arriving to scheduled appointments, increasingly accompanied by a laptop rather than a clipboard, are still the best method of all when large, complex questionnaires need patient systematic completion. This is, of course, costly, but is undoubtedly better if the data contains lots of open-ended text-based questions.

Summing up, quantitative consultation has hardly experienced dramatic improvement except at the margins, or in relation to new technology, which we discuss in detail later on. What has happened to consultation is that experienced consultors have discovered the limitations of the numbers game and have moved decisively towards qualitative methods as the mainstay of the dialogue mix.

## QUALITATIVE TECHNIQUES

What we really mean here is methods of listening to people that do not boil down to statistics. There is an academic definition that says that qualitative techniques are methods that are, in fact, non-quantitative; so now we know!

Actually, a lot of the data that is collected in a consultation is capable of being counted – it's just that it wouldn't mean very much if you did. Take a public meeting as a good example. Supposing fifteen people get up to say pretty much the same thing and a sixteenth then says something that is close but not quite the same. How would one count it? What significance would we attach to it? But let's go further and assume there are two public meetings. Our fifteen speakers might have been 75 per cent of the twenty who turned up at the first meeting, but of the fifty who came to the second meeting, only ten (or 20 per cent) took the same position. So a majority viewpoint in Meeting One was a minority viewpoint in Meeting Two. Or was it? Because what we've done is counted those who spoke and we're not sure about the others because there was no vote.

This little cautionary tale illustrates how easy it is to tie oneself in statistical knots in the search for numerical significance from processes that are essentially qualitative. Spurious analyses abound from a desire to prove one argument or another. It seems that many researchers have failed to grasp the idea that if you haven't got a statistically valid sample in the first place, there is little meaning to a statistical analysis of what they've said or done.

Yet you only have to look at the way in which most written or documentary consultations are analysed to see the confusion between the qualitative and the quantitative approach. Many will ask straightforward questions, as in other surveys. Better consultations recognise that what they are after is advice and insight from informed stakeholders who may have valid points to make about various proposals. This is quintessentially a non-statistical process, yet you will often see a nicely designed pie-chart purporting to show that '65 per cent of respondents broadly agreed with the main thrust of our proposals'. What in blazes might that mean?

The search for numbers is often aided and abetted by new technology text analysis tools. These can scan huge quantities of material and identify common themes or messages, as well as straightforward string-searching, with which most of us are familiar. These are great if you want to get a firm handle on how many people are of a similar mind, but are dangerous if statistics are produced with any suggestion that they are representative. What analysts should be doing is trying to understand who is saying what and why – the essence of qualitative assessment.

Fundamentally, qualitative consultation is subjective. There has to be someone who makes judgements about what they see and hear and who synthesises the material into coherent conclusions. The analogy with a lawyer weighing up evidence is a remarkably good one; the skill is often the ability to distil from a mass of extraneous noises the few key messages that can make a difference. If we relate this to the processing of hundreds of submissions sent to a consultor over a detailed policy consultation, the true complexity becomes apparent.

A few years ago, we agreed to act as assessors for a politically sensitive consultation that aroused strong feelings in the voluntary and community sector. We were presented with more than 200 submissions ranging from a handwritten letter, barely legible and really difficult to interpret, through to forty-page academic-style polemics that required a PhD to read, let alone comprehend. And we had everything in between. The great and the good had written. Respected professional associations explained how they had consulted their members and come to their conclusions. Local councils tried to leverage their democratic credentials and community groups made much of their voluntary status and record of good works. Then we noticed that some of the same names appeared on very different-looking documents and realised that whole paragraphs seemed to be copied by several organisations, or altered very slightly. We also noticed that some names were associated with completely contradictory positions.

It got even better – or maybe worse! The consultor, a Government department (which had sought little advice before designing the consultation document), had tabled a dozen or more questions that appeared, at first sight, to be sensible enough. But presumably it had not piloted the survey elements of the consultation and had inadvertently produced overlapping questions, whereby a respondent wishing to make a particular point could reasonably place it in one of three or four questions. It sounds great to draft open-ended questions, such as 'What do you think would contribute to better relations with the department?' But too many such questions make analysis virtually impossible.

Like many other researchers who have wrestled with similar scenarios, we devised a coding structure that sought to capture the various messages coming from the respondent base. They ran into hundreds. Any statistical analysis based on the number of 'mentions' would have been pretty insignificant. And yet. . . in the hands of well-informed assessors who knew the background thoroughly and so could contextualise the information, all this would have provided evidence from which a few clear conclusions could emerge.

Qualitative research relies upon someone somewhere making judgements about the views that consultees articulate, and deriving insights from it. Much depends upon the methods used to gather the data in the first place. So the focus group is effectively a structured facilitator-led discussion managed in such a way as to provide very specific input (hence 'focus') on a particular question. It is also an environment contrived so as to create the opportunity for people's views to be challenged or tested by others. 'Bill, what makes you think that?' 'Mary, do you agree with him?' A trained facilitator can observe how members of a focus group subtly change their positions when confronted with counter-arguments. On occasions they change their minds completely; at the very least, you see how they respond to other people's views.

Contrast this to the traditional written consultation, so beloved of Government policy-makers. What we had in the earlier example was a one-dimensional set of arguments from authors who had no reason even to consider an opposing point of view. It is remarkable how one-eyed some consultees can be. Many live in a clear-cut world where they are right and everyone else is either wrong or misinformed. The method does not provide the consultor with a mechanism to go back to the author to check if the point being made has been fully understood, or to enquire more deeply about aspects of the consultee's position. In fact, nothing would please the consultees more than to see the consultor taking a serious interest in what they've written; it would become a far more meaningful dialogue were this to happen more frequently.

If we were generous we would claim that in better consultations, this type of follow-up occurs quite frequently – but we doubt it. What is true is that qualitative consultation often means looking for a needle in a haystack; the really proficient assessor develops the skills to detect the one argument, advanced by, say, three people out of the hundreds of respondents, that can make a serious difference to the balance of the argument. Civil servants trawl through endless piles of submissions knowing that the law of unforeseen consequences has torpedoed many a worthy policy change over the years and that among those who are wise after the event, there may have been a consultee or three who had indeed spotted the flaw and articulated it.

This is why the great value of consultation for many does not lie in the numbers game; that is for headline-chasers or for those issues of mass interest or mass impact. The qualitative side of the activity is more about understanding the different shades of opinion, testing various arguments, identifying where people seem to agree and, even more importantly, where precisely the disagreements are.

One of the strengths of the recent consultation culture is that those who are professionally involved have begun to recognise the primacy of the qualitative approach and the inevitable reliance upon informed assessors who can weigh up the evidence and defend their conclusions. It has, however, contributed to the most striking area of all for new innovation – the trend towards participation-based techniques.

## PARTICIPATION-BASED TECHNIQUES

Apart from new technology (see below), this is the most obvious way in which the business of consultation has changed. There is now much greater acceptance that the best forms of consultation involve real people or real interest groups and that their participation is helpful both to the consultor organisation in the specifics of a particular issue and to the wider community, which benefits from more transparent process.

It's hardly new; witness the venerable institution of the public meeting, warts and all. In recent years, there have been many attempts to breathe new life into an old format and to address some of its weaknesses. Its image as a talking shop for the usual suspects is well deserved, especially where we have traditional chairmanship with a local worthy dangling the mayoral chain of office before a bored or sceptical audience. Television has, these days, made people familiar with charismatic personalities with inquisitorial skills and the kind of celebrity charm that helps galvanise a debate. Not every meeting can have a Dimbleby or a Paxman, but we suspect there is an emerging lucrative sideline for current affairs presenters whose faces are familiar even if only to regional audiences and who can attract a wider audience for a subject of otherwise limited appeal.

Celebrity facilitators are not the only way to attract more people to a meeting. The latest generation of hand-held devices give an audience the chance to express an instant opinion, in the style of *Who Wants to Be a Millionaire?*. 'Ask the Audience' is popular but subject to all the caveats and criticisms that apply to other unrepresentative voting formulae. But it underscores the abiding truth about participative mechanisms, which is that those who come along feel more engaged and, at least for a while, become more confident that their views are being heard.

International comparisons of political activities indicate that the British are not a particularly demonstrative people; our propensity to march in the streets is fairly low. It is doubtful whether those who urge upon us an 'empowerment agenda' of greater involvement really intend to replace our current reliance upon the slower and more bureaucratic apparatus of representative democracy with more visible forms of direct participation. But it is one risk among many, for encouraging a more participatory culture can often also fuel dangerous prejudices in sensitive areas.

The emphasis now placed on neighbourhoods has spawned a range of consultative machinery designed to make public service more accountable to residents. Area committees, area forums, neighbourhood forums and parish meetings are all, however labelled, an attempt to demystify the traditional infrastructure of committees and its attendant bureaucracy. They go hand in hand with the idea of Local Area Agreements, which are intended as a better way to link local public service providers with locally visible outcomes.

Where there is a radical place-shaping agenda, such as an urban regeneration project, there is usually a raft of parallel machinery devised to bring other stakeholders into the fold and bind them into important developments. They have a mixed track record and we often find the suggestion of machinery chasing participants rather than the other way around. But there are significant success stories where communities are getting together to debate the kind of changes they want.

One move in this direction is the creation of networks of individuals and organisations with an interest in the NHS in each town or county. These have been christened 'Local Involvement Networks' or LINks* and

---

\* Introduced in 2008, Local Involvement Networks have been created throughout England. See http://www.dh.gov.uk/en/Managingyourorganisation/PatientAndPublicinvolvement/ DH_076366.

replace Public and Patient Forums, small committees which lamentably failed to live up to their promises. Harnessing the energies of the dozens of support groups, charities and other community associations with an interest in health and social care is definitely a good idea, though it is early days and a hands-off approach by the Department of Health meant that all 180 of them have had to work out their own modus operandi. Neither is anyone really sure that the management of the UK's favourite public service is really minded to heed the views of the public! This highlights another of the risks of participative models, which is that the greater the involvement, the higher the expectations.

An emerging model which we believe has a lot going for it is the deliberative event. One version of this is a stakeholder conference. In your town, it may not carry that title, but when you see a banner above the entrance to the largest hotel in the area proclaiming 'Newtown 2020 – Your Vision Conference', it is probably what you're going to get. Inside you may find 200 or more who have applied for tickets to come along. The local Women's Institute may have sent three delegates, the British Legion another two or three; there are sixth-formers from the local comprehensive rubbing shoulders with officers from the local Federation of Small Business and the friends of the local drama society. All human life is there – or so is the intention, and they will probably hear presentations on the various issues facing the locality before splitting into breakout groups to argue about the details.

One of the virtues of this approach is its acknowledgement that society is composed of numerous varying and sometimes competing interests. It is a feature of democratic models that everyone tends to lobby upwards along the vertical plane of accountability. So pedestrians complain to the council about car drivers and cyclists. The cyclists in turn lobby the Government for harsher penalties for dangerous driving; meanwhile everyone demands better safety arrangements on our streets. Public bodies often find themselves the butt of everyone's criticisms, even though the real problems are not with them *per se*, but with other competing interests. What stakeholder conferences and similar mechanisms achieve is to force people with different agendas to sit down and argue out their debates *with each other*, rather than joust with the local authority – in other words horizontal rather than vertical dialogues.

There are umpteen varieties of deliberative process and events of this kind, of course, need careful management. We've heard the word 'choreography' used for some of them; this unfortunately gives the impression of manipulation. At their best, they provide an environment for community groups, businesses and active citizens to find common ground and seek compromises. They can even contribute to consensus-building, though that is not their main aim. The skill lies in selecting the topic matter and designing both the input and the breakout sessions so that different viewpoints can be heard and the arguments absorbed. Care has to be taken with the feedback loop, and there is often a debate about whether to use pre-assigned group facilitators or let every group organise itself. There are similar issues concerning how to allocate people to topic-specific groups – or maybe allow them to select for themselves, with the risk that everyone opts for the popular subjects and eschews the one with the hard choices.

Conferences and events like this are far more satisfying for participants than the old-style stakeholder seminar; 'Come and let us tell you about the issues and you can tell us what you think' smacks of a lecture even if, in practice, it is different. The word 'seminar' is sufficiently offputting! But if you call it a workshop, immediately the image is conjured up of rolling up your sleeves and getting down to business. We have often distinguished a workshop from a seminar by claiming that while the latter teaches you about something, the former is a problem-solving session designed to apply the same principles to a particular situation.

Some problems are really intractable and involve absorbing contentious information and weighing up complex options. These are sometimes tackled by a Citizens' Jury.* They are expensive and

---

*   A Citizens' Jury is a dialogue method whereby a small group of citizens (usually chosen on a representative basis to reflect the local population) is brought together to consider a particular issue. They receive evidence from expert witnesses and can cross-examine them. A report is then drawn up setting out the jury's views, including any differences of opinion.

not necessarily representative. However, they do offer an opportunity to consider conflicting evidence, and we can see them being used for difficult decisions such as finding the right location for a waste incinerator, or prioritising social or health issues. A round table is different again; it includes the aspect that those invited are encouraged to share their experiences and perspectives as part of the debate.

What all these methods have in common is that they seek to create the opportunity for open and transparent dialogue and differ in detail, sometimes to accommodate the subject-matter. Using new presentation technology is a popular way to spice up the process. Visualisation techniques of amazing sophistication can now show the residents of an area about to be redeveloped how it will, or may, look in a few years' time. A demonstration we recently watched featured a helicopter view of the new utopia as it swooped down among the yet-to-be-built houses.

Now we have no doubt that the discussions and debate that followed such a presentation benefited from a far greater understanding of what was proposed than the parallel consultation a decade ago. But it also brings some problems. New technical wizardry can obscure as well as enlighten; it can exaggerate – or even misrepresent, either innocently or by design. Either way, these are dangers; among them is the fear that well-funded commercial interests can exploit such tricks of the trade to skew the debate in their favour.

The trend towards participative methods is closely related to the move to more inclusive consultation. Hard-to-reach or seldom-heard groups rarely feel comfortable with written documents: for some the traditional methods are simply out of the question. Meeting such groups face to face is far more productive. Specialists in dialogues with such interest groups strive to create conditions which are favourable for them. Many bodies representing disadvantaged people or those with social or medical problems can find even overtly participative mechanisms deeply inhibiting. Stakeholder conferences or deliberative events, for all their virtues, will not appeal to some of those bodies, hence the need to devise group-specific consultative mechanisms – more than likely through, or with, the group itself. One has to watch out for the gatekeeper problem, but modern thinking is to develop such machinery while avoiding a ghettoisation or marginalisation of those interests that do not easily integrate with others.

## NEW TECHNOLOGY

About twenty years ago, when the first generation of desktop computers appeared and e-mail was in its infancy, the larger companies began to realise that there was an opportunity to gather information from all their employees without sending them all a piece of paper. Thus was born what we now know as the eSurvey. Today there are dozens of eSurvey software applications available, the market-leaders being SNAP, SPSS and SurveyMonkey. The chances are we've all responded to surveys published in this way over the internet and the technology itself can be regarded as a commodity. What a wonderful invention! Cost per response is much lower. Internet penetration is now high. The digital divide is slowly disappearing, and by now there are few qualms about the integrity of such methods. Increasingly Government consultations rely heavily on this method; where key stakeholders are mostly organisations which are certain to have broadband internet connections, there can be few objections.

But there are drawbacks. As we have mentioned before, a survey is not of itself consultation and the eSurvey possesses many of the disadvantages of the non-electronic species – if not more. Many authors of eSurveys fail to recognise that the medium is subtly different and people approach it differently. We know that survey completion rates are lower, in part because it is not always obvious to the respondent how long the survey will take or whether the questions are relevant, interesting or suitable for him or her to answer. At least with the written version, the respondent can flick through it, glance at its contents before deciding to complete it.

In an interesting experiment we handed a printed, multiple-page survey to professional consultees. Invariably they opened it from the back, scanned it and took an instant decision whether to complete it themselves or delegate it to a colleague. With an internet survey, how do they decide whether or not to respond? Will the design of the page have an influence? Do clever graphics help? How important is the way the subject is presented? Does any of this matter?

It does. One of the concerns of market research purists was always the self-selected nature of the respondent base (even though the same applies to traditional mail surveys), particularly in the early days, when they were used heavily by technophiles and shunned by the technophobes! Since those days strenuous efforts have been made to demonstrate that data obtained through eSurveys produces largely similar results to that obtained through traditional questionnaires, but the suspicion remains that these people's brains work differently and respond to different stimuli.

eSurveys have many advantages when it comes to the design of the questions and the navigation through them. 'Conditional branching' is a case in point. This is when you answer 'yes' to a question and it takes you to the next one along; answer 'no' and you skip eighteen questions or get directed to a sub-set just for you, before returning to the main agenda. On paper, it's awful; online, you're not even aware it's happened.

Form design is a real art; the designers of eSurveys now have a battery of tools and tricks equal to any challenge. For this reason alone, we caution against taking a hard-copy questionnaire and just converting it for the web. Neither is it a job for the uninitiated – although the software applications proclaim themselves as user friendly, we'd hate to see a user-unfriendly one! By offering the survey-designer a galaxy of options, they seem to us to be adding to the problem rather than providing a solution. As for data analysis, one must not confuse the attractiveness of the graphics for the soundness of the analysis, but sadly, many do exactly that.

Moving on to the more consultation-specific applications, the survey can be integrated into an electronic consultation document. We call this an online commentary, especially if it allows the respondent to make comments on the narrative itself rather than just the questions posed as a survey within it. Imagine, if possible, a split screen with the consultor's paper on the left-hand side and room for you to add your comments on the right. The beauty of this is that it's like a draft document that you scribble on and send back to your boss. Of course, Microsoft included such functionality in MS Word a long time ago, but it doesn't work to return a Word document to the consultor in such a form – partly because it is so difficult to analyse. As an alternative to the distribution of a hard-copy consultation document, the online version provides an instantly available cost-effective option; as a substitute it is more controversial.

When the Labour Party launched its Big Conversation solely as an online document, it came in for criticism as a result. In our view, any consultation seeking a mass response probably needs a printed document – even though it's more environmentally sensitive to avoid this whenever possible. Another advantage of online documents is that they can help shorten the timescale for the whole exercise. In those cases where there are relatively few stakeholders – and when they know it's coming – the technology, in principle, enables a fast-track process. Who needs three months if consultees can give their opinions in an instant?

Now this, of course, is to disregard the complexities of secondary consultation or the whole issue of how those who take part formulate their responses. But the 'transaction time' for the online process is very short and as a fast-track enabler, the case is unanswerable.

More controversial as a new technology participation tool is the eDiscussion forum or, as it is popularly called, the chat room. This is an electronic version of the conversation in the pub, according to some of its advocates, a meeting place of ideas where the cut and thrust of dialogue is not inhibited by the conventions of more traditional debate. Well, so much for the theory – in practice these chat rooms vary enormously and many are culturally closer to the entertainment industry than any variant of democracy. True, it's a democratic forum – anyone can contribute, unless it's a closed club, and the rules of engagement are normally liberal, provided correspondents do not libel or infringe standards of public decency. In many ways, these forums provide a valuable outlet for people to express their views and are used, for example, by journalists and broadcasters as a means of feedback. Indeed, the advent of 24-hour rolling news and current affairs and its insatiable appetite for material has stimulated the development of a chat room for almost every programme. 'Have Your Say' they scream. What they mean is: 'Give us some user-generated content!'

A true eDiscussion forum is much more than a receiving point for feedback – it is a live dialogue that can illuminate any debate.

Representative it is not, although many of the contributors fail to appreciate the point. The question is whether one should regard these forums as anything more than vanity publishing. In other words, is anybody out there listening?

Part of the problem for consultors is that the software does not always lend itself to meaningful analysis. Not long after the new Scottish Parliament opened, we were shown around and during the visit introduced to several innovations, one of which was the eDiscussion forum. 'What had been the most intense debate?' we asked. Proudly we were told that the subject of wind farms had attracted 400-plus postings, a source of considerable satisfaction to those who had managed this process. Suitably impressed, we enquired whether this was 200 people who had each posted twice, or maybe only twenty who had posted twenty times each. Alas, no-one knew. It seems that short of reading the entire transcript and manually analysing who had contributed, the data wasn't available. Some of the difficulty lies in the cultural tendency towards anonymity, which was the initial hallmark of such forums. The use of nicknames or aliases means that Mickey Mouse can have a heated debate with Donald Duck! But in a consultation context, can this be right? If the debate is about whether to pull down a Victorian building in order to erect a new multiplex cinema, should it be possible for someone like the property company's director to masquerade as Winnie-the-Pooh in order to influence the discussion?

It is for this reason that public bodies have been reluctant to offer this type of eDiscussion. There are ways to avoid some of the issues. Participants can pre-register and commit to particular 'rules of engagement'. Forums can be moderated or managed, either before anything is published, 'pre-moderation', or afterwards, 'post-moderation' – an onerous activity. Moderators are trained to guide a debate: 'Now that's an interesting point, Martin – have any of the rest of you had similar experiences?' They are taught when to start up a new thread of debate and when to close down one that's run its course. On occasions, it's part of the job to summarise the discussion and write up the conclusions for publication either to the participants (a good form of feedback) or to the world at large. Most importantly, such reports are of value to the consultor organisation itself – and the role is analogous to the focus group facilitator or note-taker who prepares a summary for consideration by those who are running the consultation. In management terms all this supporting activity means cost and hassle. People whose views are edited to make them decent, or who are refused publication, for whatever reason, may want to challenge the decisions of the moderator. Then an appeals mechanism gets put in place. . . before long you have more bureaucracy than with the old-fashioned methods!

The BBC actually gave up moderating its forums; no wonder public bodies are shy of such facilities. In part this is because of the fear that forums act as a magnet for the dissatisfied and the disaffected. There are not many examples of their being used by lots of highly satisfied citizens competing to voice their paeans for services they've received. It's back to the age-old conundrum – do you spend money making it easier for people to articulate their complaints or do you invest the same amount in addressing their grievances?

The whole question of using public money to provide a platform for what some may see as whingeing self-publicists grinding obscure axes is an absurd irrelevance for many in local government, and they will take some persuasion to go down this path. However, a few brave souls have done so, arguing that it is better for debates to be organised by the community as a whole rather than by fringe groups peddling their own ideas. That way, it is more transparent and it signals that it is okay to dissent. One example is the London Borough of Southwark. When we looked at its website it had managed to attract more than 1,700 postings on almost 200 different topics, many of which are far from controversial.

An alternative way for those who share an objective and make common cause is through social networking sites such as Facebook and Bebo. The Wispa chocolate bar owes its successful reintroduction to a viral marketing campaign run largely in this way. Most recently, Twitter has started to be used by individuals to nudge their 'followers' to support their latest cause.

The 10 Downing Street ePetitions site attracts thousands and has resulted in hundreds of petitions being open at any one time. In one celebrated case a campaign against road pricing attracted over a million signatures. In her 2008 White Paper 'Communities in Control',* Local Government Secretary Hazel Blears sought to make it easier for people to express their views and suggested a legal duty to respond to petitions. The Local Democracy Bill, if and when it becomes law later in 2009, will oblige every council to invest in ePetitions software.

There are safer, less contentious forms of eDialogue. We are getting familiar with what is called 'VIP-chat'. This on the surface is very much what it says on the tin, an online question-and-answer session with someone of note. But it isn't always with exactly the person you thought it was, for world leaders who have been persuaded to do this have occasionally found an inability to use a keyboard and an ignorance of the web a slight disadvantage! Still, never mind, what felt right for Vladimir Putin was bound to be okay for Gordon Brown and who cares if someone else actually operates the technology? A videoed interview session is but an extension of the same idea, but can process far fewer questions, especially given politicians' resistance to short answers.

This form of dialogue is likely to increase once civic leaders and chief officers learn to become comfortable with the medium. 'Here is your monthly opportunity to put questions to the council's chief planning officer.' It's a sort of local radio with fewer irritating presenters, if you like. One London borough has experimented with chat sessions for local councillors in an attempt to mimic traditional political surgeries, allowing private one-to-one messaging between young people and elected representatives.

In short, public officials and elected members alike are becoming accustomed to being broadcast, even at local levels. A webcast of a council meeting may not command the ratings of *EastEnders*, but where matters of genuine controversy arise, we expect to see an upsurge of interest in this.

But it isn't consultation unless there is the possibility of dialogue through some feedback messages. Television does this all the time, of course, inviting viewers to text their views or reactions using live SMS messaging. It is hardly scientific, but it does give a flavour of what some

---

people think. On Saturday evenings, a programme on BBC Radio 5 Live called *606* invites listeners to text their thoughts on football matches they've just attended. Their messages are then read out on air alongside the more familiar phone-ins, where sports fans typically joust with know-all commentators as to whether the referee in a particular game was biased or just incompetent!

Switch back to television; the whole genre of live fly-on-the-wall *Big Brother*-style programmes have spawned their own version of feedback, with enthusiasts engaged in prolonged dialogue about the minutiae of what's happened. Is this a form of consultation? Can one suppose that instead of debating whether the way Kevin spoke to Sally means that everyone should vote him out of the *Big Brother* house, the same process can work for a plan to grant a licence to a new nightclub in Bletchley? In other words, is this the modern form of public debate?

If it is, there are many possible objections. Someone 'moderates' the dialogue and the editorial decision as to which views to broadcast gives them immense power, which we know has not always been wielded impartially. TV programmes have a built-in preference for the dramatic over the boring and are systemically more inclined to prefer confrontation and controversy to consensus. On the other hand, public debate has always been susceptible to such forces. Is it, in principle, very different from the greater attention given to a flamboyant and charismatic speaker at a public meeting compared to the quietly spoken but more reflective contributor?

In 2007 and 2008, broadcasters who had been careless or capricious in their use of feedback mechanisms, such as phone-ins and competitions, got their comeuppance and only time will tell whether this is an activity which, once it has learnt its lesson, can settle down to a reasonable set of standards. Some people think that the inherent nature of the technology and the pressures for 'good television' make this an unlikely scenario. We are inclined to agree with them and are therefore sceptical about the long-term contribution these forms of vox pop will make to the consultation processes.

What is undeniable, however, is that easy-to-use messaging and snap polls will continue to be popular and may just be effective as part of a wider mix of dialogue methods. It may boil down to the subject-matter. For some serious policy-type subjects, it may look and feel like a dumbing down of debate. For other topics, especially ones with a connection to new technology or maybe particularly targeted at young people, such techniques may be very appropriate.

Finally, there is a rather different role for new technology and one which may well be more important than those we have considered so far. This is not to use the new tools for the dialogue itself, but to find and access the debate in the first place. In many ways the bigger challenge facing a stakeholder organisation that wishes to influence public bodies is to identify where the consultation and its associated papers might be found. This has led to directory applications – literally an index of consultations; one such product calls itself a Consultation Finder.

Increasing numbers of organisations now have a special section of their website entitled 'Consultations' and providing a listing of exercises that are either completed, current or planned. If you click on a particular entry it should take you to a more detailed page on the particular exercise, tell you what it's about, how to download the relevant documents and maybe how to participate in the dialogue. Here it might offer some of the new technology tools themselves, possibly an eSurvey or the opportunity to join in a discussion forum. Alternatively it might promote public meetings, seminars or other more deliberative ways of becoming involved. Where a consultation has been completed, this is the place where, ideally, visitors to the website can find out what happened. This is where the published feedback should be found, along with any reports and, if you're lucky, cross-references to other relevant public engagement.

Note our use of the phrase 'if you're lucky'. Sadly, we haven't been lucky very often! There's nothing wrong with these applications, but few organisations have mastered the art of keeping the data up to date. We think there are three reasons for this. Firstly, the people with the knowledge work in departmental silos; they are too busy with operational aspects of consultation exercises, so that putting the data on the web is a low priority and is often neglected. Secondly, there is insufficient training to give such people the confidence to use the web-publishing aspect of these systems on a continuous basis. But thirdly, there is a perception by many that such pages on the website are a just another tick in an eGovernment box and that few people pay any attention to them. Indeed if a failure to keep them up to the minute prompted lots of phone calls from irate consultees demanding to know why they could not find certain information, no doubt there would be a stronger motivation to fix the problem. As it is, many local authorities and other public bodies, having invested in such directories, have struggled to make them effective and this in turn limits their appeal.

We don't think that eConsultation will remain a minority sport for much longer. This is not because something wonderful is about to happen to the techniques we've described, but just because of the wider acceptance of new technology in the way that people work. Slowly but surely, transactions we used to undertake using traditional methods are giving way to newer, digitally based alternatives. As more and more people license their cars, book theatre tickets, apply for a grant or download a map over the internet, so they become more likely to look for similarly quick and effortless ways of being heard. It is said that we live in a cash-rich, time-poor society. In the depths of recession, the 'cash-rich' part of the description seems not to feature; it's the pressure on people's time that seems to determine their likelihood sooner or later to embrace eConsultation if they want to have influence.

This is why, of all the innovations we've described, the growth of new technology is ultimately likely to be the most telling.

## THE CHANGING DIALOGUE PROFILE

The innovations we've described are all real, and despite the drawbacks we've highlighted, are gradually becoming more widely used. But the true change that is afoot is one of those cases where the whole is greater than the sum of its parts. It is not the individual techniques, new or exciting though they may be, that matter; it's the way they can be mixed and matched for individual projects so as to produce a slightly different impact case by case.

Someone setting out to engage with the public today has a much wider range of options available – and it is this choice that is the biggest single change. It allows someone to mix a very traditional approach with something far more experimental. Planners, for example, can use a proprietary method called Planning for Real®, where consultees can physically handle models of roads, buildings and other spatial elements, alongside the ubiquitous consultation document.* The traditional exhibition can now use a games-based feature. Consultations with big budgets can mount impressive participatory conferences and small-scale specialist projects can use techniques such as peer interviews to build relationships with seldom-heard or difficult-to-access individuals or groups.

Choice is not always an unmitigated blessing. Among those who commission consultation exercises are the over-enthusiastic, who are drawn to the sexy or experimental when they might do better to stick to routine tried-and-tested methods. Despite this, a rich and diverse menu of consultation options presents the public with variety and allows imaginative organisers of public engagement to creatively design a dialogue cocktail that is right for the subject-matter in question – and for the cultural comfort zone of different stakeholders.

---

\* See Neighbourhood Initiatives, http://www.nif.co.uk/planningforreal.

# PART FOUR
# MAKING CONSULTATION
# MEANINGFUL

# 16. SILVER BULLET OR MAGIC FORMULA?

SPOT THE DIFFERENCE

The distinction between these two rather over-used phrases captures some of the debate among professionals who work in the field of public engagement.

The silver bullet is a single reliable special solution. Long ago it was held to be the only way to kill werewolves, which were immune to other forms of attack. Today it is the sole ingredient that can make a critical difference and can amount to success or failure. Is there such an element in the world of consultation? Is there a single step, which, undertaken properly, would in all probability see a consultor through to a satisfactory outcome?

The magic formula is a different idea altogether. It implies that there are lots of elements in the mix, and that, rather like baking a cake, the skill lies in devising a successful recipe, assembling the ingredients, preparing them properly and cooking competently. This is a much more complex process and things can go wrong at different stages. We think that public and stakeholder consultation is much more like this and is intrinsically a very fault-intolerant process; by this we mean that one can do almost everything right and yet fail because of one seemingly small oversight. Lots of professionals make similar claims – doctors, lawyers, teachers, architects, civil engineers, to name but a few. But many of these involve very precise technical disciplines; the field of social affairs or politics is seldom an exact science, and there has usually been a fair amount of wiggle room.

What this book seeks to demonstrate is that amid far too much mediocre or downright poor consultation, there is an emerging sense of best practice. It isn't really codified, although there have been a few faltering attempts at standards. The Government's first real attempt to lay down the ground rules for its own consultations turned out to be too ambitious. It was quietly weakened in 2003 and, when reviewed in 2008, watered down still further.

## STANDARDS

The difficulty with standards is that the diversity of methods – ranging from the very formal to completely informal – militates against very precise rules. There have been a few attempts to set standards, among which Communities Scotland deserves special mention. In 2004 it used a highly participative process to come up with a 24-page document, *National Standards for Community Engagement*, which has been found useful by many of those who have to organise consultations north of the border.* Our criticism is that many of the so-called standards carry the hallmark of 'consultation by brainstorm' and some are monumentally vague. How exactly is one supposed to judge whether participants in a consultation 'behave openly and honestly' and that the exercise has 'no hidden agendas'?

This is just one of a number of indicators from a set of ten standards: Involvement, Support, Planning, Methods, Working Together, Sharing Information, Working with Others, Improvement, Feedback and, finally, Monitoring and Evaluation. None of these are wrong or inappropriate; overall they represent a fair agenda for what needs to be done properly, as we hope to show in this section. But they suffer from being over-elaborate or too comprehensive. If we return to the recipe analogy, the list of ingredients is just too long and there isn't enough to distinguish those that are essential from those that are optional. Nonetheless, they are a useful contribution to our understanding.

When we established the Consultation Institute, we took a different approach in devising the Consultation Charter.† It seeks to be concise, consisting of seven principles: Integrity, Visibility, Accessibility,

---

\*    See http://www.scdc.org.uk/national-standards-community-engagement.

†    Available from the Consultation Institute, http://www.consultationinstitute.org.

Transparency, Disclosure, Fair Interpretation and Publication. As with the Communities Scotland standards, one can build checklists underneath each of these headings as a mechanism for evaluating whether or not a particular exercise conforms.

## ACCREDITATION OR KITEMARKS?

It may be premature to speculate which set of standards emerges as the definitive one. We are convinced that some form of recognition for best practice is inevitable. We aren't sure if a Government-backed formal accreditation scheme is needed, but there is clearly a demand for some signal that a consultation is being undertaken to a certain quality. There are several reasons for this.

One is that public bodies often find themselves in a no-win situation; they either face a vigorous debate on the substantive issue, or they have a row about the consultation process. Recently we attended a small public meeting convened by the local Member of Parliament to discuss passenger dissatisfaction with the area's railway operator. A curious thing happened. After acceptably professional presentations from the train operator, full of candid apologies and some promises of jam tomorrow, the MP as chairman sought to build an agenda of items the audience would like to discuss. A predictable list was assembled, including fares, rolling stock, car parking, timetables and the like; but by far the biggest issue was capacity, especially since the number of coaches on a popular commuter service had been halved. 'Let's start the discussion with capacity, then,' said the MP.

But before anyone could say 'standing room only', someone put up his hand to question the railway company. 'You mentioned you had consulted the passengers,' he said, 'but we didn't know about it.' There followed an animated discussion about the exercise and how it failed to engage most of the people in the room.

Soon the persistent MP tried to move on, saying: 'Let's get back to capacity issues.'

Another member of the audience immediately put up her hand. 'Going back to the consultation,' she said, 'why didn't the people of our village receive the leaflet?' A few more minutes of discussion culminated in an apology from the senior manager present, who had to admit to failures in their process and deflated much of his earlier ebullience. By the time the discussion finally moved to the issue of substance, a lot of time had already been taken – and the credibility of the service-provider compromised.

We think this scene has been played out in hundreds of similar situations. What it shows is that the process frequently gets in the way of the substance. Time and time again, consultors have been only too willing to engage in a proper discussion about a substantive issue, only to find that the intricacies of the consultation process occupy too much of the debate. Because consultees sometimes over-interpret simple administrative failures, which fuel any existing sense of injustice or resentment, many of these disputes escalate out of all proportion. It is as if attention to procedural detail becomes a litmus test for the integrity of the consultor; where the ultimate outcome is a disappointment, angry consultees point the finger at process deficiencies as proof positive that the entire exercise was tainted. An independent verification from a trusted third party can remove this from the agenda.

A second reason why standards are becoming important is the need for better expectation management. Too much is made up as people go along and the absence of best-practice benchmarks simply creates further confusion. We saw a tender invitation a short while ago where a local authority wanted to use Citizens' Juries for a particularly thorny local consultation. As there was no clear definition of what was meant by a Citizens' Jury, bidders were presumably at liberty to interpret the term any way they liked. When we enquired of the tenderer what she had in mind, she confirmed that the intention was indeed to rely upon the creativity and imagination of suppliers to offer them something interesting.

Such 'fishing trips' are not unusual and not always a bad idea. In a world of greater clarity, though, less time and money would be wasted. In more mature markets, people know what they are buying and what they are getting. Many public officials set off to conduct a consultation without much of a feel for what they are launching. In fact, we suspect that there is a culture of 'out of sight, out of mind' behind many consultations. The minister may genuinely want there to have been extensive dialogue on her proposals, but prefers not to scrutinise the details too closely. It reminds us of the words of Bertie Ahern, the former Irish Taoiseach, who commented that policy-making is rather like making sausages: one should not enquire too closely about the manufacturing process!

Without some benchmarks, agreement on key definitions and a better understanding of performance standards, it is possible for consultors and consultees to experience the same process and yet for one group to be delighted and the other depressed by the same level of performance. Is 95 per cent successful distribution of a household survey good or bad? Is a 10 per cent response rate satisfactory or unsatisfactory? Is 40 per cent unprompted awareness of a consultation acceptable? Is 1 per cent attendance at a public meeting okay? Is it reasonable to wait six months for feedback?

These questions illustrate how standards cannot just be a set of numbers. There may, however, be a need for a robust method whereby those in charge know whether what they did is defensible – a way of knowing what is below par and what is excellent.

There is a third reason why standards will become more important and that is the need to tackle the scepticism of the general public. We have repeatedly noted that trust in some consultor bodies is at a low ebb. Some of this is justified, and high-profile criticism, such as the legal challenges we discussed earlier, lodges itself in the popular memory and can take years to disappear. It means, unfortunately, that many consultations start with a built-in disadvantage, with people mistrusting the process even before it gets under way. This may be seriously unfair to conscientious managers. It may also reveal prejudice on the part of consultees, who may be as guilty of prejudging the outcome as the consultor. The fact remains that confidence in the process is not always high and the ability to rely upon a respected form of verification might at least allay some of the consultees' fears.

So we are not advocating a statutory scheme – there is just no need. It would be over the top to require every consultation to carry a best-practice accreditation. But we do see the need for the contentious ones to demonstrate that they are run properly, and we think that consultors who want to protect themselves from criticism will see the need for themselves.

# 17. THE DISCIPLINES OF SM

## DISCIPLINE!

SM, in this context, stands for 'stakeholder management' – not 'sado-masochism', although the concept of discipline appears to feature in both contexts. Those who practice stakeholder management might also reflect that in this light-hearted comparison, there may be some other parallels for it can be a painful experience with much introspection and even feelings of guilt!

For all that, we think that if the consultation culture is here to stay, one of the inevitable consequences will be the need for organisations of all kinds to understand stakeholder management better. Many will, whatever we say in this book, adopt several of its practices, either consciously or unconsciously. Some will use this terminology and, as we noted earlier, there are already people occupying such posts as Stakeholder Manager or Stakeholder Relations Officer. Others will just amend a traditional public affairs role or tweak existing jobs.

The variety of stakeholders is pretty obvious and includes customers, suppliers, investors, regulators and so forth. Companies manage their interactions with them; many use the term 'corporate social responsibility' for this activity. In the public sector it is still new, even though the stakeholder language has been in use for a while. This has been partly the result of all the consultation activity we have noted, but it has also arisen from the popularity of evidence-based policy-making. For any large organisation, the challenge is broadly the same – how to manage, as opposed to react to, what happens in your relations with stakeholders.

This requires a disciplined approach to many activities which in the past have been conducted in a largely *ad hoc* and disorganised manner. It involves a serious investment in information technology plus further development of processes and systems for capturing, storing and analysing information on stakeholder organisations.

## STAKEHOLDER MANAGEMENT TRENDS

This is not the place to describe stakeholder management in detail. But it is the place to recognise how its adoption will radically change and improve the practice of public engagement and consultation. There are three fundamental trends.

### Stakeholder identification will be more comprehensive

The hit-or-miss practices we observed earlier are the product of an age where few records were kept and where the proceedings of one exercise were rarely shared with its successor. When policy-makers sat down to design a consultation exercise, their starting point was usually a rather blank sheet with those key stakeholders who came to mind scribbled across the top. Replacing this with a more systematic effort is not in principle difficult to do, except in so far as few consultations these days fall neatly into one departmental or even geographical unit, and the question arises of who comes round the table to identify those stakeholders that need to come within the scope of the next exercise.

### Data-supported relationships

It has taken about twenty years for the commercial sector to invest in customer relationship management (CRM) and to learn how to gather and use the data it has on its customers.* The public sector found CRM applicable to its activities much later and benefited in part from the lessons learnt in the private sector. Among these was the realisation that the answer lies seldom in data of itself, but in the way it

---

\* CRM consists of the processes a company uses to track and organise its contacts with its current and prospective customers, and is particularly used to refer to software applications connected with such processes.

is used. But also there is little tradition in the public sector of keeping high-quality records of contacts with community groups and other stakeholder organisations; notes or minutes rarely confirm who said what to whom. Instead they rely on capturing the bare conclusions of the discussion.

In contrast, a stakeholder management approach recognises the importance not just of transactional data such as that, but also a wealth of important organisational information which needs to be gathered and stored if effective relationships are to be built.

### Data maintenance matters

The trouble with 'soft' data is that it is difficult to capture consistently. Unlike records of sales, where one can use a sales order-processing system, or financial transactions of any sort, the kind of information needed on stakeholder organisations is less precise. Let's take a simple example. Two of the most basic items of data about any stakeholder are 'what is it?', then 'what is it for?'. In principle this is not difficult to discover. Almost every community organisation now has a website; hopefully, under the heading 'About Us' will be found a mission statement or equivalent. Sometimes there is a more elaborate set of objectives but at this point there arises a need to look carefully and maybe read between the lines. After all, until Tony Blair came along, the Labour Party declared an intention to nationalise everything in sight, according to Clause 4 of its constitution! In another example, take membership data. Lots of consultees exaggerate – sometimes it matters, sometimes it doesn't. Our point is that the background information needed to conduct a continuous relationship with stakeholder organisations is not always what it seems to be – and much of it has a margin of error.

The most dynamic information of all is contact data. Details of individual post holders, their addresses, telephone numbers and e-mail addresses change regularly. We estimate that over the course of a year, the 'perishability' of data in this category is around 40–50 per cent. Yet without processes to keep this information current and accurate, consultors run the risk of appearing inefficient or not to care.

## A SINGLE REPOSITORY OF KNOWLEDGE

All these trends point to a clear yet elusive conclusion. Those who want to succeed in public engagement or consultation need a single stakeholder database. At first glance many will find it surprising that such a statement of the obvious is at all radical. But it is. We discussed earlier the litany of failures that stem from having a multitude of lists as department after department squirrels away its hard-won data trophies and makes heavy weather of exchanging or sharing even the most basic level of information.

Quality-conscious process-managers have learnt that one important way to reduce inaccuracy is to enter data only once. Every time someone copies an entry from one system or application to another, there is scope for error. Having several sources of data where one should suffice inevitably means that they are seldom consistent one with another. Even sophisticated data synchronisation tools cannot always overcome the physical separation of systems and in any case this is not a technical matter, but more a question of having a disciplined process. Having a single source of stakeholder information has many advantages. Not only does it reduce the scope for mistakes, but also frees up resources that are wasted duplicating data-gathering, data support and analysis effort.

An effective stakeholder database should contain three types of information:

- *Information about the stakeholder organisation itself.* We referred to its basic aims earlier – and also, where relevant, the nature and statistics on its membership. But more is needed. In particular it can be critical to understand its governance. Is there a committee? If so, who is on it? When does it meet? How frequently?
- *Relationship history.* This should be a consolidated and complete chronology of what's happened between your organisation and its stakeholders. Just as a CRM system captures the chronology of an organisation's transactions with customers, so this needs to capture the interactions with stakeholders – including correspondence, documents exchanged, minutes of meetings and so forth.

Centralising the data does not mean that the relationship has to be similarly centralised, but the record has to be kept in one place.

- *Preferred mode of consultation.* We single this out as a piece of information every organisation needs to hold in respect of those stakeholders it expects to consult. It requires you to know how consultees prefer to be contacted. Some have a preference for face-to-face meetings, others can handle the traditional big fat document – others will only respond to eConsultation. It is not that the consultor must always act in accord with these preferences – cost or other resources may make it impossible. But we think it is important for them to know the preference and appreciate the reasons for it.

## GATHERING THE DATA – THE STAKEHOLDER PORTAL

Gathering all this information for potentially large numbers of stakeholder organisations sounds a formidable task and those who anticipate building such databases recoil in horror at the spectre of armies of clerks manning the telephone to check that Mrs Smith is still the Hon. Sec. of the Townswomen's Guild.

Fear not; that was then, and this is now. The modern way to keep this type of data maintained is to transfer responsibility to the stakeholders themselves. They are the ones who know that Mrs Smith has been replaced by Mrs Brown and that the e-mail address has changed. The trick is to find a way to motivate community or business organisations to tell those bodies that might need to know and to do so in a timely fashion. We think the answer lies in building a stakeholder portal. As with other 'portals' the idea is of a gateway – but this time for individuals or organisations that want to register and therefore have certainty that the consultor knows about them. The portal for stakeholders should be built around self-registration whereby those who wish to be consulted provide such information as we have listed above. The stakeholder states its objectives, declares the membership and outlines its governance. Above all it registers which of a list of forthcoming topics it wishes to be consulted upon. A council can summarise its forthcoming programme of public engagement and ask its stakeholders to tick those boxes where they wish to have an involvement. At a stroke one can solve the problem of unwanted documents pouring into the in-trays of consultee organisations who just aren't interested. Consultation fatigue, when caused by indiscriminate 'ask everyone' methods, can be a thing of the past.

Once the stakeholder has registered and indicated the subjects upon which it wishes to be consulted, the portal can, we think, provide it with a menu of activities from the directory applications we described earlier through to the online dialogue methods such as eConsultation or eDiscussion forums. This time, however, it is possible to present the stakeholder with only those consultations in which it has an interest; the focus of concern is now understood. In today's service culture and in IT terms, they call this 'personalisation' – a valuable exercise in removing all the irrelevant clutter from one's field of vision. It's a little like programming Google Alerts to let you know of something that is of particular relevance to you.

We are not yet aware that anyone has built a stakeholder portal as such, though many of its component pieces are becoming available and are there waiting to be assembled. Many local authorities have created community directories – and there are private ones alongside. What they all have in common is a platform to inform the rest of society about what local organisations do. It's more than advertising, although it does that too. It is a local notice board and a communication tool – somewhere for people to discover mutual interests and common causes.

The stakeholder portal we see on the horizon builds upon all this but, in addition, integrates all those electronic dialogue tools which are now available. So if the chamber of trade wishes to press for a new academy in town, it can use the portal to seek people or organisations of a similar mind. It becomes a marriage between consultation and campaigning where stakeholders can find who supports and who opposes particular proposals. Note that all of this is totally transparent. If we use the portal to publish or view – either as part of a formal consultation of just as part of our normal day-to-day campaigning, it is done so openly, visible to all. It can be a one-stop shop for consultees and make it easier for one stakeholder to see or read what another is saying.

So if the benefits are so manifest, why do we not already have them in place? We think there are five reasons:

- No single supplier of eConsultation tools has yet brought a satisfactory product to market.
- Having a stakeholder portal either presupposes that there is already, or anticipates that there will be, a single stakeholder database. But as we've noted, this is not yet happening, for departmental silos still rule in many organisations; the culture of each with its own list still lingers.
- Investment is still focused on the needs of the consultor rather than the convenience of the consultee; too few organisations responsible for public engagement have recognised the need for an accurate database and the role that such portals can play in monitoring data without incurring disproportionate costs.
- Much of the eConsultation functionality comes in bits and, like other systems, has grown by addition and enhancement on a piecemeal basis. To create a stakeholder portal involves integrating many of these tools and the skills to do that are in short supply.
- There is a fear that the digital divide makes this a not quite politically correct solution. Many of those working in the field of public engagement are acutely aware that many of the seldom-heard groups do not have easy access to the internet and that many others, such as older people, do not feel comfortable with the medium. They fear that allowing some stakeholders to register their details to make their preferences, to choose which consultations to participate in and then to conduct a visible dialogue – all in full view of whoever wants to know – while others are unable or unwilling to do so is somehow wrong. They point out that although approximately 60 per cent (depending upon location) of the population has access to the internet at home or at work, this still leaves a substantial part of the community excluded. Far better, they argue, to spend limited money on more participative techniques.

The digital divide issue is a real one for individuals – but it is now largely a thing of the past as far as stakeholder organisations are concerned. There are now very few of them which do not have such access and in the private sector there are no inhibitions at all in confining the choice to an electronic one. Just try booking on a budget airline!

In the public sector, we agree there must be provision for the non-digital player – but in practice, developing and deploying a stakeholder portal will achieve so much that the small sums required to supplement this primary tool with secondary communications facilities for the non-digital should be affordable.

## IT INVESTMENT

Putting stakeholders first has not been the natural reflex of management. Yes, they want to hear their views, but making serious investment in that communications channel has thus far been difficult to justify. Until the trade in dialogue is seen to be as valuable as financial transactions, it will play second fiddle. This is why the providers of CRM software are yet to exploit this market.

Most of what's needed for the next generation of stakeholder management exists now in IT terms. The code is written and the software that carries information to the town hall about where you live, whether you receive housing benefit and whether you have paid your council tax already exists. With modest changes, these massive applications could certainly handle what in database terms are very small, if specialised, datasets of stakeholder organisations.

In fact, a mid-sized unitary authority has between 4,000 and 5,000 stakeholder organisations, so in theory a CRM system that already handles a range of services for 200,000 residents could comfortably handle this latest challenge. So why isn't it happening?

We believe that there are a number of factors which might now inhibit this path:

1. CRM system-builders haven't yet been asked to develop this application. No-one is queuing at their door saying 'please!' Few consultation or public engagement champions understand CRM very well and IT departments have seldom understood the vagaries of stakeholder management.
2. CRM applications are having a tough time out there. The complex task of business process re-engineering for hundreds of different council services and constant concomitant change management is

a perpetual challenge. There is usually a long list of improvements to make – and so far the consultation co-ordinator has scarcely been recognised, let alone permitted to join this queue.

3. CRM solutions may just be too big. Many of them were conceived for large enterprises with dozens of users and a hierarchy of roles. Consultation is, in comparison, a cottage industry. It would feel like using a sledgehammer to crack a nut – and, of course, our stakeholder managers or consultation co-ordinators aren't particularly trained to use sledgehammers. 'Can't we use MS Outlook instead?'

All this is to try to explain why, despite most public bodies and commercial companies having CRM solutions of one kind or another available, they are not used to manage public engagement.

We don't think this will necessarily remain the position. All these reasons, though valid today, may be less problematic in the future and we predict that many CRM software vendors will start to tackle the requirement of stakeholder management. A slowdown in their core activities may yet send them looking for new parallel opportunities.

What might they do differently? They might invest in the more demanding aspects of knowledge base navigation whereby those responding to stakeholder submissions or telephone calls can refer to relevant documentation directly and easily. They might also develop specialist tools such as stakeholder mapping. Right now this technique is used without the benefit of new technology; most of the variants we've examined consist of a group of managers meeting around the table to see if they can reach consensus on their view of various stakeholders. Using conventional Boston-square style analysis, usually on the two axes of Influence and Interest, they can 'position' each one so that it helps them figure out which ones are 'key stakeholders' and which are not. We have often thought that the therapeutic benefits of this process may be greater than its practical value – but investment in technology and the visualisation of stakeholder mapping is very promising. If the data produced could be integrated into a CRM database, and tracked over time, this would become a useful tool for monitoring the changing relationship with important contacts.

Other tools which can and, in our view, will be developed include consultation planning 'wizards' and effective project management functionality for public engagement – hardly rocket science in technical terms but important to reduce the extent to which the wheel gets reinvented every time. Specialist eConsultation companies have already developed valuable templates, but these are still early days in learning how to reuse consultation components.

Among the industries that could capitalise upon a standard IT-assisted approach would be civil engineering, where large infrastructure projects almost always involve stakeholder consultation as a key part of project planning. There seems to be a need for as rigorous an approach to the planning of listening exercises as to the quantity-surveying aspects of the building project itself.

We recently sat down with the people who are planning the massive project to supplement London's 150-year-old storm water system with the new Thames Tideway tunnel, a £1.7 billion project that will involve about forty construction sites disturbing the peace of many London communities for the twelve years of its duration. Organising community engagement for this, or for the Olympics, is a massive challenge. Likewise for new nuclear power stations, major road-building contracts, rail infrastructure projects and the hundreds of regeneration schemes in our towns and cities.

It seems to us that the management skills required for these demanding projects need to extend to their associated consultation activities instead of being sub-contracted or hived off to others. In other words, they should be fully integrated into overall project management.

# 18. FIRST THINGS FIRST

## STARTING POINTS

Even if many of the more obvious problems surrounding consultation manifest themselves at the end of the process, it is at the beginning that the real difficulties arise. That is because too many listening exercises start life as vague attempts to involve people; no wonder their organisers wake up months later to the realisation that they've ended up with information that either isn't what they wanted, or just isn't very useful.

Too late they conclude that the activity is only as good as the data that has been produced. If the consultation has been badly designed, no amount of elaborate analysis will change the sow's ear into a silk purse. The problems experienced in feedback, for example, are just symptomatic of the wider issue of how consultations have been conceived in the first place. If the purpose of the dialogue is sound, the various tasks that characterise the latter stages of the process will be more likely to follow a logical and predictable path towards better use of the data.

The trick is to get far better at the front end of the process.

So, borrowing from Oscar Hammerstein, 'let's start at the very beginning'. What exactly initiates a consultation exercise? We have discerned a number of scenarios – some rather more justifiable than others.

### A desire to be seen to be listening

We're not just referring to politicians; a few years ago we had a major financial institution parading itself as a 'listening bank'. People in the public eye are, however, tempted to make a virtue of their willingness to listen and recent leaders of the UK political parties have been noticeably more explicit in recent years. When Tony Blair suffered a significantly reduced Commons majority in the 2005 general election, his immediate reaction was to talk about 'listening more'. When Gordon Brown succeeded him two years later, he also used the same language. The other parties are just as concerned to press the same buttons, and all have instigated listening exercises at one stage or another. They don't always work!

More damaging is when ministers launch consultations in a speculative bid to attract favourable publicity. There may or may not be serious issues of policy lurking on the departmental agenda, but to artificially stimulate a debate when there are few if any policy proposals to consider can often be viewed as a cynical exercise in spin. In 2006, the Department for International Development launched a consultation on eliminating world poverty.* In an age when the average consultation paper is still published as a weighty tome, at first sight this was a refreshing change – a slim, almost flimsy volume containing little if anything of substance apart from an exhortation for consultees to send in their ideas so that the minister could subsequently publish a White Paper.

No doubt this was a worthy subject for debate, but smacked of 'has anyone got anything to suggest because we haven't got a clue'. We are probably being very unfair to conscientious ministers, but rightly or wrongly this is what it looked like – a consultation designed more for effect than any substantial contribution to policy-making.

Too many leaders want to be associated with a listening exercise, giving the impression that question one is 'How can we hold a consultation?' and question two is 'What do we want to know?' We have a suspicion that the true inspiration for initiatives of this kind come from marketing consultancies. From their perspective, they are perfectly logical (and profitable) ways to promote options and ideas. We will see more of this kind of activity, for social marketing† is establishing itself as a significant

---

*    See http://www.dfid.gov.uk/pubs/files/wp2006-consultation.pdf.

†    For more information about social marketing see http://www.nsmcentre.org.uk.

and useful approach to tackling lifestyle problems such as obesity, binge drinking and other health-related issues.

### We are legally obliged to consult

There are countless legal obligations to consult and they may well do more harm than good. Largely inspired by our legislators' natural desire to stimulate the consultation culture, their effect is often to induce managers to consult when there isn't a burning question with options that stakeholders or the general public can reasonably understand or offer an opinion about. Given that we are where we are and that no politician will realistically light a bonfire of such enactments, we live with the assumption that the impetus for many consultations will be a provision somewhere that this is what legally has to be done.

At least when there is a statutory obligation we can be sure that a consultation happens. It does not, however, guarantee that it is any good. We don't know of a provision that says to organisations what to do once they have obtained people's views, although there are increasing moves towards asking some, such as NHS trusts, to report on what they decided after the event. That is a move in the right direction.

### Wanting to be better informed. . . for a purpose

Ultimately this is the one that matters. Unless managers genuinely want to know something, normally one should not bother. The trouble is that few organisations are good at planning their information requirements and for many, by the time they realise they need to know something, there isn't the time to organise a proper consultation.

We have to draw a distinction between knowledge for a specific purpose and just for its own sake, somewhat akin to the difference between applied and pure science. Social science has had a long and distinguished history in both areas and one can always argue that one needs to understand the context in order to know what specific questions to pursue. The best consultations occur, however, when someone realises the causal connection between a decision that is needed and the information that should ideally underpin it. We don't think this is often done particularly well, if at all.

The great virtue of this third scenario is that the starting point is 'We need to know this'. Much of the data that is sought may be factual. If you're in the business of designating development land to allow for more housing, you might decide that you need facts and figures about the existing housing stock; or you may need estimates of likely demand; you may also need to know what's in the pipeline and so forth. Next come people's perceptions. What do residents think? What do potential buyers want? What can the building industry deliver? That then prompts a series of relevant questions such as whose views can be sought and how one should ascertain them.

This last example is the ideal. It poses the questions in the right order and is much more likely to produce a meaningful result.

## THE CONSULTATION MANDATE

There is even more to this initiation phase. For some years we have advised organisations contemplating a consultation to construct something we call the consultation mandate. We've chosen the word carefully, for we think the analogy with a political mandate is reasonable. So fed up are people with a succession of public and private bodies soliciting their views that the onus these days is on the consultor to demonstrate exactly upon what basis, or at least on what pretext, the consultation is being conducted.

Several public bodies have experimented with a control document to initiate a consultation and, following the principles of good project management, tried to capture the key elements of what's intended. Unfortunately these can run into page upon page of bureaucratic nonsense. You may know the kind of thing: 'Do you intend to comply with the provisions of the authority's gender equality scheme?' or 'Have you carried out an independent risk assessment of any activities proposed in your project plan?' They conjure images of consultation officers hesitating lest someone delivering questionnaires from house to house trip over a paving stone.

Instead we decided to strip out all bar the essentials. We reckon there are seven items of information that are 100 per cent required and they are not all as obvious as they sound.

- **Identity.** Who are you? And will those whose views you want recognise or have trust in you? Remember that public bodies have started to change their names almost as often as those in the private sector and both are equally capable of confusing their customers and stakeholders. The consultor organisation might, in any event, be someone else again. It might be a market research company. This is important because *who* you are inevitably influences the potential respondent, who might love you or loathe you, and the level of trust is a key factor in whether people bother to take part in a consultation, let alone tell the truth.

- **Target.** Obliging those who propose a consultation to state clearly whose views they want is an effective discipline and is especially valuable as an antidote to those 'let's have a general debate' ideas, which lack precision. This may not be the place for an exhaustive list, but the consultation needs to fix attention on the key priority audience.

- **Issue.** This should be the earliest clear articulation of what the consultation is meant to be about. Defining the real issue is paramount and yet it is often expressed vaguely. For a mandate to do its job there is a need for the issue to be captured succinctly and precisely.

- **Actor.** This is the term we use to describe the person or organisation that will do something as a result of the consultation. It may not be the same as the 'identity' – the party that runs the organisation; indeed we suspect that, as often as not, consultations are run so that other people can act upon them.

- **Action.** Here we encounter one of the most frequent causes of fudging – no-one is too sure what the actor will do. A favourite formula is that the actor 'will take views into account' – but we would not be happy unless it went further and stipulated what exactly would be done and in relation to what.

- **Date.** By when? Obliging consultors to put this on record at the outset helps everyone. Sometimes it highlights a mismatch between an aspirational target date and a realistic one. We are rarely happy with a wide date range; it's usually another fudge.

- **Wider aim.** By encouraging those planning the exercise to express the entire mandate in the context of a wider goal, we address the question of whether the activity proposed will accomplish what's needed. Again it can expose tenuous linkages and sometimes an alarming non-sequitur. Unless the whole mandate makes sense in terms of the wider aim, there must be serious doubt about it.

Artificial though it may be to shoehorn an exercise into a rigid formula of this kind, we think that something like it is essential if we are to curb the number of nonsense consultations that take place. Even then, a seemingly convincing proposal may not deserve to go ahead unless it fits into an overall and coherent programme. To evaluate a number of proposed mandates is, in our view, the right way to develop a good programme of public engagement. It is also the way to make progress with the challenge of joined-up government.

Comparable forms to our mandate cover the budget required, the methods to be used and so forth, while these are helpful to prioritise and schedule, we think that the value lies in focusing attention fairly and squarely on the purpose of the exercise. The reason why this matters is that it's only at the end of a consultation when the brickbats fly and the recriminations begin – and when one party or another to a debate tries to prove that the consultation did or did not actually demonstrate what others say it did.

## SEEKING WHAT EXACTLY?

These arguments only arise because consultation lends itself to too many expectations. To counter this, we find it useful to see it as being capable fundamentally of providing five things – either individually or in combination. They are all potential answers to the question 'What are we after?'

### *Proof*

Arguably this is the most ambitious objective. Here, you set off to consult in the hope that, by so doing, you can demonstrate something beyond doubt. When London was bidding for the 2012 Olympics, one of the more demanding factors likely to influence the International Olympic Committee was the degree of popular support which the bid enjoyed;

they don't like awarding the games to applicants who are half hearted. Any consultation needed to prove a high degree of enthusiasm for the project.

A supermarket seeking planning permission in contentious circumstances similarly hopes to prove that the public really wants the facility. Needless to say, setting out to prove something is hazardous and disappointed consultors are on occasions tempted to revise their objective and instead opt for a second element. . .

### Evidence

This acknowledges that there may be a debate and that the purpose of a consultation is to understand how the balance of the argument sits. Seriously divisive issues such as nuclear power generation, wind farms or fox-hunting have failed to produce consensus and the opposing sides of the argument are as far apart as they ever were. Policy-makers know, however, that sometimes subtle shifts in opinion can open up avenues of progress barely discernible to a broad-brush observer, and a legitimate goal of some consultation is simply this – to gather evidence as to the state of opinions. Who believes what? How strongly? Under what assumptions?

This is especially valuable where scientific or social change is rapid. A consultation on, say, 'green' taxes conducted fifteen years ago would have revealed a very different response to a similar exercise today. Changing perceptions affect issues such as genetic engineering, with oversight bodies such as the Human Fertilisation and Embryology Authority anxious to at least keep in touch with public opinion as it responds to new developments.

### Advice

The third element we have identified can be found when consultors appreciate the limits of their own expertise and systematically seek contributions from individuals or organisations they think might know more. Of course, once one has gone out to consultation, it is scarcely possible to confine your attention to bodies you respect. If advice is what you seek, advice is what you get, whether it be welcome or unwelcome, firmly rooted in acknowledged expertise or totally uninformed.

*Insight*

This differs from advice in that it digs deeper into an understanding of why people believe what they believe. It is one thing to receive advice, but quite another to appreciate fully the reasons why people advance the views they do. Insight is most valuable at the early stages of policy-making, when consultors have more room for manoeuvre and when there may be more options.

*Ideas*

This is the most open of all, where the consultor is merely searching for good ideas. This may be a secondary objective for many consultations, but where it is the primary goal, it is probably either highly speculative or just a PR exercise.

The significance of these five elements and the need for consultors to form a clear view of what they want are based on this: depending upon what they seek, the methods and the approach will differ. Let us take proof and evidence as one category. What these have in common is that the answer will normally be quantitative. There has to be a number. Proof will usually mean the percentage of the consultation audience that either believes something or agrees with something. The consultation therefore has to be shaped towards the delivery of that particular number.

Now contrast this with the advice element. Here it is not enough to record that 70 per cent of those consulted offered a particular flavour of advice. What matters here is not so much what is said, but who is saying it. Consider a consultation run by a health department. Advice on something technical will be answered differently if, for example, it comes from the British Medical Association, representing 139,000 doctors, than if it comes from Dr Gilbert of Basingstoke. Now at that point, hold the analysis. What if this individual was the BMA's retiring president; how much of a difference would this make? The truth is that once one moves from proof and evidence towards advice, it suddenly becomes vital to know who is giving the advice and on what basis. This requires a level of knowledge well beyond having a name and an address and is the reason why we advocate the stakeholder management approach.

The search for insight goes a step further. Where you receive advice though a written submission, that insight comes either from detailed discussion with the consultee or preferably though a focus group. The ability for members of a focus group to challenge each other or to probe into each other's position through a skilled facilitator is a great enabler of deeper insights. By this we mean an understanding of values and fundamental beliefs rather than the restatement of established positions. Insight is what you need if you're developing a new public service and where the key factor is recognising that different people might have slightly different needs. That appreciation is vital.

Good ideas, in contrast, are just that – no matter where they come from, unlike the provision of advice, where the credibility of the consultee is paramount. Quit trying to figure out who offers ideas to you; it doesn't matter. Go to the internet; advertise your interest in learning about a new idea. It matters not whether it comes from deepest Dulwich or the Isle of Skye. Be grateful for something that offers you what you need.

This analysis is useful for three reasons. Firstly, it clarifies in the mind of the consultor what exactly it is looking for. Secondly, it influences the likely choice of methods. But thirdly, and most importantly, it has a bearing upon the way in which pre-consultation is undertaken.

## PRE-CONSULTATION

Over the years, we've seen many a sardonic smile cross the faces of people for whom pre-consultation is a new concept. 'Aha', they exclaim, 'consulting about a consultation?' In fact, that is exactly what it is – a vital but often neglected part of the overall process and one which has an important bearing upon the success of the ensuing exercise.

Pre-consultation is essentially talking to key stakeholders about the forthcoming consultation. When should it take place? How wide should its scope be? Who needs to be involved? How best can you engage with them? These and other questions are legitimate issues to discuss with those who have an interest and the trick is to enter into dialogue on these matters without being drawn into the substantive debate.

It is a shame that some large organisations – and even Government departments themselves – have started to use the term 'pre-consultation' when they are canvassing ideas on the substantive question. In our view it is much better to focus on the procedural aspect, if only because so many consultees are so vocal in their complaints about the conduct of consultation exercises. Clearly it is not feasible to talk to every potential respondent before launching a consultation, but we get the impression that far too many exercises would have been more successful had the consultor bothered to get advice before proceeding.

Good pre-consultation yields a number of other benefits. It is a means of teasing out of stakeholders their likely reactions. It can secure co-operation for example in locating or assessing hard-to-reach or seldom-heard groups. It can do something else: it can neutralise certain kinds of opposition. Talking to the media may often be a good idea.

On local matters, local newspapers are extremely influential. Even without overtly taking sides, they have immense power to frame the argument – in a phrase, they 'make the weather' for a dialogue to take place. Journalists can, of course, be fickle and just because you took the local paper's editor to a good restaurant, plied her with Chablis and flattered her ego does not mean that her position on the issue will be any friendlier. But it would be exceptional for such a paper's leader writer to chastise a council for a consultation had his or her advice been sought at the outset – and heeded.

Pre-consultation is not without risks. There are dangers in being seen to talk to some groups but not others. A wise consultor is therefore careful to seek the views of more than one side in a consultation where there are deep divisions of opinion. In fact, you may receive better advice from opponents than from supporters. In a planning scenario, for example, those who are opposed to development are likely to find fault with your process whatever you do. Yet this is not reason enough to freeze them out of pre-consultation.

Their input could, for example, help you understand which aspects concern them most, and, who knows, there may be aspects of the forthcoming dialogue where allowances can be made for views that have not yet been fully considered. So, if pre-consultation is an obvious thing to do, why is it so neglected? We think that shortage of time, though certainly a factor, does not tell the whole story. Too many consultees, we feel, are fearful of what they might hear.

Imagine a consultation being planned in the way we've conceived – complete with a mandate. A series of pre-consultation discussions now takes place with organisations that have a significant stake in the issue. They have strong views. They seek to persuade you that now is not the time; there are other parallel developments, maybe being pursued by other agencies. They make a convincing case – and you're back to the drawing board. Back to the bosses to tell them that the consultation they commissioned shouldn't happen. Of course consultation staff are hardly queuing up for the privilege of bearing such views. Ministers, having committed to a consultation, are hardly likely to backtrack simply because officials have taken soundings and found flaws in the plan.

And yet this is what should happen. Far fewer consultations would be criticised and there would be fewer at risk of judicial review if the advice of those most likely to be affected was taken on board. Sadly, consultation staff seldom have the seniority to bend the ear of the ultimate decision-makers – so pre-consultation, when attempted at all, is often done in a perfunctory way. 'Ring round some of the usual suspects and share our thinking with them' may be the formula one hears.

More typically, key stakeholders will be positive about a consultation. They may well have campaigned for a change in the law or for exacting new developments and their exercise may represent a constructive step forward. Expect them, however, to be extremely interested in the scope of the consultation – for they will know that the devil is in the detail – and will use the pre-consultation dialogue to impress upon the consultor their view of the questions that should be asked.

Another reason why pre-consultation is rarely undertaken properly is the sheer difficulty of treading a narrow path between too much and too little. Talking to some but not others is always tricky to defend and yet is inevitable, so the choice has to be made in some kind of logical and defensible basis. One way is to be open and make it public that in some months' time, you intend to consult on the following subject and invite those who are interested to give you their views on how it should be conducted; those who fail to respond have less scope to complain if they aren't involved. You have to be sensible, though; if you're a local authority and decide to take soundings from one political party, you would expect a reaction unless you engaged the other parties equally!

But the biggest problem is how to confine such pre-consultation dialogues to just the process. After all, aren't the protagonists itching to debate the substantive issues? Although you may wish to focus the conversation on exactly where and when to hold the stakeholder conference, they are more interested in the questions to which the consultation seeks answers. Really experienced planners of consultation exercises have learnt to listen constructively with that inscrutable smile of Michael Dobbs's creation Francis Urquhart MP and his catch-phrase, 'You might very well think that. . . I couldn't possibly comment.'*

Why shouldn't you comment? It's because the period leading up to a consultation can be a frenetic time of lobbying for or against a particular slant to a debate. In the same way as critics of a referendum stress that everything, but everything, depends upon the question, those who dislike the outcome of a consultation will often argue that the wrong questions have been posed. If it therefore transpires that one side or another in a contentious issue appears to have had disproportionate influence over that question, the consultor is on the back foot.

Engaging in pre-consultation discussions can therefore be a hazardous occupation, but necessary. To an extent they act as an insurance against getting something totally wrong. Bureaucrats can misread the mood of the public, or even of stakeholders whose views they should value. So think of pre-consultation as a failsafe mechanism – one last chance to avoid making a very public blunder.

## ANALYSING THE ISSUES

We think the central feature of this is to understand the issue properly. Again, this sounds obvious, but it is not. More typically, policy staff – who generally do understand the subject – arrive at the door of the consultation specialists saying they need to organise a listening exercise,

---

* From Dobbs's bestselling political thriller *House of Cards*. The catch-phrase was used by Urquhart whenever he could not be seen to agree with a question, with the emphasis either on 'I' or on 'possibly', depending on the situation.

and the starting point is usually the menu of dialogue methods, or, if they have heeded our advice, a thorough grasp of the stakeholder base.

But there is something even more important and that is to thoroughly understand the issues that prompt the forthcoming discussion. Guess what? They change. Seriously, an issue that looks straightforward when first articulated by a policy-maker can magically morph into something quite different when it becomes part of a public consultation.

One of the best examples we know happened in Scotland. One of the country's regional health boards got into such financial difficulties that an exasperated Scottish Executive decided to pull the plug and merge it with a neighbouring board or boards. But which? The problem was all about geography, for we are discussing a huge area of rural western Scotland, from the tip of the Mull of Kintyre right up to Oban and beyond, including the islands of Mull, Jura and other rather wonderful, if inaccessible, places. For good measure it also included populous parts of the Clyde valley within a stone's throw of Glasgow. Indeed, how that area was put together in the first place is a mystery to us.

We attended a briefing at the Department of Health, which had little room for manoeuvre as its minister had already committed to abolishing the existing board and just wished to go through as sound a process as possible to elicit people's views as to how to carve up the area among the neighbouring boards. So we were shown a variety of maps – you would not believe how many ways there are to draw lines on a map! One followed geographical logic; another was based on populations; others again were based upon administrative boundaries, except that there were several and they were different. All this was fascinating and we were assured that this would be the stuff of a good consultation, as it was so important for citizens to feel comfortable about the source of the health service upon which they depended.

Then an officer asked if the quality of care and the funding behind it would be affected. 'Oh no,' came the reply. 'This will only be about the boundaries.' But someone else pointed out that the reason why they were in the situation in the first place was because the health board had run out of money. If the NHS in this area was taken over by an adjacent administration, would there be more resources available? Or fewer? And what difference would it make to the delivered service on the ground? It was immediately apparent to us that the dialogue would mostly be about one thing and one thing only – money.

The civil servants were horrified. How could we have misunderstood the brief? They asserted that people would be told that financial issues were not on the table. 'This is about lines on a map,' they repeated.

Well, that consultation went ahead and in fairness was undertaken very professionally, at a cost of over £200,000. As we predicted, it was much more about money than about boundaries. The high-profile independent facilitator, brought in by the Department of Health to run public meetings up and down the area, was scathing in her subsequent report about lack of financial data available for the debate; in fact meaningful figures only arrived at the eleventh hour and reasonable questions posed by concerned residents just could not be answered. Some regarded this as management incompetence, but we think it just reflected the fact that those who conceived the consultation were too close to the subject to see objectively where the focus of debate was likely to be. It is a classic case of not seeing the wood for the trees.

As a tool of better understanding, we use an issue analysis grid, with two different but related dimensions. One axis represents the amount of discretion available to the consultor. Rarely is this an absolute 'yes' or 'no'. There are degrees of discretion. Take a situation where a mobile phone operator looking for a site for a mast in a congested area, where, try as they might, they have only found one reasonable and one marginal site that seem appropriate. There is admittedly some scope here, but not much; if there were four or five equally viable sites, it would be a different matter altogether and the consultor would have far more discretion. Fundamentally, those about to consult need to break down the subject matter into its component aspects and in respect of each one, ask the question 'How much room for manoeuvre do we really have here?' If there is very little, we score it to the left-hand side of the grid; if there is ample scope, then it scores to the right.

The vertical axis records something more subtle – we call it the propensity to listen, or the scope one has to listen to a particular voice, such as the general public. Maybe the best analogy is to consider the airwaves. How crowded are they in this debate? Are there many voices clamouring to be heard? Or is it pretty quiet so that one set of messages can be heard. Let's go back to the mobile phone mast example. In that case, once the technical assessments have been made, other than the local planning authority, the decision-makers can be largely guided by the public response – there are few competing voices.

**Issue analysis matrix, showing eight typical positions of hypothetical consultees**

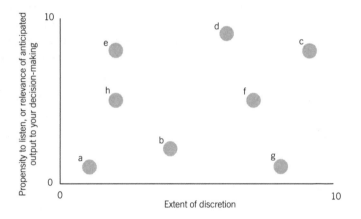

Other cases are, however, more complex. In many public consultations, those who ultimately decide have to take account of a whole raft of considerations other than the public they've consulted. There may be advice coming from Government sources, from regulators or long-term planners. Financial issues may loom large and all manner of other factors might need to be taken into account. In other words the ability of the consultor – its propensity if you like – to listen to this audience is heavily constrained.

Score the components of an issue on this grid and you can quickly see those that will lend themselves best to an honest consultation. By this we mean a debate that can result in genuine action to respond to what people have said. If the policy aspect is at the top right of our matrix, then there is a lot of discretion and a good chance that the voices will be listened to.

Focus your dialogue on these issues and stakeholders are reasonably well placed to exert meaningful influence. If policy aspects lurk towards the bottom left, take this as a serious warning. Here the subject-matter is one where the consultor frankly has very little discretion and, furthermore, your voices have to compete with lots of others anyway.

Using this grid helps organisations focus their consultations on the issues where the debate is likely to make a real difference; on too many occasions in the past, a failure of analysis has led to the launch of exercises which ask people's views on issues where there is very little scope to influence. These are sadly doomed to disappoint. Had our friends in the Scottish example undertaken this kind of analysis, they might have recognised that some of the financial issues were ones where those consulting had little scope to change the inherited resource-levels. A consultation based on this would therefore be problematic. On the other hand, there were aspects of the issue where there was far more opportunity to influence. A simplistic example, but important in the context of regional identity, would be the name of the realigned NHS board. Frankly, there was almost complete discretion here and few competing voices. The will of the people could be pretty conclusive. In between were a variety of issue components where a reasonable debate could be held.

## PERCEIVED DISCRETION

Such an analysis reveals something else and this is really important. Sometimes, as in the Scottish health case, there is a mismatch between what the consultor regards as being its level of discretion and the public's perception. Here we encounter our theory of perceived discretion, which, unfortunately for many in management, states that when it comes to the nature of the debate, it is not the amount of discretion you actually have that matters, it's the amount consultees think you have! In fact it is worse than that, for on occasion what's paramount is the amount of discretion they think you *ought* to have.

From the public sector, there are innumerable examples where civil servants or local government officers can point to the small print in statutes or regulations that show exactly what they can and can't do. There is no reason why even key stakeholders would necessarily appreciate such niceties and, no matter how clearly they are articulated in the consultation paper, these are constraints which consultees find convenient to overlook. If challenged, respondents to consultations will either deny that they knew about the constraints, or just argue that there shouldn't be any. Two-tier local government, and the public's congenital failure to understand who does what, regularly give rise to situations where a district council asks advice and receives a barrage of submissions all assuming it has responsibilities which in fact are vested elsewhere.

Let's take another scenario from the regulated private sector. A train operating company consults about the future of a particular service only to find that one of the most contentious issues is the level of car parking charges. What follows is classic 'not me, guv' dialogue. 'Now if it was up to us, of course we'd provide an incentive for you to park your car and ride on public transport, but it's our regulator, see. . . needs us to make as much money as possible to subsidise the painting of the station.'

What's happening here is that consultees have debated the issue on a perception that the train company had a discretion it does not in fact have. And if approached, most travelling commuters would solidly assert that 'it jolly well should have that discretion'. All this can be really frustrating for an organisation seeking to consult on those matters it sees as being within its jurisdiction. Of course, it can take steps to influence the perception. The district council can invest in publicising what it does and what does not do; the train company can mobilise its PR machine to explain why it cannot slash car parking fees. But we have concluded that such moves make only a marginal difference. The general public has an innate sense of what is at the root of many debates and we advise consultors to accept this and work within that expectation.

One way to do this is to think forward and try to visualise the dialogue before it happens. Give those planning a consultation a clean sheet of paper and ask them to describe what will happen. Who is likely to argue one way and who will argue the opposite? What will be the most telling arguments? Who will get better coverage in the media? Who will have the loudest voice? Whose voice will struggle to be heard?

Thinking aloud on such questions will often highlight how key figures in a project have very different ideas on the way the debate will develop.

Rather like stakeholder mapping, the exercise can be highly therapeutic in forcing those responsible to think through the detailed planning of a consultation.

When this is carried out in the light of a proper stakeholder analysis, with a clear view of whether the ultimate objective is to determine proof, evidence, advice or insight or to search for ideas, and after a thorough bout of pre-consultation talks with key consultees, then, and only then, would we expect the groundwork to be properly laid for an effective consultation.

# 19. FIXING THE FEEDBACK. . .
# AND LEARNING TO FEED FORWARD

REPORTER OR RECOMMENDER?

Those who conduct effective and meaningful consultations have in their possession something really valuable. But it's an asset that is under-valued and under-exploited.

Earlier, in Part Two, we bemoaned the dearth of good feedback, but this is in fact part of a much wider malaise, which is that insufficient thought and resource is given to what happens after a consultation. So in addition to feeding back into the consultee channel or to the public at large, we are also talking about the all-important task of feeding forward to decision-makers. This is the exertion of influence.

Sometimes there is a confusion of roles. Those organising a consultation exercise are unclear as to whether their job is merely to report or to make recommendations. The reporter/recommender debate rages because the role can vary from one exercise to another. Where there is a specialist consultation unit its primary task may be to organise a dialogue on behalf of a policy department that has commissioned it. They may see their role as gathering all the data, assessing it and then presenting it in the most effective way that meets their client's requirements. Many third-party consultancies would probably work in a similar way – used merely as analysts and presenters of information. Occasionally, however, the policy people might acknowledge that experience gained in listening to stakeholders might give consultation professionals an insight into the strength of feelings expressed and the drift of finely balanced argument. If the issue is non-technical it may indeed be tempting to ask those who organise a dialogue to make recommendations. Whichever happens, what is important is to settle upon the accountability at the start. One reason why this matters is that during the consultation itself those with a message to transmit want to know who to target for their comments. There is mistrust of decision-makers who hide behind consultants or make themselves scarce when matters of controversy are debated in the public domain. Very often those who compile the consultation report have a significant influence over the end result and we feel that those engaged in dialogue have a right to know who is writing it up.

Remember that the challenging part of consultation analysis is the need to integrate into one set of messages the output from a variety of different dialogue mechanisms. Putting together the results of public meetings, questionnaires, focus groups, deliberative events and an eDiscussion forum is almost impossible – it's like combining apples with oranges and the desire to be concise can only be fulfilled at a price. Winston Churchill was famous for requiring everything to be put on one side of a sheet of paper, but we wonder how one can do justice to complex consultations in this way – though neither do we advocate long, indigestible reports which cannot be read by busy decision-makers.

## DELIVERY VEHICLES

Presenting the evidence is probably about accommodating the whims and culture of the decision-making body. There are some who want a regular supply of evidence from an ongoing consultation. If the subject is of continuous interest and maybe has a bearing upon other decisions which an organisation is taking in parallel, it might be wise to obtain regular updates of how a dialogue is progressing. We call this the 'wheelbarrow' method: it is a bit like weeding the garden – you accumulate a quantity of stuff and once you have filled up the container you take it to the back of the garden. The analogy is loose, but imagine receiving dozens of written submissions, undertaking several one-to-one meetings with interested groups, holding public meetings and at every month's end summarising it all for the management team so that they get a feel for what's going on.

There is much to be said for this method of feeding forward. It obliges those in charge of the dialogue to monitor and assess its key messages on a regular basis. It keeps the top brass better informed of the progress of a debate. It can prompt changes or improvements mid-exercise so that a wider range of views can be heard.

Of course, one can go further and some organisations publish feedback and feed-forward on a continuous basis. Instead of a wheelbarrow, think conveyor belt. As soon as a new submission is received or a new survey result compiled, off it goes to those who need to know. Instant publication on the internet means that every twist and turn of the dialogue becomes apparent to anyone who cares to find out.

A more likely scenario, however, is neither of these, and here the analogy is with a pantechnicon. Nothing is sent to those who decide until it is all gathered together, nailed down in a sealed container and delivered door to door on a 'just in time' basis. This influencing vehicle is designed specifically to be tamper-proof and to limit possible interference with the data mid-consultation. Okay, 'interference' may be a little strong, but partial information can of course be misleading and it is always possible that well-meaning managers, actively monitoring the emerging output of an active dialogue, could find early unrepresentative views appearing more significant than they will be in the fullness of time.

There is no particular right or wrong method of packaging the consultation output for consideration by decision-makers. It's another case of horses for courses. But we believe that good consultors will spend more time thinking about the best way to handle this, for it is the critical point of any consultation.

This is where even the most transparent process tends to become a little hazy and where there are doubts about claims to be 'reporter' rather than 'recommender'. This is because of the fine line between analysis and interpretation. The former is about finding out what the data says – the latter is what the data means, so this involves a conscious injection of context and insight into the mix.

## INTERPRETATION AND INFLUENCE

Conflicts of interpretation are found in all organisations. When service delivery managers ponder declining satisfaction levels there is often a difference of view between the pessimists, who argue that standards are worsening, and the optimists, who insist that the market, or society, is changing and with it the expectation levels. Same data, different interpretation.

As with performance data, so is it also with consultation output. Interpretations can vary according to the perspective of the assessor. It suggests that there are occasions where it is right and proper for the ultimate decision-makers to have direct access to the raw data – and to be able to interrogate it. At other times, as in quasi-judicial processes such as planning, it may best to let independent people address the evidence and present it impartially to those who have to decide.

It can be very difficult to be wholly objective. If, as a consultation specialist, you have taken great pains to ensure that hard-to-reach or seldom-heard groups are fully engaged in the dialogue, you could be acting pretty inconsistently if you did not also try your hardest to ensure that those voices were properly heard. Handing over a great wodge of data is a pretty unsatisfying thing to do under these circumstances and we suspect that consultation staff with wide experience know how to win friends and influence people at this stage of the game.

So much depends upon the style of the decision-making in the consultor organisation. In workshops we have run, we have invited participants to select from a range of adjectives to describe those that most accurately portray the way in which decisions are taken where they work. We offer them words such as 'democratic', 'considered', 'evidence-based', or phrases like 'on the nod' and 'based on papers'. What emerges is that there are different views of the same process according to where people sit in the organisation. Not surprising really, but what strikes us was that there's a difference between what ought to be happening and what really happens.

How often is the decision-making body nominally a committee of some sort? And how often is the gathering in reality but a rubber stamp for a powerful committee chairman whose will is 95 per cent bound to prevail? Collective accountability in theory, but harsh political reality in practice, where one person carries more authority than the rest put together.

Now in situations such as these, does the consultation manager sit back and submit the output – with or without recommendations through the agenda paper factory? Or does a proactive officer seek out the person who matters and talk him or her through the key messages that come from the consultation? For those who interpret their task as not merely obtaining the views of stakeholders but also of ensuring that they are properly fed forward to those who take the decisions, this is the only honourable course to take.

Another way to describe this would be 'political nous', and this is an invaluable talent for those who have to handle the output from consultations. For 'nous' you could substitute the word 'nose', for what's needed is an instinct that can smell trouble or, conversely, navigate the right way forward though a bureaucratic maze. This rare but valuable skill includes the ability to read a large number of submissions and maybe notice in just one of them an argument, fact or proposition that makes a difference to the balance of the debate – or, as it was put by one of our delegates from Scotland recently, 'the vital wee nugget'.

It needs more than knowledge of the subject and also more than an understanding of the stakeholders concerned – though both of these help greatly. What is most in demand is an appreciation of the factors likely to sway decision-makers; that's tough, because too few of them bother to get involved in the nitty-gritty of planning a consultation and in sharing their thoughts with those who will manage the dialogue.

Ideally, before planning a public consultation, one would sit down with the ultimate decision-makers to try to understand what might lead them to select one option rather than another. It is a disturbing thought, but we suspect that were this conversation to take place, there would be occasions when it became impossible to identify anything that would alter an already almost-decided position. If taken, however, this step would be really significant and effectively empower the consultation assessors to focus on those messages likely to have greatest influence on decision-makers.

Because there are so many different types of consultation scenarios it follows that there are different models of action that take place as a result. There are times when the advice obtained may not sway a decision that has to be taken today, but could be profoundly influential in determining an organisation's future direction. It may therefore not be entirely fair to judge a consultation merely on its immediate impact and over that one particular decision. Indeed, who can calibrate the cumulative effect of a series of dialogues on a body of decision-makers?

In Part Two we pointed out how disappointing are the results of the 'one year after' test, but it could well be that for some subjects and for some organisations, it is unrealistic to expect rapid results and that it makes far more sense to wait a little longer and assess the impact of consultations over a series of iterative discussions. In other words, the feeding forward of consultation outputs may need to be viewed on a programme basis rather than on a project basis.

We suspect this is the crux of the matter. Organisations that are truly consultation minded should plan their work in such a way that they have pre-determined which tasks and which decisions require formal consultation and which do not. For those that do, the timetable leading up to the decision can provide for the planning, implementation and reporting on the relevant consultation. For greater transparency, this can all be published in advance.

Some local authorities do this already. Executive Cabinets publish in advance the decisions they expect to take at a particular meeting and may specify which inputs will inform their decisions. These may be technical reports, minutes of meetings with partner organisations or the results of a consultation. We think this is commendable good practice and effectively provides an audit trail between the end of a consultation itself and its consideration by those who commissioned it.

## TRANSPARENCY

That audit trail is important. Many otherwise sober and sane consultees subscribe to all manner of sinister conspiracy theories when it comes to speculating about the output that's given to decision-makers.

They saw and studied the output feedback and broadly had no quarrel with it. But they suspect that in between the objective assessment of what stakeholders said, there was an intermediate layer of consideration where the data was reinterpreted for presentation to the powers that be. This is not necessarily wrong; in large multi-layered organisations it may be inevitable. It is rarely transparent. One day soon a disgruntled stakeholder will try to use the Freedom of Information Act to obtain copies of these intermediate documents. Success is not assured, however, as Section 35 of the Act* protects certain policy-making processes and advice to ministers.

But there is more to the audit trail than meets the eye. If Churchill required everything summarised for him on one side of paper, we've heard of decision-makers for whom even this could be considered far too verbose – who demand the output of a consultation to be encapsulated in a paragraph, or a sentence! This is a bit rough on those who have to work through the mass of material submitted in a deliberative consultation – and who, to do their jobs properly, need to capture some of the nuances of the message. The trouble with some decision-makers, however, is that they don't really want any nuances. They are looking for simple uncomplicated messages and an effective dialogue on a serious issue is not always likely to give them such clarity.

Unless one is careful, therefore, the progress of documenting the results of a consultation can easily become an exercise in de-nuancing. Reducing complex arguments from slightly different perspectives and packaging them into comprehensible conclusions inevitably risks under-reporting something important. No doubt it can be done, but for this you need someone with an ultra-developed sense of political judgement, who can spot what's likely to become significant well beyond the immediate policy horizon. In short, it is a job for a clairvoyant!

Back to the Freedom of Information Act. To our knowledge, no-one has yet tested the ability of the law to lift the veil of secrecy that surrounds the magical process whereby tons of paper and hundreds of e-mails

---

*    This is one of twenty-six categories of exemption to the Freedom of Information Act 2000. Guidance is available from the Information Commissioner's Office.

(not to mention survey results – but that's the easy bit!) are synthesised into a concise set of recommendations. We therefore think that smart organisations will start to work on the assumption that they have to be clean as a whistle in this area. One lawyer we know believes that if push comes to legal shove, at judicial review, a court would have little hesitation in ordering production of documents or any evidence that suggested that officials had discounted, or failed to pass on, significant views expressed by relevant stakeholders.

In a world where people simply won't bother to take part or to give their views unless they have confidence in the way their opinions will be passed on, failure to clean up this part of the act will reduce the credibility of an organisation's consultation. That is why, and also for greatest transparency, we think best-practice organisations will put all analysis and reporting summaries into the public domain. If that is done, it will act as a critical check and balance on the overall process.

But at heart, it isn't really about process, is it? Genuine consultations are usually about something that matters – at least to some people. So the biggest problem in the aftermath of a dialogue is that asking people will have raised all manner of difficult or uncomfortable issues which those who commissioned the consultation might prefer not to address.

## AFTER THE CONSULTATION
There are several kinds of scenario which emerge.

One is simple enough to identify – where the process produces what the decision-makers regard as the wrong answer! Of course, this breaks the immutable rule of integrity: you must never consult if you have already made up your mind – but sadly, it happens. This is extremely inconvenient, but may have been foreseen by those in authority, who may well have tried hard to manage the expectations of all concerned; indeed they may only have consulted because they were either legally or politically bound to do so. The classic case is probably the Energy Review consultation of 2006, which led to the Government's embarrassing defeat in the courts, but there are many others. One can imagine a hapless civil servant having to tell a minister that unfortunately the consultation output is entirely opposed to his or her wishes!

There are a number of sensible approaches to this problem. Best of all is to force a visible and transparent rethink, or at least to publish a reasoned explanation why the minister or whoever rejects the advice of the consultation. Other tactics include postponing a decision, at least until the dust has settled, or making cosmetic adjustments such as might appear to respond to representations without making significant difference to the overall decision. What is not recommended, and yet is surprisingly often considered, is just to launch a repeat performance in the hope that consultees come to a more palatable answer. Here is a parallel with the European Union's perceived approach to similar issues. When countries were seen as having delivered the wrong answer in a referendum, they were effectively told to try again ('and please will you do better this time around'). On EU enlargement, Ireland did!

A local authority we know confounded its own officials when councillors rejected their advice and turned down a planning growth option that the professionals had recommended. Although opinion was pretty evenly divided, the political arithmetic meant that the decision went against the officials' preferred strategy. What ensued was high farce, as the officials fled to their chief officers, who prepared a paper for elected members that called upon the collective forces of central government, the courts and previous precedent – all but Mother Teresa and the Pope – plus a touch of blackmail, to convince them to change their minds. Guess what? Elected members dug in their heels and reaffirmed their previous decision!

A second scenario is where opinion is evenly divided. In many ways this is the archetypal consultation outcome, for if a subject is worthy of substantial dialogue, it is likely to be because there is more than one view. This is also the easiest for decision-makers to deal with, for they have some basis for veering in either direction and can point to a body of support for their choice. The real question is whether to invest any time or resource in seeking to bring opposing views together. In the ideal world, this is the natural response to a vigorous dialogue. 'Now we understand where everyone stands, let's see what common ground we can find.' Specialists in conflict resolution and consensus-building point out that the starting point is not just to gather everyone's stated position, but to understand the underlying forces that shape their positions. It is people's interests that, in the main, drive their positions. So back again we come to our main message about stakeholder management – the key skill lies in understanding that stakeholder base.

The decision whether to invest in a consensus-building exercise obviously depends to an extent on a judgement that there is a realistic chance of achieving something by so doing; if the chances are zero, little is accomplished. Where two sides of an industrial dispute remain poles apart after consulting their respective members, there is still normally an impetus for some form of negotiation; too much is at stake if the stand-off continues.

Now apply this to a more conventional consultation exercise. The dialogue phase is over; everyone has had their say. There are many opposing views. There's some common ground, but not a lot. Is it worth trying to bring the parties together or finding a middle way? We think that it is. For one thing, stakeholders may have adopted a more extreme stance in order to impress or appease members, as in the employee relations example above. For another, once people feel they are being genuinely listened to, they become more flexible. Most importantly, an attempt to find a collective way forward gives a very positive message about the intentions of the consultor, who is seen as wanting to solve a problem through consensus rather than forcing one view through to the bitter end in the face of opposition.

Usually there is little to lose; honourable failure to achieve consensus rarely attracts criticism, unless bungled. If you're going to have a go, it must be done properly, with discretion and showing respect for all the participants. There are skilful mediators and facilitators who know how to do this; indeed the skills of settling a planning, education or health dispute are not much different from those deployed in international conflict resolution and if you have the opportunity, and the budget, to involve respected third parties, there may be good reasons to do so.

The third scenario worth mentioning in the post-consultation phase is where the dialogue uncovers significant minority views. To take a legalistic analogy, it is fair to reflect on the way English law has, over the years, been shaped and influenced by important dissenting judgments from High Court judges. Outvoted by their colleagues on a particular case, their ability to articulate and publish an alternative view can have a significant impact.

Good consultations can achieve similar results. Maybe 90 per cent – or even 99 per cent – of those involved share the conventional wisdom, but suddenly a different view begins to get noticed. In the chemistry of the earth's atmosphere, we know that subtle changes to carbon dioxide levels can alter our global climate, even though it makes up just a tiny proportion of the atmosphere. In a similar way, trace elements of opinion can have a disproportionate effect on the overall debate; well-informed consultor organisations will be alive to their potential impact. The question is how to handle minority views of this kind.

One approach is to acknowledge their significance and enter into direct dialogue. The danger here is that there are times when the majority take umbrage at what they view as unjustifiable favourable treatment for a smaller body of opinion. This is easier to explain and defend if there is already an active programme of pursuing strands of thinking with a number of stakeholders in the wake of the formal stages of the consultation. We certainly believe that significant minority views should be reported to the decision-makers. This is particularly important if the minority view represents a clearly defined special or protected interest: 'Everyone is in favour of building houses there, except for the Wildlife Trust, which is concerned about the great crested newt.'

Equality and diversity policies should by now have drummed it into the psyche of public officials that it is necessary to explore fully any special views that stem from some communities' status as an ethnic, linguistic, religious or other minority. In a consultation, it may be necessary to ensure that enough is known about respondents and participants so that minority views can be identified and taken into account. Basically, if you don't ask whether a survey respondent is disabled, you are never going to know whether, as a group, their views are any different.

There is one final scenario that is sadly all too prevalent. We will call it 'Pandora's box'. An accurate sub-title might be 'Good heavens, what have we done?', for this is where those who commission a consultation come to think they made a big mistake, if the process has unleashed a welter of issues and problems that may either defy solution or raise expectations which cannot be fulfilled. There are countless areas of public or corporate policies or practice where lurk some awkward unaddressed problems. Sleeping dogs might be best left to lie, but once public consultations expose them, they are difficult for managers and policy-makers to ignore.

This is why some long-promised consultations disappoint many who have campaigned for them. Cautious mandarins in Whitehall may have curbed their terms of reference to avoid them straying too close to Pandora's box, for fear of uncovering issues which can no longer be ignored. In reality, and in the tradition of *Yes Minister* bureaucracy, the favoured reaction is to mount a further inquiry, investigation or other diagnostic device in the hope that kicking an issue into such long grass postpones the evil day when the subject has to be tackled.

In summary, feeding forward is a highly political process where those in charge of a consultation have ample scope to mismanage. Avoiding embarrassing mistakes requires political skills – occasionally with a large 'P', but normally with a small 'p'. It also depends upon your having anticipated that it is an essential and demanding part of the overall consultative process and having budgeted for it – in terms of having the right people, funds and the right access to decision-makers so that they can be truly involved in what happens.

# 20. MAKING SURE IT'S WORTH IT

## BUT ARE WE SERIOUS?

Any management toolkit, and this applies to virtually any technical or professional discipline, will have a chapter called 'Evaluation'. It's deeply embedded into project management; in an age of 'cover my backside', anyone who spends public money on a large scale knows that, sooner or later, questions may be asked and a failure in evaluation will make them look fools or knaves – or both.

Under the surface, however, lies a serious case of double-think, for sadly these provisions are often ignored. Lip service prevails and, despite good intentions, people never quite get around to evaluation. In some cases, there is a box to be ticked, but the minimum possible for compliance gets a token effort and that's it.

We're sure there are honourable exceptions to this generalisation. However, as a cultural phenomenon of modern management, there are too many managers investing time in developing new ways of doing things, and there is less emphasis in finding out whether existing methods work well enough. It is actually part of the disease afflicting performance management – you measure what you can count, rather than what matters.

There is a classic, but sadly typical, example from the world of Government consultation. The Cabinet Office, under its Code of Practice issued in April 2004,* committed itself to review the operation of the code. A good idea, as the code laid down some demanding

---

* Now superseded by the 2008 Code of Practice.

standards upon Government departments and their agencies. Its best-known requirement was that consultations should last twelve weeks unless there were minister-approved derogations. It also insisted that there should be feedback from every consultation – a bit basic but who was going to quarrel with that? Going further, it said that at the end of every consultation there should be an explanation of how the consultation had influenced the eventual outcome. Now that's really good – absolutely excellent news and truly best practice.

Eagerly, we reached for the annual report published by the Government to see how well it had done in meeting these standards. We were impressed to find that the twelve-week rule had been observed in more than 90 per cent of consultations. That was, until we realised that this statistic was based upon a sample of only those consultation co-ordinators who had bothered to respond to the questionnaire. Banana republic time! More significantly, there had been no attempt whatever to measure whether the consultations had led to proper feedback. Nor had the Government looked to see how many of them had explained how policy had been influenced. Imagine – some civil servant or minister, or both, in the UK political machine had sat down and taken a decision to measure the twelve-week bit of the guidance but not the aspects of the code that really made a difference.

So in examining how best to evaluate consultations, we shall not look to the British Government for advice! It's a shame, really, because there has never been a stronger case for devoting resources to the proper evaluation of consultation. In 2007 a *Times* editorial complained that there was, 'scant evidence that consultations produced anything new nor are listened to by Government'. We might disagree with that conclusion, but the fact is that this is a widely held view.

One reason why there is now a need to focus on evaluation is the sheer amount of money spent on consultation. Most chief executives in the public sector have no idea how much their organisations spend on these processes. If they do, they quote a minimal figure of bought-out services such as printing or the use of specialist consultants. One local council tried to claim that the only cost of a public meeting was the tea and biscuits! This is because they exclude the cost of paying their staff, using their own buildings or other 'in-house' facilities; a neat bit of public sector accounting, but some distance away from a real world where these are paid for by the taxpayer. It is time to do some realistic evaluation, just to see if this money is well spent.

There is another motive and that arises from the proliferation of dialogue methods: the greater the choice, the more the need to evaluate what works best. After all, some of the most popular forms of dialogue are expensive to organise and take significant non-cash resources. Many organisations have empirically discovered what works for them, but we think there are lots who have lapsed into a practice of using the same methods year in, year out with little or no objective assessment of their value or effectiveness. Where organisations seek outside help, or invite tenders for conducting a consultation, it should be part of the procurement process to examine the effectiveness of the operation at its conclusion. We have seen examples of contractors being invited to evaluate themselves – a form of marking one's own homework, which is asking for trouble, but even that is better than no evaluation at all.

For public bodies, we think there is a further reason why evaluation is seldom properly undertaken. The silo mentality ensures that departments are reluctant to share their work with others from elsewhere in the organisation and while this is true for consultations as a whole, nowhere is it more sensitive than in their evaluation. Having embarrassing responses may be a cause for reticence, but an evaluation that suggests that the exercise as a whole was flawed is doubly so.

In consequence, we have the theory that at a time when there should be more evaluation, in practice there may be less. This won't last, for we think the overwhelming logic of evaluation will win through.

One factor that has held back the practice of consultation evaluation is that there is no universally agreed set of criteria. Unlike the earlier discussion on standards, evaluation in this context is about looking at the overall process and determining what value it has added. A simplistic but effective way to do this might be to ask the decision-makers right at the outset to stipulate exactly what they are looking for; in the last chapter we illustrated the various qualities they might have in mind. At the end of the process, one might simply approach the same people and ask them about the extent to which their requirements have been fulfilled.

Looking more objectively, there are three different but related types of evaluation tests and although they can be used discretely they will, in practice, be more valuable if used together. For a consultation programme as a whole the use of all three is essential.

### Decision audit

Has the consultation made a significant difference to the decision? Note that the answer does not have to be a 'yes' or 'no', for few decisions are that clear cut. Perhaps it would be better to rephrase the text to read 'Has the consultation had an influence. . .?'

Of course, to answer this question one needs to know what the decision might have been had there not been a consultation and only on rare occasions is this easy to discern. Macho managements like to play down any influence that others have exerted on their activities, but more modern stakeholder-sensitive organisations tend towards the opposite. In order to appear to have listened, they will go to some lengths to attribute changes to the wise words of those whom they have consulted. In undertaking a decision audit one has to guard against spin.

It is in evaluating the impact on decisions that the value of the audit trail described earlier is most visible. If consultors can demonstrate that views and opinions expressed in the dialogue phase led to additional analysis, a reconsideration of certain aspects, or maybe a modification here and there, they have solid grounds to claim that they made a difference. Documents can chronicle these and that is why the audit trail is useful. Minutes of meetings or an exchange of e-mails might constitute excellent evidence that consultation output made its presence felt. Of course, they could prove the reverse!

### Process compliance

The second test is ostensibly about procedure, but at a deeper level it is about the whole process from start to finish. The question here is: 'Was the consultation carried out with such professionalism as would indicate to the public or to stakeholders that its organisers were truly genuine in seeking to understand and listen to their views?'

It's not a bad approach, for there is a world of difference between a hastily assembled focus group, badly facilitated with questions biased towards a pre-determined answer, and the real thing. Retrospective evaluation of some techniques is easier than others. The success of a public meeting, for example, may be difficult to assess objectively, but one could look at the attendance figures, or its profile, the nature of the questioning and the quality of the contributions. The shortcomings of surveys and other quantitative methods have been covered earlier and become quite visible when a formal evaluation is attempted. It is at this point that one thinks of the killer question no-one dreamt up at the time – or the hard-to-reach group the sample somehow excluded.

There are always lessons to learn from looking back at the dialogue phase of consultations. We know very few where conscientious organisers claim to have got everything right – it is just not that exact a science. But there are failures and failures. Some procedural errors can go to the heart of the matter and would be analogous to what lawyers call 'fundamental breach'. Those could include changing the key questions mid-way through a consultation, or maybe allowing insufficient time for reasonable responses. Relying on incomplete stakeholder lists, or exhibiting bias when inviting people or organisations to participate, might all cause serious concern. Again, there is no 'yes'/'no' answer.

Compliance with best practice standards is a judgement best made by someone independent. Where an organisation publishes its own standards, it is a matter of auditing against those standards; an internal audit function in some larger agencies might be geared up to do this. More likely, an organisation would invite outsiders in after the event to assess whether or not good practice has been followed.

### Stakeholder reactions

We're tempted to call this test 'stakeholder satisfaction', but that raises uncomfortable issues. It's rather like asking a terminally ill patient if he or she is 'satisfied' with the treatment. No doubt this can be done with suitable sensitivity and we're sure our local hospice would be a case in point; however, if this is mishandled it could cause distress as well as produce dubious data.

Consultees are bound to be influenced by the outcome, are they not? They would be less than human were their views not coloured to some extent by what resulted from a public engagement exercise that mattered to them. If they have contributed to a consultation on an issue that affects them, asking their reaction to it afterwards is bound to produce an answer that reflects at least in part their satisfaction or otherwise with its result.

Despite this, however, we think this is a valuable ingredient in an evaluation. After all, if you see consultation as just an episode in a wider, longer-term relationship with stakeholders, it is clear that their reaction to that one event is important – if only because it will have a bearing upon that broader relationship. Measuring their reaction is not a function of a conventional satisfaction survey. We would not be impressed by a routine phone call from a market researcher asking if we were 'satisfied' with the consultation process. Better than nothing, maybe, but not a lot better!

And yet. . . when it comes to consultation, we repeatedly find that consultees appreciate most those elements in the process that bring them face to face with those in authority. It is one reason why the remoteness and impersonality of traditional written or documentary consultation turns people off. Eyeball-to-eyeball, when it's possible, creates a much better impression and leads those involved towards a perception that they've been genuinely heard. A good method of evaluation using the stakeholder reaction test is to separate those who, generally speaking, were satisfied with the outcome from those who were not. Both categories should be asked for their reactions to the process overall (preferably in an insight-generating method, such as a focus group) and the resulting analysis should enable a judgement to be made as to the extent to which satisfaction with the outcome influenced their satisfaction with the process.

### *Using the tests together*

Put these three overlapping tests together and we might find some interesting profiles. Typically a consultation that had real impact should, all things being equal, have reasonably content stakeholders, but that assumes the impact was broadly in tune with their opinions and sometimes it's not! There is less correlation between the process compliance test and the decision audit test. Many a perfectly well-executed dialogue has had negligible influence and, impressive though the mechanics may have been, there is no guarantee that swish and sexy processes convince sceptical stakeholders.

**The three overlapping tests of evaluation**

What we like most is an evaluation not just of a single consultation – valuable as that may be at times – but a regular assessment of a consultation programme. This is because we defend the right of a one-off consultation to result in an unchanged decision. Neither do we think a consultor organisation becomes inept when one or more of the dialogue methods fails to function perfectly once in a while. It is when those things happen too often that eyebrows will rightly be raised.

As we have stressed, consultation is not joint decision-making. The decision is not democratic and those with responsibility for taking it are perfectly at liberty to reject the advice offered to them. Note we say 'reject' and not 'disregard' or 'ignore'. If, however, the evaluation of a whole programme shows managers or elected members routinely rejecting the output from public engagement, then we would conclude that their approaches were flawed. Either they were not serious and were indulging in classic going-through-the-motions, or else they were deceiving themselves into thinking they were listening when they weren't!

## VALUE FOR MONEY

Occasionally the Government redeems itself and commissions a thorough evaluation. One such exercise was done by Diane Warburton, of Shared Practice, who undertook the assessment of a 2006 NHS consultation, entitled *Your Heath, Your Care, Your Say*.* This was by any yardstick a massive consultation. Although Warburton's conclusions were generally positive there was one area that was not covered in the report – and which guaranteed a hostile reception for her findings. No-one has volunteered the overall cost of this consultation, though it is rumoured to have been in excess of £2 million. So here is the issue. To what extent should one add yet another test to an evaluation? Simply, is there a value-for-money, or cost-effectiveness, test? If we asked the Audit Commission, the National Audit Office or, for that matter, most members of the general public, the answer would probably be a resounding 'Yes!'

It rarely happens. One reason is the tendency not to count – or care – how much a consultation costs. When Shailesh Vara MP asked each Whitehall ministry what individual consultations cost in March 2009, replies were either evasive or blatantly misleading;† adding it up seems

---

\* This was one of the most extensive and expensive Government consultations in recent years and was subject to full published evaluation. See http://www.dh.gov.uk/en/ Publicationsandstatistics/Publications/PublicationsPolicyAndGuidance/ DH_4127357.

† Shailesh Vara, Conservative MP for North West Cambridgeshire, asked the same question of more than twenty departments. A few provided the requested information, but others claimed that it would cost too much to compile the data. And even when provided, many of the costs such as staff time were ignored.

either too difficult or too sensitive. More frequently, no-one asks. We think this is a real shame, for unlike the NHS mega-consultation, we believe a great many exercises are very cost effective and yield useful results for modest expenditure.

What we need is to adopt the commercial idea of a return on investment or ROI. We could call it a 'return on consultation investment'; while it is always difficult to convert these things into financial terms, it is not impossible. Avoiding the unforeseen consequences of some policy decisions can be measured in cash terms, especially now that Impact Assessments are required for options placed before consultees. In any case, it would be a sound discipline to encourage proper costing of consultation activities. It might also force organisers to think seriously about the value obtained from the exercise.

## SUCCESSIVE DIALOGUES

If consultations themselves are frequently iterative, it follows that evaluations should also be so. Challenging social issues are often about changing values and evolving public understanding. Consider traffic management in our larger towns and cities. For car-drivers to accept workplace parking restrictions, or a whole range of other measures, is a very slow process. There can be many consultations over several years before the logical culmination of a policy direction emerges. So congestion charging finally becomes the high-profile dialogue – but it has been preceded by half a dozen less visible consultations, involving fewer people and exciting less interest.

Evaluation should help make these consultations progressively better. Successive exercises ought, at least in theory, help remove gaps in the identified stakeholder base; they should highlight which methods work and which don't in respect of this issue. Best of all, they should demonstrate what influence, if any, has been exerted on the debate. Successful consultations move the argument forward in some ways; they become a dynamic dialogue, and effective evaluations find ways to chronicle this movement.

In practice, when dialogues are spread over many years, expectations also change. Aspects that are hardly contentious one year can easily become controversial a few years later, for much depends upon the political backcloth. Attempts to build on the green belt, for example, are hardly new and have prompted a standard level of participation for years. Suddenly in the first decade of the new millennium, the issue shoots up the agenda and becomes proxy for a whole raft of green-related causes that inspire far more people to show an interest.

Those evaluating a consultation in these latter occasions have to be careful not to confuse the success of the methods employed with a latent and greater propensity to involvement which has been triggered by other factors. Indeed a common danger of evaluation – a little like consultation itself – is over-interpretation. So prone is the turnout at public meetings or other consultation events to serendipitous accidents of the calendar or the mood of a community that it is rarely wise to rely too much on counting heads in a public consultation. A more qualitative assessment of the dialogue is far more likely to reveal the nature of what's been happening. Have new issues come to light? Have new arguments been advanced? Has there been new insight into the implications of options or proposals? Have alternative options been identified? If so, by whom? We might call this the 'added-value test'.

Clearly such judgements cannot be made by bean-counters – or, in the case of public participation, by head-counters. In fact, the only people capable of making the judgement are those who have a reasonably strong grasp of the subject itself. But, surprise, surprise, these are likely to be the very people who either run the consultation – or are committed to one course of action or another. Finding independent experts who can look at the content of a debate, understand its context and determine the contribution made is far from easy and is yet another reason why formal evaluation is rare.

## BUILT IN, NOT BOLTED ON

Our preference is for evaluation to be built into an organisation's public engagement strategy right from the start. Public bodies should, in effect, be saying: 'We want to take account of the views of our stakeholders in all the major decisions we make – and to prove that we are doing this for real, there will be an annual evaluation of our performance in this area.' Might it be a regular feature in an annual report? Perhaps an appendix detailing what consultations or other forms of dialogue have been organised, and with what results?

Evaluations need to be transparent; declaring that a consultation achieved this or that result is of limited value unless criteria are set out clearly and measurement against these criteria shown to be made objectively. As we pointed out above, many of the most valuable parts of an evaluation involve making subjective judgements and therefore the identity and credibility of those making them are an important factor. That is the whole principle of auditing – knowing that professionally trained specialists have underwritten the numbers, or in this case the judgements.

So we come back to standards again, for an evaluation has to ask key questions of an engagement exercise – and to do so in a way that elicits meaningful answers.

Ultimately the beneficiaries of sound evaluation practices are the stakeholders themselves. They, more than anyone else, yearn for processes that let them express their views and interact with decision-makers. It is they who want to see consultors learn from their mistakes. Process improvement is a painstaking iterative set of actions at the best of times, but the therapy of noting what went wrong is always helpful. Taking active steps to rectify failures should, of course, be reward itself, but, ideally, one makes this highly visible to the stakeholders – so that they can see for themselves that lessons are being absorbed.

So much is accepted wisdom and axiomatic in quality management. What makes it particularly relevant to public engagement and consultation is that here we have an activity where so many participants are openly sceptical and where the failures that we have sought to chronicle in this book have damaged the credibility of many organisations. In such an environment, evidence of a genuine attempt to evaluate may be of some solace to long-suffering consultees.

Part of that comes not from the evaluation itself but from its destination. In other words, who gets to see it? Who is the recipient of the evaluation itself? Self-commissioned reports occasionally have a habit of remaining on the desks of managers whose work is criticised, so the better process is always to ensure it goes to someone else. In a local authority, might the obvious recipient be the relevant overview and scrutiny committee? In other major organisations, should they not be examined by non-executive directors?

Evaluation must become neither ritualised nor routine. This is the danger with bureaucratic mechanisms such as the Audit Commission's successive schemes. Although we advocate using a third-party assessor, a university or professional body, dangers lurk even there that relationships can become too close for comfort and there is a case for changing to another evaluation source every few years.

Maybe the optimum situation is for the industry as a whole to adopt a transparent set of evaluation standards and to publicise them, so that interested stakeholders and others can make a reasoned judgement as to whether an organisation that consults has examined its practices as objectively and constructively as it might.

# 21. SKILLS FOR PARTICIPATION

Much earlier in our argument, we claimed that consultation skills were becoming a core competence for many organisations. Few would challenge this assertion. But what exactly does this mean? And is it really possible? The difficulty here is that the ability to organise and leverage public or stakeholder consultations is itself part of a wider range of communications and relationship-building skills which are also used in other environments.

In 2003, Sir John Egan was commissioned to examine the skills needed for the UK to be more successful in delivering 'sustainable communities'.* The commission arose from a suspicion that those responsible for the built environment were still predominantly preoccupied with professional skills, many of which had been honed years ago and might not have kept pace with the emerging challenges of the sustainability agenda. What emerged was a fascinating analysis of skills shortages and cultural/behavioural practices which were at odds with the requirements of politicians, civic leaders and the public itself.

Egan's focus was on those occupations which play a part in what has since become known as place-shaping. His team found there were rather a lot of them – in fact well over 100. They included architects, planners, engineers, surveyors, landscape designers, builders, property speculators and developers. They found a multitude of public bodies, their responsibilities criss-crossing the subject-matter like a spaghetti

---

\*    *The Egan Review: Skills for Sustainable Communities.* See http://www.communities.gov.uk/
     documents/communities/pdf/152086.pdf.

junction of overlapping accountabilities, with jobs requiring delicate negotiation between many of them.

They then noted the thousands of elected members at all levels of local government who have an influence over key decisions, and added civil servants in Government regional offices of the regions and in central Whitehall ministries. They also highlighted a range of 'generic skills' they thought it necessary to develop for the future. Some of these looked straightforward and probably in plentiful supply. But others were far from commonplace and comprised the classic 'soft skills' – those needed to make the 'hard skills' succeed.

Here we are at that point where skills development shades into culture change. Egan concluded: 'Attempting to upskill these professionals in isolation will not produce the outcomes we are seeking. Instead success will lie in changing the behaviour, attitudes and knowledge of everyone involved, many of whom may not have realised in the past that they had anything to do with each other, or with sustainable communities.'*

So there we have it – the whole is greater than the sum of its parts.

What interests us about this analysis is that so much of what Egan diagnoses about sustainable communities is also true about many other aspects of modern life – health, education, economic development or the arts. The technicalities of treating people's ailments, teaching children, running a business or even performing a play are all known skills. Today's challenge lies not just in learning how to perform these tasks, but in relating the effort to the expectations of the community.

That is why we find that many of the 'generic skills' identified by Egan are directly relevant to the world of consultation and public engagement. Egan identified thirteen in total:

- Inclusive visioning
- Project management
- Leadership in sustainable communities

---

\* *Egan Review*, p. 54.

- Breakthrough thinking/brokerage
- Team/partnership working
- Making it happen, given constraints
- Process management/change management
- Financial management and appraisal
- Stakeholder management
- Analysis, decision-making, learning from mistakes, evaluation
- Communication
- Conflict resolution
- Customer awareness and how to secure feedback.

Let's look at some of them.

### Team/partnership working

It is not difficult to see why Egan placed such emphasis on this, for the built environment is the product of many agencies' efforts and examples of unco-ordinated thinking have been responsible for some of our more spectacular planning failures. But learning how to operate in a truly joined-up environment means learning how to cope with conflicting goals, plus the small change of having to put your own immediate objectives on one side in order to achieve a more ambitious outcome for the many.

Overbearing bosses who charge their staff to safeguard their own narrow interests at all costs and who send them to partnership forums with a mission 'to win' become curiously out of place in a world of multi-agency partnerships. Team-working is about understanding the other person's roles, goals and constraints. But it is one thing to meet around the table as a management team within a single organisation and quite another to operate across different agencies. Complexity is a big barrier here. Imagine going into a room with ten other organisations as diverse as health trusts, police forces, courts, universities, social service providers and so on. Team-working requires knowledge that few currently possess plus a degree of political (mostly small 'p', but occasionally capital 'P') intuition as to where they can effectively work together and where they cannot.

### Stakeholder management

We welcome its inclusion in the Egan list of generic skills, for it confirms much that we have been preaching for some time. The ability to place oneself in the shoes of those who will be most affected by all kinds of developments is an important attribute and clearly underpins a more comprehensive approach to sustainability.

Stakeholder management relies heavily on gathering and using the right data, but there is more to helping people become excellent stakeholder managers. It means developing insight into the way that organisations and individuals behave and predicting their response to different situations. We defy anyone to teach these skills without using lots of examples from a wide range of environments and helping to distil common patterns from an intrinsically variable set of scenarios.

Maybe more emphasis should be on the word 'management', for we think too few people appreciate the need to manage the relationships that are inherent in the stakeholder analysis. Too many relationships just happen; they are not subject to any planning or effective monitoring. Teaching professionals that, in addition to their technical skills, they also have to build and sustain relationships to achieve certain objectives has strangely been absent from the curriculum in a number of disciplines. In practice it has fallen to employers to design courses or request help from those who are most experienced from within their own staff.

The best form of stakeholder management amounts less to a skill set and more to well-developed processes that embed relationship management norms into the way that key activities are undertaken inside an organisation.

### Analysis, decision-making, learning from mistakes, evaluation

Egan meant this bundle of skills to act as a counterweight to the creative aspects of many tasks in the built environment. To match the instinctive, there is a need for the analytical – another variant, we think, of evidence-based policy-making.

Rigorous analysis certainly forms part of any defined skills inventory for those who have to deal with quantitative or qualitative data, but, of course, this does not always go alongside decision-making, which can be a far less organised process. There are far more variables involved in public (or for that matter, private sector) policy-making than the data that is submitted in support of key choices. What can loosely be termed 'experience' or what we regard as political nous is all about the interpretation of information provided with an insight into its likely underlying meaning. What people mean is not always what they say!

The skills that are needed by those who organise public engagement include being able to define what analysis is most relevant and being able to present it to decision-makers in a way that helps rather than hinders responsive decision-making. Indeed so much analysis is really presentation and the ability to distinguish peripherally relevant facts from those that are central to an argument.

### Conflict resolution

This is becoming an absolutely pivotal skill; without it one misses much of the point of public consultation. Issues that matter will, as often as not, provoke a range of views and it is seldom sufficient just to capture them. If we take conflict resolution and consensus-building together (they're not quite the same, but are closely associated), they amount to a whole block of capabilities which are essential to community cohesion and to building structures that command the support of stakeholders.

Trying to defuse situations that have become emotionally charged requires patience and an ability to empathise with different protagonists. We are here talking about understanding the forces that lie behind people's declared views or opinions. Sometimes these are deeply hidden beneath layers of prejudice, misinformation, confused expectations or previous unsatisfactory experiences. Delayering them can be a slow process; the best in the business recognise that people cannot shed years of conditioned thinking without undertaking tortuous self-assessment and a reappraisal of much they have previously accepted without question.

Engaging with the public on matters of heightened sensitivity demands very clear thinking and runs the risk of unleashing forces that can be difficult to control. Imagine a scenario of ethnic or religious tension in some of our inner cities, or maybe look at scenes of public anger which erupt when cherished institutions are threatened with closure. What distinguishes the best at public participation from the average town hall bureaucrat is an ability to spot the emerging conflict and to initiate discussions that can diffuse the emotional quotient in the row, while finding practical ways to resolve as many aspects of disagreement as possible.

### Customer awareness and how to secure feedback

Egan's final generic skill is all about consultation – and is probably central to many service delivery roles. Just as the best private companies are genetically programmed to be customer conscious, Egan wants to see those who influence the built environment similarly motivated.

In the public realm, people as customers experience the results of decisions taken by those who commission or procure services. One of the major achievements in recent years has been to acknowledge the distinction between commissioning and delivery. As long as these two roles were lumped together, one experienced the sensation that maybe the service was designed with the interests of the service-provider uppermost in mind, while those of the customer, patient or passenger came a poor second.

Separating the two roles is intended to eliminate this risk: to let those whose job it is to commission services concentrate fully on understanding the customer, prioritising various customer needs and converting them into service specifications. It can be a revealing process and commissioners often find themselves in danger of specifying services which are beyond available resources or the will to deliver. But just to capture and articulate service requirements is, of itself, a major step forward.

We are still in the early days of public services commissioning and the skills and knowledge are still being developed. Clearly knowing how to seek the views of service users forms a major part of what's required.

This canter through some of what the Egan Review called 'generic skills' is a useful benchmark against which to test our own theories that consultation requires all sorts of capabilities that are not always easy to find. In some ways, we're talking about a basket of skills that are individually not rocket science but taken together form a demanding set that have seldom been comprehensively defined, let alone structured into real jobs.

## NEW ROLES

New roles have emerged and many are becoming established and recognised.

One such is the *consultation officer*. This is the person who organises consultations, but whose most challenging task is to devise the programme in the first place. It means critically examining each and every occasion when someone thinks it's a good idea to have a survey or ask customers what they think. He or she has to know how to prepare a consultation document, and how to buy in or organise oneself the most popular or relevant dialogue methods, and has to ensure that the stakeholders have been properly identified and engaged in the process. Responsibility for analysis and the dissemination of feedback rests here, as does the constant updating of information about the consultation programme on the organisation's website.

Full-time consultation officers can increasingly be found in public bodies and private companies who recognise that there are a significant number of projects to be run. The dilemma is whether to train functional professionals to be able to turn their hand to running consultations or whether to employ dedicated specialists in this role. Right now we are witnessing a dramatic increase in the number of consultation officers, while simultaneously seeing an upsurge in training initiatives to ensure that those who need to undertake these exercises as part of a wider role still have enough know-how to go ahead.

A variation is the *consultation co-ordinator*. Here the job is not so much to execute or organise consultations but more to make sure they happen – and to the right standards. Although we might imagine that this is the obvious role for a Local Strategic Partnership, in practice most post-holders undertaking this task are there to try to produce some coherence *within* an organisation. One county council we know estimated that it had well over 100 people organising one form of consultation or another in its various departments. Sounds crazy, doesn't it? But bear in mind the huge range of responsibilities, covering the caring services, education, highways, planning and so on, and the tendency for good managers everywhere to try to understand their stakeholders or customers. Then one sees the immense task.

No-one seems to have definitive figures as to exactly how many consultations are organised in a large local authority, but we think it easily exceeds 200 per annum. Soon, however, we should find out, for consultation co-ordinators have been put in place to try to sort out the mess. Without this, they just won't succeed in the joined-up consultation that the government is pressing public agencies to deliver. The co-ordinator's job is to find out all the public engagement activities that are being organised and to try to hone them into a sensible programme that will minimise consultation fatigue and make the best use of multi-purpose dialogue mechanisms such as citizen's panels.

Many departments will resent such interference. Departmental managers will feel that they should be free to undertake whatever dialogues they like with people they may regard as 'their' customers. Rightly they may claim that any restriction on their discretion to engage with their stakeholders runs counter to the principle of devolving management accountability as close as possible to the front line. Moreover, many of course do a perfectly satisfactory job; why interfere? How on earth can we therefore recommend that public bodies claw back some of this autonomy and try to co-ordinate that which has been previously delegated?

The answer lies in costs and resources. For everyone to do their own thing, to their own standards, carries a cost – as well as an opportunity cost. Local or national organisations that are consultees for these purposes become totally exasperated at the different kinds of approach they must follow in order to participate in dialogue with different parts of the same organisation.

Clever consultation co-ordinators will wield a classic mixture of carrot and stick. They will induce departments who know how to conduct a professional consultation to continue and to observe house rules which lay down minimum standards; they will retain operational autonomy in their project management of public dialogues. But this has to be earned by effective use of these techniques and by a fully transparent approach. Departments that have failed to invest in the necessary skills or who rely upon *ad hoc* projects in a hit-or-miss style will be denied the right to undertake them until such training or process deficiencies have been made good.

Obviously this is a role where the ability to build and maintain decent relationships is paramount. Co-ordinators without internal credibility will fail and so must not be too junior. Whitehall ministries appointed consultation co-ordinators some years ago and they act as custodians of the Code of Practice we discussed previously; their success has been limited due to their fairly lowly status and the few sanctions available to them where their advice is ignored. This is a role that will need considerable further development.

A third job that is emerging is the *stakeholder-manager*. This is entirely a relationship management role and can be compared with key account executives in the private sector. Much of this surrounds data management and is sometimes of a very sensitive nature, but the mechanics are secondary to the basic challenge of ensuring that stakeholders have been properly identified and that the contact points, the preferred dialogue methods and their priority concerns are known.

This role carries a heavy responsibility and one that might well need to report at a senior level – possibly to the chief executive. He or she might be the bearer of bad news, for this is the post that should, on a regular basis, survey key stakeholders to track their opinions of the organisation as a whole. Companies whose business imperative involves maintaining a favourable image among key groups take this very seriously. Typical examples include companies with share-price sensitivity, where the published views of financial journalists can dramatically change the value of the enterprise overnight.

Public bodies face not dissimilar risks to their reputations. Before summer 2007, who had heard of the Pirbright Agricultural Laboratory?[*] Poor maintenance of a disposal pipe resulted in an outbreak of foot and mouth disease and immediately led to the resignations of key senior management. In the autumn of the same year, the notorious and wholly indefensible loss of data by HM Revenue & Customs led to its chairman

---

[*]    See http://www.iah.bbsrc.ac.uk/about/lab_p.shtml.

falling on his sword. Little wonder that public agencies, large and small, have to take crisis management seriously and that a critical part of this agenda is to ensure that key stakeholders are kept well informed and sympathetic to the challenges they face.

Supportive stakeholders cannot save incompetent managers from their fate, but they can make a difference at the margin. Rather like executive directors, at their best they can act as a critical friend, watching out for changes in the business or political environment and able to use their external perspective to warn, guide or advise on required changes or development strategies. None of this happens without effective dialogue mechanisms and the job of a stakeholder manager is to figure out the best channels of communication for these purposes.

Mechanisms to create, support and derive value from dialogues with these groups can be resource-intensive and may be sub-contracted to specialists, but someone somewhere has to be responsible for ensuring that it is done. Stakeholder managers are therefore often to be found reporting to a director of communications and while this can work well, there is one big danger. It is this. Not everywhere has corporate communications developed into the open-minded two-way process that organisations need if they are to listen well and act upon what they hear. Too many firms – and public bodies – use this function to push their own messages and to promote their own self-image through a significant emphasis on public relations and media management activities. Ninety per cent promotion and 10 per cent listening will make the stakeholder manager less effective than he or she needs to be, for it underplays the necessary focus on understanding and absorbing what stakeholders tell you.

In Chapter 17, we went into detail on emerging best practices for a single stakeholder database and the opportunities to use technology to manage these relationships. It goes without saying that a top-class, pro-active stakeholder manager will be the prime mover in developing and exploiting such facilities. Whether organisations themselves will grasp quite how pivotal a strategic asset this could become remains a more open question, for this may boil down to the mindset of the boss. In short, stakeholder managers may need to rely for their ultimate success upon commitment and leadership from the top of the organisation.

## LEADERSHIP

This brings us back to our overall conclusion that consultation and participation is ultimately a matter of corporate culture and that unless those at the top are committed to the principle, no amount of effort by those lower down will deliver to their potential.

This sounds like yet another whinge from specialist functions who claim that their particular roles in life do not receive sufficient backing from on high. Finance managers complain that the managing director is so besotted with technology and the latest products turned out by the R&D boffins that she never looks at the bottom-line figures. Or the marketing director thinks the boss is so cost conscious that he won't approve sensible spend on promotion and advertising. Then there's the quality manager tearing out his hair because the products aren't good enough, and the HR manager who thinks that the company treats its employees badly and that a poor example is being set by an internecine board and a fratricidal chairman.

It is only too easy to blame chief executives for a failure to provide a lead in all the myriad aspects of modern management. In the public sector, there are additional dimensions of political imperatives overlaying all the normal obligations of sound management. One chairman of a NHS primary care trust confided this year that he had been given fifty-seven 'top priorities'! Hilarious – but sadly true.

How on earth can one make the case for elevating public consultation or stakeholder management anywhere close to the top of an organisational leader's agenda? Well, here goes! In a nutshell, success in business or in public service will increasingly be seen as delivering outcomes and not outputs. To achieve such outcomes almost always involves insightful understanding of the detailed circumstances of various stakeholders – and an ability to hear what they are telling you in time to act upon it. With very few exceptions, top managers will need to carry people with them, or at least secure a minimum level of acquiescence to their plans and activities. Losing the confidence of key parts of the stakeholder base will, in future, be as fatal for leaders as a failure of performance and consequently astute chairmen and chief executives will pay at least as much attention to their public engagement programmes as to other aspects of their jobs. So it matters.

## 22. CULTURE CHANGE OR CULTURE SHOCK? THE FUTURE OF CONSULTATION

Some things just won't happen.

For example, we don't buy into a vision of mass democratic involvement in the minutiae of public administration or a resurgence of political activism on the back of internet-driven obsessives all eager to make wonderfully useful contributions to everything that is debated in the public domain. Neither do we foresee the demise of consultation – to be replaced by more ambitious, if ill-defined, concepts of involvement, engagement, participation or the Government's catch-word of 2008 – empowerment. We believe there will always be a role for a process that enables decision-makers to gather views that matter and to broaden the information base upon which they make choices and allocate resources.

In fact, we see a future where decision-makers become more assertive and eschew the more spurious 'look-over-your-shoulder' type of consultation, done as a defensive reflex and contributing little to better decisions. Arguably, the coming years will see only small, though valuable, improvements in the methodologies of dialogue.

Here are five predictions.

### 1. *The best organisations will make a strategic investment in consultation and engagement*

Obviously this cannot cover everyone and, no matter how vociferously the press bang on about a postcode lottery, those that take the listening role seriously won't fall into any obvious geographical or functional pattern. So we will find local authorities with a smashing record of public engagement co-existing alongside neighbouring councils which just don't see the point.

But an increasing number of the better-managed public bodies, companies and third-sector organisations will get the message and make the appropriate investment. Some will do so at the behest of strong leaders who have become personally convinced. Others will have a bad experience at the hands of a vengeful electorate or incur the show-stopping wrath of key stakeholders – and resolve that it never happen again. Some, we dare say, may get there by happy accident.

Those who set out to invest in making their organisations truly excellent at consultation and engagement will derive a significant return on that investment. There won't be a linear pattern of cause and effect, for the forces at work are too complex for such a simplistic answer. But an organisation that has inculcated into its employees the awareness that everything they hear from customers or from other stakeholders has a value, and provides them with mechanisms to record and use this information, has a wealth of knowledge that others do not. In the commercial world we call this 'market intelligence', but in public services it is called 'citizen intelligence' – a phrase recently adopted by the Audit Commission to describe what it will look for in assessing whether councils are truly aware of what their communities think and what they need.

Organisations that make this step-change will probably adopt a twin-track approach. On one hand they will become good at running formal consultation and engagement exercises, with demonstrable results that should impress their customers or citizens. On the other, they will cultivate a culture of informal consultation where every front-line employee acts as its eyes and ears. These approaches complement each other and serve to change the organisation's ethos fundamentally.

### 2. The public will remain sceptical and ambivalent about consultation

Much as we would like there to be enough organisations that make the strategic investments we promote, there will still be others who continue to make a hash of the whole process. It may be pessimistic to suggest that in another ten years, much of what we've written in Part Two may still be valid. But that may well be the case, for this is a business where there are often two steps back for three steps forward and not everyone will sustain an investment in public engagement year in, year out.

As in other walks of life, good practice may be obscured by the bad. The media will always find a better story from a consultation that seems to be going wrong. When BAA consulted on its proposed expansion of Heathrow airport, the *Sunday Times* gleefully reported a Freedom of Information request, the result of which appeared to suggest that the consultor had been capriciously selective in its use of certain statistics in the consultation document.* This and similar stories fuel a public mistrust that even when the process seems to be beyond criticism, the content of the consultation narrative is suspect and powerful bodies can spin the story to influence the dialogue, steering respondents towards the answer they want.

The public can also be very fickle, prone to accept the process warts and all when the outcome they wish is the result. The same people can be thoroughly disgusted by a similar process that delivers them something less acceptable. This ambivalence spreads from the public through to their political representatives and to those who serve them as civil servants, local government officers or executives. For in the human psyche, we acknowledge the need to listen professionally, but we struggle to separate our commitment to such process from our preference for certain outcomes.

All of this means that those who organise consultations must continue to strive to communicate better, must constantly seek to persuade people that the exercise is genuine and that the organisation responsible indisputably wants to hear from those whose views it seeks.

### 3. *The Government may finally learn how to do it!*
Despite all the criticism – most of it abundantly justified – we think that the Government stands every chance of getting it right in the future. Part of our argument is that it just cannot afford the political embarrassment of continuing to get it wrong. Policy-making processes are already reasonably consultative in their overall approach; best practice

---

\*    See 'Evidence fix led to third runway being approved', *Sunday Times*, 9 March 2008.

is sufficiently established in some central government departments and agencies. Belatedly, the high chiefs of the National School of Government, no less, have stumbled upon the need for policy-makers to involve what they call the 'front line' rather more.*

What is actually needed is just a more concerted effort to apply good consultation practice consistently; better observance of the latest Code of Practice might help. What might assist even more is for governments to acknowledge the difference between general and specific consultations.

General consultations are popular with administrations that want the public to engage in a thorough-going debate about something they think is important. A good example is the education debate 'Time to Talk',† kicked off by Ed Balls when he was appointed Secretary of State for Children, Schools and Families. Rumoured to have cost over £1 million, it featured a travelling roadshow and large-scale deliberative events addressing such questions as 'What are the biggest challenges facing. . .?' Now there is little wrong in raising such issues, provided that those who take part recognise that the contribution they are making is towards a better overall understanding of a subject rather than developing detailed policies. These background debates can be valuable for policy-makers who need to appreciate the landscape so that they can then develop firmer ideas. And the scale of such 'involvement' surely gladdens the hearts of those for whom the highest priority is just to engage as many as possible. However, these are quite different from specific consultations, when options can be laid out for open discussions and hard choices may have to be made.

General debates can be long-winded affairs and can benefit from having sufficient time for opinion to evolve. Tight deadlines can be avoided and a high-wide-and-handsome approach can be taken to stakeholder identification and engagement. Specific consultations, we

---

\* See *Engagement and Aspiration: Reconnecting Policy Making with Front Line Professionals*, produced by the National School of Government's Sunningdale Institute for the Cabinet Office (March 2009), http://www.nationalschool.gov.uk/downloads/EngagementandAspirationReport.pdf.

† See http://publications.dcsf.gov.uk/eOrderingDownload/TimetoTalk.pdf.

think, should be more focused – with processes selected to produce the level of informed, detailed debate that is appropriate for often complex problems. For these, a shorter timescale with relevant, motivated and knowledgeable stakeholders committed to participate is perfectly feasible.

Confusing these two very different types of exercises cause governments untold problems, but we think they will gradually learn to distinguish between them. What might be useful is an opposition that is alert to the importance of good consultation and harries errant ministers to abandon eccentric departures from best practice.

### 4. Standards will emerge. . . but from the bottom up, not the top down

What works best is far more visible on the ground than in centralised think tanks or even in academia. That is why we are somewhat cautious about well-meaning attempts to codify best practice through published standards. In time, there will be such codification, of course, but it is worth remembering that it took more than a decade to develop the ISO 9000 quality standard* and subsequently the BS 8477 customer service standard.

Instead, many organisations that will prioritise public engagement will adopt their own standards – usually adaptations of other published efforts, quite possibly our own Consultation Institute Charter.† It will be an iterative process. Sometimes attempts to promote a set of standards will evaporate with the enthusiasm of one advocate; at other times, pressure of events may collide with the more demanding rules.

One particular standards-conscious manager recently explained how he had agreed a number of non-negotiables within his local authority – conventions that were backed by senior management and including the edict that no formal consultation should proceed without his personal involvement. Six months later, he told us how the director of education had totally ignored this rule and ran her own exercise over the contentious issue of closing rural schools. She broke so many best-practice standards

---

* See http://www.iso.org/iso/iso_catalogue/management_standards.htm.

† See http://www.consultationinstitute.org.

that, by rights, she should probably have been fired. She wasn't and our doughty consultation champion fights on to instil a sense of discipline in an area of traditionally happy chaos.

What is interesting about this story is that, at first glance, it seems to make the case for top-down standards. If only the rule had the force of a nationwide compact! Might not departmental managers think twice before stepping outside the safety zone of complying with universal standards? Well, maybe. But we think that observance of such standards is often tokenistic and minimal. Believe us when we assert that the trauma of a blazing row with local residents who consider themselves badly consulted is a far more effective learning experience for those in charge of this particular council.

And that is the point of standards. All they are, ultimately, is a benchmark that chronicles what's recognised at a particular moment in history as being satisfactory performance. As such they are dynamic and in this sphere they will have to chart the growing sophistication of a sceptical public and better-informed stakeholders. We think a proliferation of standards probably inevitable, but accept that there is a highly therapeutic benefit from lots of people worrying about what makes a good standard; is it best to shoot for a standard of responding to an e-mail in forty-eight hours or five days? Time spent deciding upon such details is not wasted, for, over time those who have to scratch their heads become more proficient at what they do. So that's why we welcome the emerging concern with consultation standards; it will slowly but surely lead to improvements.

### 5. Specialists in public engagement and consultation will gain more recognition

The people we have just described probably don't see themselves as part of any defined profession right now, but we think that will also change as consultation and public engagement rise in the political and managerial stream of consciousness. Some may argue that practitioners already form part of the public relations profession; others may lean towards the market research field. But we think that the issues tackled in this book cover a wider and subtly broader canvas; maybe a touch of market research, a significant dollop of public relations, with politics and psychology thrown in for good measure.

One exercise we undertook a few years ago identified no fewer than seventy – yes, seventy – skills and capabilities which consultation professionals needed. What this demonstrated was that this is a truly multi-disciplinary role and, as we showed in the last chapter, the Egan Review and other initiatives continually reinforce this claim. Consultation champions cannot be boring, narrow-minded, narrowly educated specialists. They have to be worldly-wise, politically sensitive and extraordinarily attuned to the environment around them. Let's remember that these are the people that we will rely upon to detect shifts in public and stakeholder opinions and who need to find ways to probe, prompt and capture often difficult messages and then convey them to decision-makers.

One of our first consultation champions was the lady who organised public consultations for the Metropolitan Police in New Scotland Yard. She proudly displayed her Certificate of Professional Development in her office and a few days later received a visit from one of the Met's senior commissioners. He expressed surprise. 'I never knew you could get a qualification in consultation,' he said. And of course he is right, for it is not (at least at the time of writing) a *recognised* qualification. Neither can you, to our knowledge, take a degree in the subject. And until this book, neither would you have found much written specifically about the topic.

But the point is not whether a qualification is recognised. It is whether the person is recognised. Are there ways of ensuring that other people in an organisation come to understand what is involved in the public engagement role, and can they be assisted to see how these roles contribute to the overall enterprise?

We think the activities we have described – or the art of consultation – will warrant better recognition. It is why we originally set up the Consultation Institute and we believe there are upwards of 10,000 people in the UK public sector alone who spend significant amounts of their working time on these tasks. They deserve better recognition, and will, in our view, receive it.

# APPENDIX 1: TEN TOP TIPS FOR ORGANISERS OF CONSULTATIONS

1. *Check that the consultation is really necessary.* Far too often, a consultation is used as a surrogate for other processes such as conflict resolution, consensus-building, negotiation or mediation. Is there a sensible problem or proposition that can be the subject of meaningful dialogue?

2. *Get to the heart of the issue* – and identify those parts where you have discretion, and the scope to be influenced by the views you hear. Avoid generalised aspirational wish-list issues and try to find meaty substantive questions where a consultation can help clarify the position and expose areas of agreement and disagreement.

3. *Observe a rigorous process in commissioning a consultation exercise* – so that its audiences, objectives and the timescale for acting upon its output is clearly understood. People will respond more positively to being asked if its purpose is clear and makes sense.

4. *Devote sufficient attention to identifying the audience* – and think deeply about their likely interest in what you wish to propose. Citizens, customers and all kinds of stakeholder groups vary enormously and their different characteristics make a difference when it comes to planning the consultation.

5. *Use modern communications techniques* – but ensure that key parts of your audience aren't left out. Unless the target audience is uncharacteristically homogeneous, a one-size-fits-all approach won't work, and there will be a need for a mixture of methods both for publishing the consultation narrative and for managing the dialogue.

6. *Expect the unexpected.* If consultations were so predictable, there

probably would be no need for them. Ensure that budgets and processes can be kept under constant review throughout and be prepared to go back and do it again if essential voices have not been heard.

7.  *Anticipate a sceptical public* – and be prepared to demonstrate that you are observing best practice. Remember that the process can come in for as much criticism as the substance, and that the onus is on you to prove the integrity of what you do. Be prepared to use independent third parties on occasions.

8.  *Treat feedback as if it's the most important part of the project* – and budget accordingly. This is the acid test by which respondents and participants judge whether to bother entering into any future dialogue.

9.  *Ensure that consultee views are fully considered* – it's your fiduciary duty to those whose views you've gathered. Right or wrong, it's your job to act as their advocate.

10. *Remember that ultimately it's about trust* – and that your relationship with those you consult is long term. A poorly executed consultation can quickly damage relationships that have taken years to build. So pay attention to detail; small mistakes can cause significant problems.

# APPENDIX 2: TEN TOP TIPS FOR RESPONDERS TO CONSULTATIONS

1. *Be selective.* Devote resources only to those consultations where the consultor is genuinely open to being influenced. Unless you have a membership who expect you to go through the motions in a lost cause, be pragmatic, and focus elsewhere.

2. *Understand the context.* Invest in ensuring you know what problem the consultor is seeking to solve. There may well be more than one version of the context. Gather intelligence and try hard to learn exactly where there is scope to make a difference.

3. *Anticipate the consultation by engaging early with the consultor.* Persuade the organisation that will consult to discuss the scope, the timing and the methods of the exercise with you during the pre-consultation phase. Key stakeholders have considerable opportunities to influence the forthcoming dialogues. Be helpful and offer positive suggestions that can help them organise an even better consultation.

4. *Use the consultation to work out your own policy position.* Few respondents have agreed positions on all aspects of a complex issue. Wise consultees recognise where they need to work harder on refining and thinking through their own positions; consultations provide the perfect opportunities to undertake this work.

5. *If you need to take the views of your own members, start early.* Secondary consultation can be critical but needs time and sometimes serious money. When you consult your own people, you still need to observe best practice, and that includes feedback.

6. *Make sure you answer the consultor's question and use the consultor's preferred method of response.* Even if you disapprove of either or both, you need to do as you are told if you are to have the influence you seek. Nothing prevents you from supplementing these with other matters – or responding in other ways.

7. *Play to your strengths* – focus on those dialogue methods you're best at. You may face a choice of making traditional documentary responses, participating in consultation events or a range of other methods. Choose what suits your organisation.

8. *Ask to meet key people if this is appropriate* – nothing beats a direct face-to-face dialogue, and if you don't ask, you won't have the opportunity. You have little to lose by asking. . . and even if you can't meet the key people, you may be offered an alternative. Never decline, for every meeting brings you to the attention of those that are consulting.

9. *Find fellow-travellers and make common cause with them* – credible collaborators can add weight to your arguments. Making joint submissions or joining forces to present your case need not compromise your position. Respond individually too.

10. *Monitor the consultation and its outcome* – and complain loudly if best practice standards are not observed. Consultees have the right to expect good treatment, but may only get it if they care enough to protest when corners are cut. Be eagle eyed and show you take consultation seriously.

# APPENDIX 3: WHAT GOVERNMENT SHOULD DO

Consultation should not be a party political matter, though there may be a genuine advantage to those who can demonstrate a will and a commitment to do it better. As a starting point, here's a list of seven things that could be done immediately.

1. *Treat consultation as a key component of our democracy* – not just a technical tool for officials. It should have featured in the constitutional reform programme, and still has a role to play in rebalancing the democratic system to allow greater public involvement between elections. Referenda may have a place, but consultations also play a role.

2. *Articulate a consistent rationale as to when consultation will and will not be undertaken* – right now it often feels as if the rules are being made up as they go along. Political parties might make it clearer in their manifestos whether they intend to consult about various proposals.

3. *Institute a better culture of informal consultations and consult formally on fewer occasions* – but do it better every time. When it crosses the formality threshold, a consultation needs to meet demanding standards. 'Fewer but better' is long overdue.

4. *Adopt one set of standards for public sector consultations* – and abandon the current policy of letting public bodies opt in or out of observing them. Hundreds of public bodies are not bound by the standards, so stakeholders cannot be sure that they will be heard properly.

5. *Monitor compliance with the standards* – there's no point in having them unless they are enforced. Giving this role to the National Audit Office may be the only way to stop civil servants 'marking their own homework'.

6. *Appoint more senior consultation co-ordinators* – so they have real clout in Government departments. These departmentally based custodians of consultation standards are often too junior to fight for best practice; we need to stiffen their resolve and raise their status.

7. *Provide an effective one-stop shop* – where citizens can see consultations past and present. There once was such a website, but it was closed to save money and allegedly because of lack of traffic! In truth, its information was so patchy and incomplete that few professional stakeholder organisations bothered with it. Bring it back.

None of these ideas are particularly radical. They do not compromise ambitious talk of 'going beyond consultation' or 'citizen empowerment'. But governments will lack credibility with any such notions unless they can strengthen their reputation for consultation itself. These seven proposals would help.

# APPENDIX 4: WHAT OTHERS SHOULD DO

- *Backbench Members of Parliament* regularly complain that their constituents' opinions are ignored. They could do better by acting as champions of superior consultation processes.
- *Civil servants* must embrace the new culture of consultative policy-making and the transparency that goes with it. They need leadership and training in new skills and techniques.
- *Hard-to-reach or seldom-heard groups* have a particular opportunity to be heard as consultation gradually becomes more inclusive. But they should not be complacent and expect the dialogue to come to them; they must still organise themselves to participate fully.
- *Local councillors and elected members* should wrest control of the local engagement strategy from officials, and assume real leadership. They should reconcile their traditional reliance on the customs of representative democracy with the positive advantages of consultative democracy.
- *The media* plays an important part in covering public debate, and conditions much of the environment for public engagement. But journalists often miss the best stories and could focus more on investigating what impact consultations have on policy-making.
- *The NHS* needs to practise what it preaches about public and patient involvement and tackle the traditional culture of the expert. It has to take LINks and foundation trust membership structures seriously and invest in the joint design of new and reconfigured services.
- *Police authorities* and police forces can build on a decade of respectable progress in public engagement by further strengthening

their neighbourhood and community policing dialogues. Better inter-working with other local service providers does not always come easily but should be made a high priority.

■ *Political parties* should stop using consultation as a tool to secure short-term tactical advantage. Demanding consultation only when it's politically expedient reinforces cynicism among the public.

■ *Pressure groups and campaigners* are still uncertain in their use of consultation to advance their arguments. They need to anticipate forthcoming engagement exercises better and use the media more creatively.

■ *Third sector* organisations increasingly find themselves acting as hybrid consultors/consultees – and probably need to improve in both roles. They must shed the gatekeeper image and observe themselves the standards they seek in others.

# INDEX